Palgrave Fan Studies

Series Editors
Louise Geddes
Adelphi University
Garden City, NY, USA

Lincoln Geraghty
University of Portsmouth
Portsmouth, UK

This book series represents the interdisciplinary field of fan studies. It considers the different ways in which fan studies exists at the intersection of media (old and new), cultural studies, and reception studies and as a result, rethinks the production of the fields of literature, art, philosophy, theater and performance, film and television, and beyond. The series welcomes a diverse set of methodological approaches including Marxism, race theory, gender studies, affect theory, the history of print, convergence theory, digital studies, material culture, and participatory culture, as well as geographies, historical periods, and disciplines. The aim of the series is to showcase how fan studies can offer new theoretical frameworks for understanding significant artistic, literary, historical, and cultural movements, and in turn, how these innovative approaches to representing contemporary culture and media theory have expanded the Humanities.

More information about this series at
https://link.springer.com/bookseries/16367

Neta Yodovich

Women Negotiating Feminism and Science Fiction Fandom

The Case of the "Good" Fan

palgrave
macmillan

Neta Yodovich
Faculty of Social Sciences
University of Haifa
Haifa, Israel

ISSN 2662-2807   ISSN 2662-2815   (electronic)
Palgrave Fan Studies
ISBN 978-3-031-04078-8   ISBN 978-3-031-04079-5   (eBook)
https://doi.org/10.1007/978-3-031-04079-5

Cover illustration: GeorgePeter / Getty Images

This Palgrave Macmillan imprint is published by the registered company Springer Nature
Switzerland AG.
The registered company address is: Gewerbestrasse 11, 6330 Cham, Switzerland

ACKNOWLEDGMENTS

Working on this book was a remarkable experience, and I would like to use this opportunity to thank everyone who took part in this journey. First and foremost, I am forever indebted to the incredible women I have interviewed for this study. Any wittiness, profoundness, or intelligence this book might offer is because of you. Thank you for opening up to me and for providing me with a glimpse into your fascinating lives.

I am full of gratitude to the academic mentors who have guided me throughout the years. To my PhD supervisors, Prof. Sophie Woodward and Prof. Penny Tinkler, thank you for your guidance and support. Working alongside you has helped me become a better researcher, scholar, and writer. To Prof. Tally Katz-Gerro whose brilliance is only secondary to her kindness. To Dr. Kinneret Lahad, who believed in me and showed me my potential. I am forever your fan. Thank you to the brilliant scholars who inspired me and provided feedback to my work throughout the years: Prof. Sarah Banet-Weiser, Prof. Vanessa May, Dr. Owen Abbott, Dr. Cristiana Olcese, Dr. Alina Rzepnikowska-Phillips, Dr. Kathryn Telling, Dr. Petra Nordqvist, and Dr. Maddy Abbas. To my wonderful colleagues and friends who celebrated moments of success and joy but were also happy to hear me complain: Dr. Natalie Anne-Hall, Dr. Rachel Katz, Dr. Jaime Garcia-Iglesias, Emma Fàbrega Domènech, Dr. Jinju Kim, Geffen Ben David, and Yeala Hazut-Yanuka. To the entire INVENT team for exposing me to new ways of thinking and researching. To the Academic College Tel Aviv-Yaffo, Tel Aviv University, University of Manchester, and the University of Haifa for being my intellectual homes.

To my family—I would not have been able to do what I love if it was not for you. I thank my parents for encouraging and believing in me. I miss and love you every day. To my brother, sister, sister-in-law, and my lovely nieces and nephew—thank you for enjoying popular culture with me. To Apollo, who crossed oceans with me, you are the best dog I would ever have.

To my friends—Lilach, Natasha, Michal, Maya, Maayan, Henna, Inna, Hilla, Rinat, Yuval, and Mandy—thank you for being awesome. I am so proud to have you all as my friends. You are the best people I know.

Lastly, to my love, Fabían, thank you from the bottom of my heart. Thank you for being my geeky companion, for expanding my horizons, and for encouraging me to chase my dreams. I could not wish for a better partner than you. Thank you for being my home.

CONTENTS

CHAPTER 1

Introducing Feminism and Fandom

For almost two decades I thought that my fandom was free from being what is commonly termed in popular culture, "problematic." I became a fan of *Buffy the Vampire Slayer* (*BtVS*; 1997–2003) when I was ten years old and still hold the show in high regard to this day. I was conscious of certain troubling storylines that involved the sexual abuse of women, the demonizing depiction of fans and geeks (almost literally!), and the frequent artistic decisions to dispose of much-loved women characters for dramatic effect. I was also aware of the series' lack of diversity and its overall whiteness. Nevertheless, in comparison to other franchises that became popular after *BtVS*, I boasted of my fandom: "my Buffy would never!" I took pride in the feminist icon that is Buffy Summers and kept referring back to her when constructing my narrative of becoming a feminist.

Gradually, my appreciation of the Buffyverse, and particularly of its creator, Joss Whedon, waned. As I learned about Whedon's systematic abuse of women and people of marginalized ethnicity on set, I realized that my fandom, like many others, was flawed. For years, there was speculation about Whedon's difficult behavior and faux feminism. Such accounts reached their peak when Warner Brothers opened an official investigation into Whedon's misconduct during the reshoots of *Justice League* (2017), which included the racism-induced bullying of actor Ray Fisher (Guttmann, 2021; Masters, 2021). Following the investigation, in February 2021,

N. Yodovich, *Women Negotiating Feminism and Science Fiction Fandom*, Palgrave Fan Studies, https://doi.org/10.1007/978-3-031-04079-5_1

1

actress Charisma Carpenter released a statement on Twitter where she depicted the ongoing abuse she underwent while filming *BtVS* and its spinoff series, *Angel* (Vary, 2021). Carpenter's disclosure of her experiences with Joss Whedon opened a floodgate of confessions by other cast members and crew who shared their own sour recollections of working on the series, illustrating an overall toxic work environment (Alter, 2021; Exposito, 2021). Learning that my favorite, most beloved series, the show that had shaped my life, inflicted pain on actors whose work I hold dear was a difficult pill to swallow.

This book, however, is not about *Buffy the Vampire Slayer*. Nevertheless, it is very much inspired by the recurring negotiations of my feminist identity and my passionate involvement with popular culture. As a film buff, I grew up enjoying the works of Roman Polanski and Woody Allen, whose films I will never watch or support again. I am also currently trying to tone down my avid consumption of true crime and crime fiction series, having reached the limit of the number of dead women's naked bodies I can look at and accept as having "entertainment value." At the same time, I have had multiple experiences of cheering certain content for its feminist approach and refreshing diversity, only to learn through online discussions that this text should not be regarded as feminist at all and that it is, in fact, problematic. I have also experienced the heartache of supporting supposedly feminist artistic decisions to cast women, people of marginalized ethnicity, or trans individuals in roles that are traditionally inhabited by white, cishet men, only to see them face an overwhelming backlash. I have similarly internalized that I should not be vocal about being a feminist, or even a woman, in some online fan spaces. This messiness and frequent fractious interactions between fans and the object of their fandom, fans, and feminist notions, and between various fans are the quandary I aim to unravel through this book.

My concerns and inner conflicts are not exclusively my personal dilemma, but a common predicament shared by many other feminists. Feminist women who engage with popular culture frequently debate whether a particular popular culture content is "truly" feminist and if they are "allowed" to identify as fans of "problematic," sexist, or anti-feminist content (Gay, 2014; Krachenfels, 2017; Walsh, 2017). Countless opinion pieces are posted online by feminist writers, debating questions, such as "are you a bad feminist for enjoying misogynistic pop culture" (Krachenfels, 2017), or flat out determining that feminism ruined their ability to consume popular culture as "mindless" fun (Walsh, 2017). Other pieces discuss "problematic faves": popular culture figures, either real or fictional, who are adored despite their racist, homophobic, transphobic, sexist, or ableist attitudes (Melis, 2020; Oluo, 2015; Reed, 2021). One of the most notable works written about feminist guilt is Roxane Gay's book *Bad Feminist* (2014), in which Gay details her shameful engagement with "bad" popular culture contents, such as misogynistic hip-hop music. Gay's work serves as one of the main inspirations of this book.

The main objective of my research is to explore how women negotiate, navigate, and reconcile their feminist stances and become involved with fandoms that are not necessarily feminist. This book unpacks women's negotiation of feminism and fandom by scrutinizing how they define and practice identities and their criteria for a "good" and "real" feminist fan. It examines feminist women fans' encounters with stigma and exclusion by other members in the fan community and their unease with various characters and storylines that are featured in their fandom. Ultimately, after reviewing the frictions and inner tensions, this book also examines the tactics women employ to ameliorate tensions between feminism and fandom.

This research centers on women who explicitly identify as fans and feminists that differ in their age and ethnic and national background. Such women encounter various barriers and discords. Women fans are disregarded by producers and creators who prefer to appease men audiences, are frequently disappointed by the lack of equal women representation in their object of fandom, are constantly policed and silenced in men-dominated fandom communities, and are considered "fake" fans who fawn over the "wrong" things. Linking feminism and fandom provides the opportunity to explore how women navigate between two identities that can be challenging on their own and can potentially be even more burdensome when espoused together.

The scholarly contributions of this book are manifold. First, the book unpacks the ways in which women negotiate complex identities through different stages of forming and honing their identities—from becoming a feminist and fan to belonging in fan and feminist communities and negotiating their versatile identities in fannish and feminist spaces. By doing so, the book highlights the different layers of rifts and struggles that feminist women encounter among themselves, between themselves and other fans or feminists, and with the object of their fandom. Second, this book focuses on women who explicitly identify as fans and feminists. Feminism is not a title that women normally openly espouse. Nevertheless, it is an identity that researchers sometimes attach to fannish practices, without confirming that those who practice it indeed identify as such. Therefore, exploring the discords experienced by women who openly identify as feminist fans presents a fresh and important perspective that reveals practices of gatekeeping and toxicity that women who openly identify as feminist experience. Third, this book also explores the intersection of gender, ethnicity, and age. It acknowledges that "women" are not a homogeneous group, but one that includes various levels of discrimination and privilege. This intersectional perspective accords with current discourses and calls in both fan studies and feminist literature to diversify the literature and step away from using white subjects as our default. Lastly, this book stresses that fandom and feminism are identities that matter to those who espouse them, despite the conflicts in their intersection. It advocates for the unabashed pleasure of popular culture while unraveling the complexity of engaging with it as a feminist woman.

In the following sections, I introduce the theoretical framework that foregrounds my study. Because I am examining complex identities—feminism and fandom—and exploring how women reconcile them, I analyze them through the literature on identity and belonging. As my findings reveal, "feminist" and "fan" are identities that rely on the approval and acceptance of other members of the community to be perceived as legitimate and authentic by the individual espousing them. Therefore, the identity theories I rely on primarily focus on the shaping of identities through social interactions (Cooley, 1992; Goffman, 1956; Mead, 1972; Scott, 2015). Due to the importance of involvement with the community, especially with fandom, I combine identity theories with the scholarship on belonging. Belonging involves the holistic standpoint of the individual, scrutinizes social and communal connections, and examines the implications of processes of inclusion and exclusion (Jenkins, 2014; May, 2013; Stryker & Burke, 2000; Davis, 2011). Thus, it is necessary to integrate identity and belonging in order to fully comprehend the social processes that impact how feminist women fans evaluate their identities.

The feminist and fandom literature I use identifies the rifts and tensions within each community; these clashes also potentially hinder women's ability to identify as fans and feminists. Both fandom and feminism are historically stigmatized identities, which gradually shifted from the margins of society to the mainstream. Fandom, for instance, has slowly become more popular and accepted as a valid lifestyle and identity (Bell, 2013; Orme, 2016; Reinhard, 2018; Salter & Blodgett, 2017). However, the overall acceptance of fandom is given primarily to white, cishet men, while others, such as women, people of marginalized ethnicity, members of the LGBT+ community, or the disabled, remain excluded (Busse, 2013; De Kosnik & carrington, 2019; Larsen & Zubernis, 2011; Morimoto, 2019a; Pande, 2018; Salter & Blodgett, 2017; Wanzo, 2015; Woo, 2018). The literature demonstrates that fan communities are not open and inclusive but, in fact, frequently enforce policing regimes on women fans. Somewhat parallel to fandom, feminism currently enjoys relative popularity and support from news outlets, celebrities, and other public figures (Gay, 2014; Rivers, 2017; Zeisler, 2016). However, despite its appearance as more inviting and inclusionary, feminist thought and feminist communities remain dictated by white women, who tend to ignore the needs and challenges that face marginalized identities (Ahmed, 2004, 2017; Hill Collins, 1990; hooks, 1981; Mohanty, 1988; Ortega, 2006). Such inner rifts, accompanied by a plethora of feminist strands that sometimes contradict each other, contribute to the confusion of women fans in their effort to be "good" feminists (Genz, 2009; Gill & Scharff, 2011; Pugh, 2000; Redfern & Aune, 2010).

My study adds two more lenses to the scrutiny of feminist women fans: ethnicity and age. The inclusion of these factors provides a more nuanced understanding of the experiences of feminist women fans. In both communities and bodies of work, ethnicity and age are seldom considered (Bailey, 1997; De Kosnik & carrington, 2019; Gill, Hamad, Kauser, Negra and Roshini, 2016; Martin, 2019; Pande, 2018; Stanfill, 2018). Therefore, women of marginalized ethnicity and those who are considered "old" in their respective communities experience are added with layers of discrimination and belittlement. Understanding the lack of sufficient scholarly engagement with ethnicity and age in relation to feminism and fandom and their importance to the ways in which women navigate the two communities motivated me to include these social categories in this study.

This chapter is structured as follows. First, I review the primary bodies of literature I engage with, including the research on identity, fandom, and feminism, with particular attention to ethnicity and age in each community and identity. Next, I provide a brief overview of my methodology of interviewing 40 women who identified as feminist fans of *Doctor Who* or *Star Wars*. I then briefly reflect on the terminology I use. I conclude this chapter with an overview of the following chapters and the main arguments they propose.

1.1   The I in Belonging: Introducing Identity and the Literature on Belonging

In her book, *Identity*, Lawler (2014) claims that "identity" is difficult to define, despite its centrality in sociological inquiry: "More or less everyone knows more or less what it means, and yet its precise definition proves slippery" (p. 1). Identity is an amalgamation of the social and structural categories that the individual relates to and with, such as gender, religion, ethnicity, class, and nationality, among others (Hall, 1996; Lawler, 2014; Scott, 2015). It is the lens through which people see and internalize the roles they play in society (Schwalbe & Mason-Schrock, 1996; Williams, 2000). Regardless of changes that might occur in our social surroundings, such as immigrating to a new country or changing occupations, identity provides the reliable foundations on which we construct, perceive, and understand who we are (Hacking, 1999; Hall, 1996; Williams, 2000).

Despite foregrounding the perception of oneself, identity is not theoretically defined as a stable, fixed construct but as a flexible, dynamic process, in which the individual regularly reconfigures the elements that make up who s/he is (Bauman, 2004; Frith, 1996; Giddens, 1991; Hall, 1996; Weir, 2013). Due to its fluidity and complexity, identity is a project that requires tending, developing, and reinforcing in order to feel authentic[1] and be perceived as such by others. As Schwalbe and Mason-Schrock (1996) argue, "Once an identity is defined [...] it is necessary to create opportunities for enacting and reaffirming it" (p. 126). Thus, the approval of the "audience" is imperative in the construction and affirmation of one's identity.

The three major works that acknowledged the importance of the "other" in the construction of one's identity are those of Erving Goffman (1956), George Herbert Mead (1972), and Charles Horton Cooley (1992). In *The Presentation of the Self in Everyday Life* (1956), Goffman offers a dramaturgical theory through which he argues that individuals act as if in a play, continuously performing and externalizing their identities for various audiences. Performance is a two-sided arrangement in which the "performer" can control the situation and the way the audience perceives her. The audience, on their part, receives comprehensive

---

[1] Throughout this book, authenticity is understood as the stamp of approval given to a "successful" performance, which passes as an effortless, coherent externalization of one's values, norms, and beliefs (Bargh et al., 2002; Erickson, 1995; Peterson, 2005).

information regarding the performer and understands how they are expected to respond to the performance. Even though Goffman's theory provides some room for choice and freedom in one's performance, he stresses that many social roles are already established and strictly defined. The individual is obligated to perform her chosen social role accurately and in accordance with the set expectations. If the individual fails to represent her identity correctly, s/he will be in danger of what Goffman (1967) called "losing face."

Attention to the role of the audience in one's performance is also essential to the works of Mead (1972) and Cooley (1992). While Goffman theorized about the representations of the self in interactions with other social players, Mead (1972) focused on interactions with an abstract, imagined "generalized other." Mead contended that the self is a social product. He argued that the individual develops his/her identity to the fullest only when considering how others perceive him/her. However, when Mead reflects on the "other," he does not refer to a specific but rather to a generalized other. The generalized other incorporates attitudes and perceptions by members of society toward the individual. "Only by taking the attitude of the generalized other toward himself, in one or another of these ways, can he think at all," Mead reckoned (1972, p. 156). The individual is never free from the influence of the generalized other; one can fully grasp his/her own identity only through the perceptions of others. In parallel to Mead's theory, Cooley (1992) articulated the concept of the "looking-glass self" to explain how individuals learn about themselves through society's attitudes toward them. According to Cooley, our sense of self and ability to perceive our identities as authentic and coherent are contingent on how we imagine ourselves through the eyes of others.

While the theories of Cooley, Mead, and Goffman have clear implications for women's identities, these theorists neglected to consider how different identity makeups facilitate or hinder one's performance. In other words, such seminal theories ignore gender, ethnicity, age, and other social categories that could impact one's acceptance or rejection by their audience. Nevertheless, and despite their flaws, these theories remain quite relevant. With this research, I add to them by emphasizing the importance of gender, ethnicity, and age to the representation of the self (Goffman) and the generalized other (Mead) through the case of feminist women fans.

The literature on belonging is also helpful in framing the negotiation of one's identity in reference to others. Belonging is a relational process of "identification with, or connection to, cultures, people, places and material objects" (May, 2013, p. 3). Though it may appear to resemble the concept of identity, May (2013) argues that belonging provides a holistic methodological and theoretical approach in which all elements of one's identity are taken into consideration, in contrast to being scrutinized separately, as occurs in most identity-focused studies. It is through our belonging to various communities and social categories that we are able to construct our identities and learn about ourselves (Jenkins, 2014; May, 2013; Stryker & Burke, 2000; Davis, 2011).

Even though belonging is traditionally associated with a sense of well-being and comfort (May, 2013; Miller, 2003), it also creates interpersonal and intrapersonal tensions. Through intrinsic processes of inclusion and exclusion, belonging connotes the differentiation between who is included and who is not. This distinction occurs at both the individual and collective levels where "we" define ourselves and what "we" have in common that separates us from other collectives (Goodin, 1996; Hall, 1996; Jenkins, 2014; May, 2013; Scott, 2015). Inclusion consists of exclusion by default. "We cannot have one without the other," according to Jenkins (2014, p. 21). Processes of inclusion and exclusion are clearly connected to Mead's and Cooley's theories. By marrying these scholarships together, we learn that one needs to feel included, approved of, and embraced by the community, which plays the part of the generalized other, in order to think of oneself in a positive light.

Having introduced the theoretical framework that frames the identities featured in this book, I now discuss them in depth, starting with feminism.

1.2   The I in Feminism? Finding Oneself in the Feminist Community

Feminism, according to hooks (2000), is "a movement to end sexism, sexist exploitation, and oppression" (p. viii). Feminism changes consciousness and develops the awareness of social injustice (Green, 1979; Sowards & Renegar, 2004; Vergès, 2021). It claims the freedom to define oneself (Budgeon, 2011; Faludi, 1991), turns every social "fact" into an opportunity to practice critical thinking (Ahmed, 2017; hooks, 2000;

Weiner-Mahfuz, 2002), and creates a sense of solidarity between women (Dean, 1998; Olufemi, 2020; Ringrose & Renold, 2016; Sweetman, 2013). Despite its significance, "feminist" is not an easy identity to proclaim; it is messy and confusing and can lead to stigma and exclusion (Gay, 2014; Genz, 2009; Green, 1979; McRobbie, 2004; Redfern & Aune, 2010; Walter, 1999). The exact interpretations and paths to achieve feminism's goals are often unclear to many feminists. What should women endorse or reject? What should they consider empowering? How do we achieve social equality? For women of marginalized ethnicity, for instance, these questions are only secondary to other profound questions, such as the following: can feminism be an intellectual and social home for them? Can they identify with a movement that has repeatedly ignored their needs and particular challenges? The uncertainty and fuzzy boundaries between what are appropriate feminist practices and values, and what are not, what is expected from feminists and what feminists should reject, are the questions this book aims to unpack and problematize.

The following section provides a brief overview of historical moments of fissures within the feminist movement, the contrast between feminist waves, and the controversial coverage of feminism in the media. This review is by no means comprehensive but instead presents the primary literature needed to establish the tensions that have led to women's ambivalence toward feminism. It allows to demonstrate how complex, contradictory schools of thought could be confusing for women and raise doubts about their ability to become authentic or "good" feminists.

When discussing feminist waves and strands, I am careful not to overgeneralize and acknowledge that women from disparate historical periods, countries, and cultural backgrounds engage with feminism differently. Even though this review focuses on the UK and the USA—two geographical areas that receive the most academic and media attention in the Western world—I am aware that women from various countries undergo different struggles. This insight is also potentially true for women who live in the same neighborhood but differ in terms of their religion, ethnicity, age, or sexuality. Nevertheless, some distinctions and generalizations are made in order to untangle the historical tensions and differences between feminist schools of thought. To do so, I explore the leading feminist voices related to each period and strand.

I begin the overview with a discussion of the feminist movement in the 1960s and 1970s. These decades are commonly associated with thriving feminist activism (Bailey, 1997; Faludi, 1991; Friedan, 1963; Pugh, 2000).

The inception of the second wave of feminism is traditionally marked by the release of Betty Friedan's book, *The Feminine Mystique*, in 1963 in the USA and the first women's liberation conference at Ruskin College in 1970 in the UK (Pugh, 2000). Backed by a plethora of academic scholarship (Dworkin, 1987; Firestone, 1980; Friedan, 1963; Millett, 1970; Oakley, 1972), and the ethos of "the personal is political," feminists fought against job discrimination, rape, and sexual assault and advocated for women's liberation from the chains of patriarchy.

The thriving feminist activity in the 1960s and 1970s was often besmirched by sensationalized news coverage and demonizing portrayals in popular culture. This includes the vilification of feminist protesters during the Miss America pageant in Atlantic City in 1967, which cemented the trope of the angry, bra-burning feminist in popular culture (Faludi, 1991; Genz, 2009). Other prominent examples of the deprecation of feminist women that occurred in the media during the 1980s include notorious and successful films such as *Fatal Attraction* (1987) and *Kramer vs. Kramer* (1979) (Faludi, 1991; Genz, 2009; Tyler, 2007). The women featured in these movies reflected the moral panic regarding the ramifications of the feminist movement by portraying negligent mothers or careerists who obsessively pursue married men. These movies prompted common accusations that women's emancipation undermined the "natural" social order by emasculating men and increasing divorce rates (ibid.).

The feminist movement not only faced scrutiny from the outside but also was questioned from the inside. Notions such as those expressed in Friedan's seminal book, which called for women to seek self-fulfillment in the workforce, were criticized by women of marginalized ethnicities who were already part of it, employed in exploitative jobs. There is ample research demonstrating white women's blindness to their role in excluding, belittling, and taking advantage of women of marginalized ethnicity and their faux promise of sisterhood (Amos & Parmar, 1984; Hill Collins, 1990; hooks, 1981; Lorde, 1984; Mohanty, 1988; Suleri, 1992). Such academics and activists revealed inherent flaws in the feminist movement in which white women's needs are prioritized and their achievements are gained at the expense of women of marginalized ethnicities. By focusing on themselves, white, middle-class women have become the point of reference for all women, turning those who do not resemble them into an excluded "Other." By setting up the patriarchy as its main rival, feminism neglects to reflect on racism and colonialism, and it ignores white women's contribution to reinforcing such structures (ibid.).

Acknowledging its flawed homogeneity, the third wave of feminism, beginning in the late 1980s and early 1990s, emphasized inclusion, diversity, and pluralism (Budgeon, 2011; Gillis et al., 2004; Heywood & Drake, 1997; Walker, 1995). Third wave feminists were uninterested in dictating a unified list of values and goals of the movement. Instead, they championed individualism and questioned essentialist assumptions about gender, sex, and sexuality (Butler, 1990; Mann & Huffman, 2005; Walker, 1995). With their attempts to stretch the boundaries of feminist discourse, third wavers turned to discuss so-called mundane topics that circulate in everyday life (Kalogeropoulos Householder, 2019; Looft, 2017; Purvis, 2004).

An important term introduced during the third wave of feminism is intersectionality. This wave of feminism used this concept, which is traditionally associated with Kimberlé Crenshaw, to capture the matrix of oppressions that individuals experience due to social categories such as gender, ethnicity, class, and sexuality (Alarcón, 1990; Crenshaw, 1990; Hill Collins & Bilge, 1996). In light of its popularity and prevalence, Cho et al. (2013) asserted that as researchers, it is not enough to simply use the term in order for the analysis to be intersectional. We should explore what intersectionality *does* rather than what it *is* (p. 795). Given their claim, one of the primary goals of this research is to examine the intersection of feminism, fandom, gender, ethnicity, and age and its impact on the ways in which women construct, perceive, and maneuver among their identities.

Simultaneously with the third wave of feminism, postfeminist notions gained prominence during the 1990s and early 2000s. For some of the young women who were born in and after the 1980s, feminism was an outdated movement that had exhausted its goals (Faludi, 1991; Genz, 2009; Pugh, 2000; Redfern & Aune, 2010; Walker, 1995). Therefore, the term "postfeminism" was used to mark the departure from feminism, making it obsolete. Stemming from neoliberal notions, postfeminism's tenets are freedom of choice, individualism, and the desire to "have it all" (Banet-Weiser et al., 2020; Genz, 2009; Gill, 2007; McRobbie, 2004; Rottenberg, 2014). Postfeminists rejected earlier feminist discourses that portrayed women as victims of the patriarchy and instead focused on feeling empowered (Baker, 2010; Genz, 2008; Sorisio, 1997). While 1960s and 1970s radical feminism appeared critical of "feminine" practices, such as mothering children or caring for one's physical appearance, postfeminism did not. The postfeminist stance promoted women's autonomy over their bodies, interests, and passions, and did not condemn traditional feminine roles (Baker, 2010; Banyard, 2010; Gay, 2014; Genz, 2009; Moran,

2013; Munford & Waters, 2014). Consequently, postfeminism provided a contemporary, flexible, accessible home for young women who did not relate to traditional feminist standpoints.

The attempt to turn feminism into a more accessible and alluring notion to women is also prominent in the popular feminism strand. Beginning with books such as *Fear of Flying* (Jong, 1973) and *The Women's Room* (French, 1977) and gaining more recognition in recent years with authors such as Caitlin Moran (2013), Roxane Gay (2014), and Mikki Kendall (2021), popular feminism is a term describing the export of feminism from its academic ivory tower to non-academic audiences. It is led by high-profile journalists, writers, and celebrities who strive to spread feminist thought via an effervescent approach and an unapologetic embrace of femininity and sexuality (Banet-Weiser et al., 2020; Gay, 2014; Moran, 2013; Walter, 1999). While older generations of feminists were outsiders who operated at the fringes of society (whether by forced exclusion or their own volition), younger feminists want to be celebrated in the mainstream (Banet-Weiser, 2018; Walter, 1999). From successful singers jovially parading their feminist identities to decorated tote bags and T-shirts proclaiming that "this is what a feminist looks like," feminism has, arguably, never been more out in the open (Banet-Weiser, 2018; Hobson, 2017; Keller & Ringrose, 2015; Zeisler, 2016).

The permeation of popular feminism expanded alongside the burgeoning of the fourth wave of feminism. Relatively new, the inception of the fourth wave of feminism began around the 2010s, in conjunction with the increased use of social media. In fact, scholars indicate that what separates the fourth wave from its precedents is not its ideologies but the environment in which it operates (Looft, 2017; Rivers, 2017; Winch et al., 2016). Alongside conventional activism in physical spaces, the fourth wave of feminism is characterized by online campaigns, such as #MeToo, #BringBackOurGirls, or #SolidarityIsForWhiteWomen (Bates, 2016; Boyle, 2019; Carter Olson, 2016; Kendall, 2013; Looft, 2017; Mahoney, 2020; Rivers, 2017). Virtual spaces such as LiveJournal, Tumblr, and Twitter provide room for ongoing discussions on feminist issues and the goals that have yet to be achieved.

Feminism's apparent newfound popularity, however, does not mean that the movement has overcome its long-standing challenges. In fact, as Banet-Weiser (2018) argues, due to its current prominence, feminism has attracted strong retaliation from those who oppose the subversion of the status quo, leading to extreme cases of misogyny and sexism. A prominent pop culture example from recent years is the GamerGate controversy, which occurred in 2014. GamerGate marked a surge of ferocious attacks against women gamers, developers, and critics who wanted to be treated as equal members in the video games community, while offering feminist and gender-focused takes on the medium (Chess & Shaw, 2015; Mortensen, 2018; Salter, 2018; Todd, 2015).

In parallel to past decades, the feminist movement not only is criticized and scrutinized by outsiders but also continues to experience inner discord. To start, feminist scholars warn of the drawbacks of pluralism and individualism in feminism (Budgeon, 2011; Favaro & Gill, 2018; hooks, 2000). Accepting all values and practices, finding empowerment in any behavior by women, and refusing to dictate any rules of conduct turns feminism into a fragmented, "floating signifier" (Favaro & Gill, 2018, p. 56), which lacks clear arguments and direction. Banyard (2010) cautions against a "dead-end situation whereby almost anything can be justified as feminist simply by identifying that individual 'choice' and 'agency' were involved" (p. 206). If anything, according to Budgeon (2011), agency or choice must involve some sense of revolt to be considered political or as having activist integrity. Following the dictation of social norms is not necessarily an active choice but a potential act of conforming.

Another cause for concern is the shift to a commodified, apolitical, lighthearted feminism. According to some scholars, turning feminism into a fun, consumable product flattens and dilutes its intellectual gravitas and removes it from its political roots (Banet-Weiser, 2018; Mahoney, 2020; Zeisler, 2016). Certain feminists are suspicious of the marriage between popular culture and feminism. The intertwining of feminism with everyday issues such as fashion, celebrities, video games, or comic books could be perceived as a distraction from traditional political topics that are still in need of political activism. Others argue in favor of this tie, finding popular culture a crucial environment for feminist scrutiny (Gay, 2014; Hobson, 2017; Redfern & Aune, 2010; Sowards & Renegar, 2004; Wood, 2016). The push to criticize popular culture emerges from the understanding that it is not a niche interest of a minuscule group, but a site that attracts the attention of millions worldwide, and reflects, informs, and shapes our perceptions and attitudes (ibid.).

In addition to these ongoing disagreements, scholars call attention to the fact that strands and waves that are depicted as neatly separated exist simultaneously in actuality (Banet-Weiser et al., 2020; Rivers, 2017). Over time, new generations of young women join the feminist movement with novel approaches that perhaps contradict those that veteran feminists still hold. Such generational encounters are frequently depicted as confrontational (Bailey, 1997; Budgeon, 2011; Gill, Hamad, Kauser, Negra, and Roshini, 2016; Whelehan, 2007; Winch, 2015), in which the young reject veteran feminists in a manner described as "bad girls rebelling against dowdy feminist mothers".

In light of the plethora of contrasting feminist strands, women are potentially left with uncertainty regarding the "right" way to practice and perceive feminism. In other cases, women question which of the available feminisms is a suitable intellectual and social home that reflects their identities and particular struggles. In the particular context of this book, women who are also deeply engaged with popular culture, such as science fiction fans, might find themselves unsure if their fandom is harmonious with their feminist identity. For example, as Dow (1996) shared: "To love television as I do and be a committed feminist, as I believe myself to be, will seem oxymoronic to many" (p. xii). In a different example, Roxane Gay famously dubbed herself a "bad feminist" due to the content she enjoyed. Gay (2014) felt ashamed of her passions and interests, which she thought contradicted her feminist identity: "I fall short as a feminist. I feel like […] I am not living up to feminist ideals because of who and how I choose to be" (p. 303). Dow and Gay are not alone here; many feminists have expressed shame and guilt for enjoying popular culture content with sexist or misogynistic undertones (Gay, 2014; Petersen, 2011; Redfern & Aune, 2010; Walker, 1995). The following study is dedicated to unraveling such fissure between feminism and fandom.

1.3   There Is No I in Fandom: Gatekeeping in Science Fiction Fan Communities

Fandom, much like feminism, is a difficult concept to define. Many definitions involve gatekeeping practices that attempt to distinguish between "real" and fake fans and between fans and non-fans (Busse & Gray, 2014; Click & Scott, 2018; Hills, 2002, 2017; Linden & Linden, 2016; Pande, 2020; Reinhard, 2018; Wirman, 2007). Among the plethora of conceptualizations for fandom suggested throughout the years, I concur with the one proposed by Reinhard (2018):

> A fan is someone who repeatedly engages with an object of affection […] the act of repeatedly returning to that object demonstrates cognitive and/

or affective needs that exceeds those of a person who could be classified as a viewer, reader, or player. Being a fan involves bringing together cognitive, affective, and behavioral intentions and orientations to a specific "thing." (p. 4)

Reinhard's definition incorporates the main components of fannish experience: cognitive, affective, and behavioral. To define and grasp fandom, I begin by unpacking Reinhard's model. Scrutinizing each facet of fannish identity is essential for my exploration of how women employ, embrace, or reject each facet in their effort to reconcile feminism and fandom.

Fandom could be interpreted as a cognitive or intellectual engagement with popular culture content. As Hills (2002, p. xiii) describes, fans "produce reams of information on their object of fandom": memorizing quotes, lyrics, stats, names, or filming locations, and demonstrating their connoisseurship with pride (Brown, 1997; Jenkins, 2007; Linden & Linden, 2016; Reinhard, 2018). With details and facts meticulously curated over the years, fans approach the object of their fandom as experts who can professionally analyze the text and reveal its hidden meanings, a practice also known as "forensic fandom" (Hills, 2015; Mittell, 2015; Scott, 2017). The curation of such knowledge is considered, according to Fiske (1992), cultural capital wherein fans gain acclaim and recognition in the community by demonstrating their extensive knowledge of their fandom.

Fans' involvement with the object of their fandom promotes intellectual engagement as well as emotional stimulation (Grossberg, 1992; Lamerichs, 2018; Stein, 2015). Fans' emotional investment includes a deep identification with their beloved content or artist (Brough & Shresthova, 2012; Jenkins, 1992; Jenson, 1992; Linden & Linden, 2016). As Sandvoss (2005) maintains: "The object of fandom [...] is intrinsically interwoven with our sense of self, with who we are, would like to be, and think we are" (p. 96). Furthermore, according to Reinhard (2018), the object of one's fandom embodies their set of values, including religious and political inclinations.

Scholars often use the "behavioral" aspect of fandom, as Reinhard terms it, to distinguish fans from "everyday" popular culture consumers (Abercrombie & Longhurst, 1998; Bacon-Smith, 1992; Jenkins, 2018; Wirman, 2007). The literature on fan studies frequently depicts fans, unlike passive, idle viewers, as very involved in their fandom through various practices. As Bacon-Smith (1992) asserts: "Enjoyment does not arise

out of passive reception but out of active engagement" (p. 16). Many
"behavioral" practices fall under the umbrella term of "transformative
practices," which include the likes of fan fiction[2] (Bacon-Smith, 1992;
Bowman, 2011; de Kosnik, 2013; Larsen & Zubernis, 2011; Pande,
2018; Salter & Blodgett, 2017), fan videos (Brough & Shresthova, 2012),
and cosplay[3] (Lamerichs, 2011, 2018; Rahman et al., 2012; Reagle,
2015). Such transformative practices are traditionally associated with
women fans, whereas intellectual engagement and knowledge curation are
linked with men fans (Bacon-Smith, 1992; Jenkins, 1988; Orme, 2016;
Salter & Blodgett, 2017). I will revisit this gender-based distinction and
its implications for fan hierarchies later in the book.

Despite, or perhaps because of, the plethora of fannish practices that fans
use and their devotion to their fandom, fandom has been heavily stigmatized since its inception. The term "fan" is derived from the Latin word
"fanaticus," which describes fervent belonging to a sacred temple (Jenkins,
2006), associating fandom with exaggerated, senseless devotion (Ali, 2002;
Davidson, 2007). Throughout the years, fans have been regularly patholo-
gized by the media and society as a whole. They have been thought of as
childish, uninhibited, lonely, socially deprived, obsessive individuals (Jenkins,
1988, 1992; Jenson, 1992; Kozinets, 2001; Larsen & Zubernis, 2011;
Lopes, 2006; Salter & Blodgett, 2017). Fans have historically been treated
as "a problem to be solved, a mystery to be understood" (Jenkins, 1988,
p. 470) due to their "improper [...] commitment to something as seemingly unimportant and 'trivial' as a film or TV series" (Hills, 2002, p. x).
Based on fans' passionate adoration of popular culture texts, they have traditionally been regarded as cultural dupes, passive, blind followers, who are
brainwashed by the media (Gray, 2003; Jenkins, 1992; Jenson, 1992).

Over time, with pioneering scholarly work (Bacon-Smith, 1992; Bobo,
1995; Fiske, 1992; Hills, 2002; Jenkins, 1992; Jenson, 1992; Penley,
1992), the development of digital media (another "geeky" interest) and
the normalization of fannish practices such as binge-watching, fandom has
become more mainstream.[4] Science fiction fandom, for instance,

[2] Fan-made storylines inspired by the original diegesis.
[3] Creating costumes and dressing up as characters from the fan content.
[4] Terms such as "nerd," "geek," and "fans" are frequently used interchangeably in scholarship despite their different meanings. A nerd is typically an "odd" outsider who lacks social
skills, a geek is the "brainy" type who is interested in science and technology, and a fan is a
passionate consumer of popular culture content. My focus is on fans, but I will sometimes
use affiliated terms such as geeks and nerds when citing other works or using quotes by my
interviewees, as these terms are frequently intertwined with each other.

constitutes part of a novel "geeky" masculinity, which gradually became accepted as appealing and attractive (Bell, 2013; Orme, 2016; Reinhard, 2018; Salter & Blodgett, 2017). Famous geeky men, such as Mark Zuckerberg (the founder of Facebook), Elon Musk (the founder of Tesla and SpaceX), or Evan Spiegel (the founder of Snapchat), demonstrated the potential of translating geeky interests in science and technology into financial success and popularity with the opposite sex. In popular media, men fans gained recognition through successful television series such as *The Big Bang Theory* (2007–2019), *Silicon Valley* (2014–2019), and *The IT Crowd* (2006–2013), which feature geeky men characters who work in STEM, identify as science fiction fans, and ultimately have long-term relationships with women. After years of scorn and castigation, the stigma associated with science fiction men fans has ameliorated, and they have slowly gained the power to dictate the social fabric of fan communities.

"Fanboys [...] are to some extent enjoying the new cachet of being a nerd [...] no such work yet exists for the fangirls," argue Larsen and Zubernis (2011, p. 9). When it comes to the current normalized status of science fiction fandom, it appears exclusive to white, cishet, abled men. Others who do not fit that category such as women and people who identify with a marginalized ethnicity remain stigmatized (Busse, 2013; Gerrard, 2021; Orme, 2016; Pande, 2018; Scott, 2013; Wanzo, 2015). Scholar Sheryl Garratt (1990) explains that "the word 'fan,' when applied to women, is derogatory. It is always assumed that [...] they are uncritical and stupid" (p. 409). Scholars assert that the stigma on women fans is unique and distinct from that of men fans. While men are considered trivia-obsessed outcasts who spend hours analyzing and memorizing facts regarding their fandom, "fangirls" are perceived as hysterical and emotional. It is assumed that women are drawn to the object of their fandom for shallow reasons, such as the star's good looks, while completely lacking the analytical skills that men possess in order to think critically about their fandom (Busse, 2013; Cohen, Seate, Anderson and Tindage, 2017; Driscoll, 2002; Fan, 2012; Gerrard, 2021; McRobbie, 1991; Salter & Blodgett, 2017; Scott, 2019).

To further complicate the inequality in the social embrace of fans, one must consider other social categories besides gender, such as ethnicity. In general, scholars have drawn attention to the fact that fan studies as a whole rarely reflect on ethnicity and the particular experiences of fans who identify with a marginalized ethnicity (Bobo, 1995; De Kosnik & carrington, 2019; Martin, 2019; Pande, 2018; Stanfill, 2018; Wanzo, 2015; Warner, 2015; Woo, 2018). As Woo (2018) explains, "One reason race has been marginal is because gender and sexuality have been the center of attention" (p. 247). When fandom scholarship examines the discrimination against women in fan communities, it usually misses the fact that "women" are not a homogeneous category but one that includes the intersection of many other identities, such as ethnicity. Even worse, without an intersectional examination of or a particular focus on ethnicity, "fans" are read as exclusively white, thereby erasing the existence of fans of marginalized ethnicity (De Kosnik & carrington, 2019; Pande, 2018; Stanfill, 2018). By ignoring ethnicity, fandom continues to be synonymous with whiteness, and whiteness continues to be unnamed, unmarked, and unarticulated.

Fans of marginalized ethnicity are invisible not only in fan studies but also in fan communities. As Martin (2019) indicates, because fandom, especially science fiction fandom, is considered predominately white, fans of marginalized ethnicity are apprehensive about attending fannish spaces. In other cases, fans of marginalized ethnicity are forced to adjust to the white majority or risk being cast out (Pande, 2018; Rendell, 2019; Thomas & Stornaiuolo, 2019). As Pande (2018) describes, such fans are often considered "fandom killjoys" when they try to challenge the boundaries of fandom, suggest an alternative reading of a beloved text, or critique the treatment of characters of marginalized ethnicity. According to Pande (2018),

> To be a fandom killjoy as a nonwhite fan is a deeply alienating experience, as it involved either the internalized acceptance that certain pleasures and explorations are simply unavailable, or the identification of being someone who consistently brings unwanted drama to fan spaces. (p. 13)

Because white fans coopted otherness and turned it into a "cool" and alternative identity, fans of marginalized ethnicity, who are already othered and marginalized, do not get to enjoy this "mainstreamization" of fandom (Wanzo, 2015).

Another social category that does not receive enough scholarly attention is age, particularly the ways in which it intersects with gender. Bennett (2006), for instance, explained that he had difficulties finding older punk women for his research when examining older punk fans. This statement implies that as women become older, they cease their fannish interests. In other words, older women fans are thought of as a minuscule, almost non-existent sector in fandom. In contrast to this impression, fandom is not experienced exclusively in childhood but continues as fans get older (Ewens, 2020; Harrington et al., 2011, 2014; Way, 2021). In fact, Petersen (2017) found that fandom can even increase in intensity and practical engagement when fans are older because they are less preoccupied with child-rearing or developing their careers. Therefore, Harrington and Bielby (2018) advocate for the inclusion of age and aging in fan scholarship, based on the understanding that fandom changes over time.

Having reviewed the lack of acknowledgment of fan communities' diverse social and cultural makeup, some of the questions that remain open regard the processes contribute to the erasure of certain sectors and their effect on such excluded individuals. Fans discriminate against each other and create hierarchies based on the content they endorse and the practices in which they take part. Thus, they treat certain fans, like women and people of marginalized ethnicity, as suspects until they prove their authenticity (Booth & Kelly, 2013; Fiske, 1992; Hills, 2002, 2015; Larsen & Zubernis, 2011; Linden & Linden, 2016; Van de Goor, 2015). According to Salter and Blodgett (2017), years of stigma and exclusion before moving from the fringes of society to its mainstream have made those who see themselves as veteran science fiction fans hostile to so-called newcomers:

> Geeks used to the marginalization of the chosen media and fandoms have been given a choice: embrace the new popularity and surge of interest [...] or defend the terrain from those less dedicated, who have never suffered from their geekdom. Many geeks have visibly chosen the latter. (p. 11)

Geekdom has only recently become a legitimate form of masculinity. Therefore, allowing women to identify as geeks and as science fiction fans might, yet again, turn fandom into a hobby or interest that is not masculine. As Banet-Weiser asserts (2018), "Women are framed within toxic geek masculinity as the central problematic issue" (p. 154). She goes on to argue that it is not only that women, in general, are considered a "problem" and that "feminism is a threat to geeks" (2018, p. 159). Scholars like Banet-Weiser, Scott (2019), and Salter and Blodgett (2017) have all discussed toxic geek masculinity and its antagonism toward women and feminism. What is missing in these insightful works is the experiences of feminist women fans who participate in fan communities, told from their perspectives and their own voices.

1.4   BRINGING FEMINISM AND FANDOM TOGETHER

Juxtaposing feminism and fandom reveals the similarities between the two identities. Identifying as "fan" and "feminist" might mean carrying a burden of stigma and criticism, as both appear "too" passionate, hysterical, and obsessed (Ali, 2002; Driscoll, 2002; Faludi, 1991; Pugh, 2000; Walter, 1999). Once deciding to embrace the labels of feminists or fans, women also have to prove they are authentic. As described earlier, feminist women are sometimes overwhelmed by the abundance of feminist discourses and cannot discern the "right" way to practice feminism (Gay, 2014; Genz, 2009; Gill, 2007; McRobbie, 2004; Moran, 2013). On the other hand, women fans must also deal with opposition from their male counterparts, who are eager to keep their fan community exclusive (Bacon-Smith, 1992; Orme, 2016; Reagle, 2015). While these impasses are prominent in both identities individually, I maintain that they are amplified when women proclaim both identities in conjunction. Moreover, fandom and feminism are similar in the contrast between their subversive, nonconformist appearance and inherent exclusionary practices toward those who do not align with the predominant social fabric (Findlen, 1995; Hill Collins, 1996; hooks, 1981; Lugones, 2010; Pande, 2018; Phipps, 2020; Reinhard, 2018; Wanzo, 2015).

It is acceptable to argue that the academic scrutiny of fandom was built upon feminist foundations, with a particular interest in women fans' practices and spaces (Bacon-Smith, 1992; Click & Scott, 2018; Hannell, 2020; Penley, 1992). Studies about women-focused spaces and practices, such as fan fiction communities or reading groups, imbued fan studies with feminist motifs such as political activism and camaraderie (Ang, 2013 [1982]; Bacon-Smith, 1992; Bury, 2005; Busse, 2015; Hannell, 2020; Penley, 1992; Radway, 1984). This tradition has carried on throughout the years with scholars who identify as feminists and incorporate feminist lenses and literature into their work (Busse, 2005, 2013, 2015; Scott, 2013, 2017, 2019; Stein, 2015). At the same time, Penley (1992) shared that the women fans in her study were hesitant to identify as feminists. In other cases, research subjects were not asked directly if they regarded their actions as feminist. Instead, it was the scholars who injected feminist meaning into women fans' practices and communities. As Phillips (2020) argues, feminism is conventionally "projected onto the bodies of dissenting folks that happen to be nearby" (p. 64). In other words, the mere act of resistance and critique in fan communities is translated as a feminist act, regardless of how the individuals engaging in these actions see themselves. Identifying as a feminist is a complex, messy, ambivalent process, which is frequently accompanied by the social price of stigma and ridicule. Therefore, it would not be a stretch to assume that the women in previous studies might have not identified as feminists. As a result, the significance of this study is contributing to the current body of work that engages with fandom and feminism by exploring women who explicitly identify as fans and feminists and how they negotiate the two identities, as depicted in their own words.

1.5   METHODOLOGY

This book is based on 40 semi-structured in-depth interviews with women who identify as feminists and fans of *Doctor Who* or *Star Wars*. In the following section, I review the feminist methodology that guided this research. I explain my decision to focus on *Doctor Who* and *Star Wars* as my primary case studies and the demographics of my interviewees. In addition, I reflect on the challenges that arose throughout the study and my position in the field.

My study espouses a feminist methodology. Like many theories and concepts, the umbrella term "feminist methodology" is often questioned and contested. Ramazanoglu and Holland (2002) depict its fuzziness by arguing that no method or research topic is distinctively feminist. Nevertheless, they explain that a methodology could be considered feminist when grounding its inquiry in its participants' experiences and making a political and ethical commitment to ensuring that their voices are heard. Feminist explorations recognize that women's perspectives and stories are frequently absent in what is regarded as "common" knowledge (Hesse-Biber, 2007; Maynard, 1994). This is no different in science fiction fandoms, where women are still underrepresented and excluded from meaning-making processes (Brown, 1997; Linden & Linden, 2016; Nyberg, 1995; Orme, 2016; Salter & Blodgett, 2017; Stanfill, 2018). Therefore, I tried to provide women with the opportunity to construct narratives about their identities.

To communicate women's stories through their own perspectives, those who use feminist methodology usually turn to qualitative research

(Denzin & Lincoln, 1998; Oakley, 1981; Olesen, 1988, 2005; Punch, 1988; Reinharz & Davidman, 1992). Qualitative in-depth interviews, in general, and semi-structured interviews, in particular, are considered as being well-suited to a nuanced exploration of the participants' subjectivities, as they encourage them to open up and elaborate on their thoughts, opinions, and personal experiences (Kvale, 2007; Punch, 1988). As stated, one of my main motivations in conducting semi-structured interviews was speaking *with* feminist women fans, not *about* or *for* them (Zakaria, 2021).

Participants were recruited online and offline through a poster calling for women who identified as feminists and fans of *Doctor Who* or *Star Wars*. The interviewees' self-identification was imperative in the recruitment process because I conducted the interviews only with women who explicitly identified as both feminists and fans. The definitions of and terms for fandom and feminism were open to the participants' interpretations. While Duffett (2013) wondered whether his participants were "actual" fans (p. 256), I accepted all of the interviewees at face value. In accordance with feminist methodology (Ramazanoglu & Holland, 2002), I did not force my definitions or expectations on the participants. They did not have to fit a specific theoretical definition of fandom and feminism. In fact, part of the analysis focused on the interviewees' terminology for feminism and fandom and the practices in which they engaged to perform these identities and ensure that they were seen as authentic by other members of their communities.

For the purpose of this research, I had to choose fandoms and franchises that might not align with women's feminist values. I was interested in focusing on texts in the "gray," blurry area of feminist reception, which could be empowering to some and contested by others. These fuzzy moments in which feminist women fans are unsure if they should commend or condone their fandom are the exact tensions I was keen to unpack.

Based on these considerations, this study centered on two case studies: the fandoms of *Star Wars* and *Doctor Who*. *Star Wars* was first released in 1977 and has become a cultural phenomenon and a major blockbuster. So far, the franchise includes three cinematic trilogies (1977–1983, 1999–2005, and 2015–2019), animated movies and television series, spinoff novels, comic books, video games, and more. The space opera's first trilogy (1977–1983) centered on Luke Skywalker's journey of self-revelation and becoming a Jedi, with the purpose of defeating Darth Vader and the evil galactic empire. Throughout the movies, Luke was accompanied by the charismatic Han Solo and the fierce Princess Leia. The prequel trilogy (1999–2005) detailed the origin of Darth Vader and his transformation from Jedi to Sith Lord. The third trilogy (2015–2019) developed the storyline of the first trilogy. The sequels included a woman protagonist, Rey, and featured Luke, Han Solo, and Leia from the original films. The success of *Star Wars* was and still is a worldwide cultural phenomenon, with overall box office revenues of more than nine billion US dollars (The Numbers, n.d.).

Like *Star Wars*, *Doctor Who* also gained prestige in popular culture over the years. Debuting on BBC in 1963, *Doctor Who* is the longest-running science fiction television series of all time.[5] *Doctor Who* is interwoven in British culture and has received high acclaim and success worldwide. The series follows a human-formed alien called the Doctor and his adventures through time and space. The Doctor is frequently joined by a human "companion" (the Doctor's sidekick, formally known as "assistant," and currently called "friend"), who is, more often than not, a young woman. Every few years, the Doctor regenerates into a new human form (the starring actor is replaced by a new one) and teams up with new companion/s. As a long-running series, *Doctor Who*'s ratings have fluctuated over the years, but the series has nevertheless continued to attract millions of viewers across the world each season (Doctor Who Guide, n.d.).

I selected these case studies not only due to their popularity but also because of their perceived male-dominated fandoms (Hadas, 2013; Harrison, 2020; Jowett, 2014; Widmayer, 2017). Despite their cultural status, with almost unparalleled success, *Doctor Who* and *Star Wars* are traditionally coopted by white, cishet men. At the same time, other audiences, such as women and people who identify with a marginalized identity, are not considered target audiences. For instance, I experienced firsthand men fans' dominance over the *Star Wars* fandom on several occasions while recruiting my participants. After posting my call for participants in an online forum, I received the following message:

Um … this is a sausage disco. The last girl on this forum turned about to be an American male long haul lorry driver. The one before that is still in her hospital bedroom theatre set in Scotland.

---

[5] The series was canceled in 1989, returned as a television film in 1996, and then rebooted in 2005 and has been airing ever since.

Other belittling, hateful messages were also sent my way regarding my interest in studying women, feminism, and marginalized ethnicities, terms, and populations that frequently trigger venomous reactions in some online spaces. Such responses exemplify the policing regimes and overall dismissal that marginalized fans encounter.

Doctor Who and *Star Wars* have also recently cast women in leading roles alongside new characters of a marginalized ethnicity. These new characters generated a massive backlash and exposed fractures in their respective fan communities (Belam, 2018; Blay, 2017; Chichizola, 2018; Duff, 2017). Such significant changes and the uproar that followed provided a fascinating opportunity to explore how feminist women fans navigated the backlash and the retaliation against inclusion and diversity. Lastly, choosing *Star Wars* and *Doctor Who* was also a practical decision. Since I was interested in incorporating feminist women fans from a wide age range, *Star Wars* and *Doctor Who* provided suitable case studies. Despite debuting in the 1960s (*Doctor Who*) and 1970s (*Star Wars*), both franchises still release new content. Thanks to their longevity in popular culture, I was able to recruit women from different age groups.

Ultimately, 40 women participated in the study. Of them, 16 interviewees identified as *Doctor Who* fans, 13 were *Star Wars* fans, and 11 defined themselves as fans of both franchises. In accordance with Hills' (2002) claim regarding fans' multiplicity of fandoms, the participants did not exclusively identify as fans of *Star Wars* and *Doctor Who*, but of many other franchises. Therefore, the analysis and findings focus on the interviewees' readings of *Doctor Who* and *Star Wars* but address other franchises when relevant. The interviewees' ages ranged from 19 to 55, and their average age was 36.5. The participants were from various countries, such as the UK, the USA, Australia, Ireland, Spain, France, Germany, Italy, and Switzerland. Of 40 interviewees, 29 were white, while 11 participants self-identified as Indian, Chinese, Latina/Chicana, African American/Black, and mixed.

I conducted the fieldwork between 2017 and 2020. Most of the interviews took place at the end of 2017, followed by email correspondence with some of the interviewees from the first round in 2018. Another round of recruitment and interviews occurred in late 2020. Most interviews were conducted online, via Skype and Zoom, and 15 interviews were face-to-face. The interviews were divided into three sections and themes: fandom, feminism, and being feminist fans of *Doctor Who* and *Star Wars*. Questions focused on the interviewees' process of becoming fans and feminists, their motivations to identify as such, and the challenges associated with these identities. The structure of the interview required the participants to provide retrospective reports, starting from their childhoods, the time they started identifying as fans, until today. The motivation to create a detailed biographical account of each participant's life was inspired by the literature on identity, which sees it as an ongoing, constructive process (Bauman, 2004; Frith, 1996; Giddens, 1991; Hall, 1996; Weir, 2013). The interviewees' past reflections told of who they were in the past and informed how they perceived themselves in the present, based on the details and examples they chose to emphasize.

Having presented the details of the methodology, I also want to reflect on my positionality and the limitations of this research. As I shared in the introduction, I, too, am a feminist and a fan. A fan researching other fans is not an anomaly in fan studies. In fact, many fandom scholars are fans themselves (Anderson, 2012; Bacon-Smith, 1992; Hills, 2002; Pande, 2018; Scott, 2019). Given this common phenomenon, researchers have coined the term "aca-fan" to conceptualize the frequency of such a pairing between fandom and academia (Hills, 2002; Jenkins, 2006). Nevertheless, over the years, and as I delved deeper into the scholarly exploration and conceptualization of fandom, I felt like an outsider. I related to Williams' contemplations on the definition of "aca-fan" on Morimoto's podcast, *It's a Thing*:

> I, in many ways, feel sometimes like an outlier in fan studies [...] I've never written fan fiction. I've never made fan videos [...] So, for me, I've always felt like the way that I think about my fandom is much more about me as an individual. I feel like I kind of flirt around the periphery of fandoms [...] I think I'm probably more a scholar-fan rather than a fan-scholar, in that my academic interests sometimes come first. (Morimoto, 2019b, 3:50)

Like Williams, I also experience fandom as an individual, emotional, almost monogamous connection with popular culture. I do not associate with many fandoms, and I rarely feel the need to share them with others or express my love toward them through artistic channels. This position means that I am close enough to fandom to have insider knowledge but also distant enough to question it.

Another aspect of my identity I must reflect on is my whiteness. As previously reviewed, fan scholars often shy away from scrutinizing ethnicity in relation to fandom. According to Pande (2020), white scholars usually confess on feeling unequipped to discuss race or worrying about "getting it wrong." By refraining from addressing such vital topics, they continue the erasure of fans of marginalized ethnicity, and the scholars who are marginalized themselves are left with this cumbersome duty (Chin et al., 2017; De Kosnik & carrington, 2019; Pande, 2020; Woo, 2018). Understanding the importance of engaging with ethnicity in relation to fandom and feminism motivated me to incorporate this prism in my study. At the same time, I, too, am wary of "getting it wrong." Using a qualitative methodology and conducting in-depth interviews allowed me to hone in on the participants' accounts and ground my findings and arguments in their narratives. Therefore, the following chapters are primarily based on a careful reading and illustrations of the experiences shared with me in the interviews.

With this book, I do not attempt to speak for all women, nor can I do so. While I tried to undertake intersectional research, the majority of the participants lived in Western countries and were white-identified, educated, abled, cisgender, and middle class. I am also conscious of the limited generalizability of a study with "only" 40 participants. Yet, as the following chapters indicate, the interviews produced rich, detailed, rigorous portrayals of women's navigation of feminism and fandom. Even though gender, ethnicity, and age are my main prisms for studying feminist fans, I weave into my analysis moments where these identities intersect with working-class background, queerness, and asexuality, based on other identities that the interviewees disclosed to me. Although I cannot provide a grand theory or a depiction of all feminist women fans, I hope that readers find themselves among the voices included in this book.

1.6   Terminology

Since identity is a vital prism through which I frame my findings, it is essential to discuss the terminology used for some of the identities that are scrutinized in this book. Focusing on gender rather than sex, I defined my participants as "women fans," even though "female fans" is more common in fan studies (Crawford & Gosling, 2004; Jenkins, 1992; Larsen & Zubernis, 2011; Orme, 2016; Reinhard, 2018; Scott, 2013). Because this study is driven by an interest in the cultural and social meanings of being a woman who engages in a men-dominated identity and community, "woman fan" was more suitable.

Defining the participants' ethnicity and race was more challenging because many related terms are considered essentialist, flattening, or simply "problematic" (Fields, 2001; Hochman, 2019; Jenkins, 2008; Nayak, 2006; Pande, 2018, 2020; Rai, 2021). In both of her books, Pande pondered about the appropriate term to define her participants, including concepts such as "fans of color" and "nonwhite fans." These were also accompanied by definitions such as racial minority, racialized people, or BIPOC. Ultimately, I chose the umbrella term "women of marginalized ethnicities." Ethnicity symbolizes a shared meaning that is embedded in one's "everyday" culture. It is used to mark differences between social groups based on their distinct historical and geographical background. Ethnicity is considered a flexible term, encompassing the identification processes of an individual or a collective that are produced and reproduced through social interactions and self-identification (Ghai, 2000; Hall, 2017; Jenkins, 2008; Purkayastha, 2005). Using "ethnicity" allowed me to address the diverse cultural backgrounds of my participants without "othering" anyone (a risk that could occur with terms such as "nonwhite" or "people of color," which perpetuate whiteness as the norm). Furthermore, by using the prefix "marginalized," I addressed the active practices to push certain ethnicities to the periphery and turn them into outsiders. Such ethnicities are not minorities in objective numbers, nor did they choose to be marginal; they are purposively and structurally marginal*ized*. I am aware that the term "fans of marginalized ethnicities" is not perfect. Like other concepts, it ties together ethnicities that are inherently different from each other. While I wanted to provide a nuanced analysis of my interviewees' particular challenges, I was also eager to demonstrate their similar struggles with facing stigma and exclusion in fan and feminist communities through this umbrella definition.

The last identity I examined, age, also necessitated reflection on the terminology. Since I was also interested in exploring the particular experiences of women fans from a wide array of age groups, I had to decide who was considered "young" and "old" among my interviewees. Like other concepts, age, too, is a contextual social construct (Hazan, 1994; Riley et al., 1972; Ward, 2010). For example, as my study found, in fan communities, fans age relatively quickly and are considered "old" as early as when they reach their 20s or 30s. Therefore, the participants described as "old" or "older" in this book are those who referred to themselves as such or encountered ageism in their respective fan communities. These interviewees include women who are in their 30s, as well as those who are over

50. The term "old" or "older" is often written in quoatation marks to emphasize that the term is biased, socially constructed, and far from marking one's identity objectively.

To conclude, choosing the terminology to use in this book brought with it a number of issues and concerns. Because this study focuses on gatekeeping and exclusion, it was my goal to ensure that the terms I espouse were inclusionary, non-judgmental, and conscious of social constructs and their implications for our everyday lives. In some cases, the chosen concepts led to "wordy" articulation, and in others, they might not be the perfect fit. Nevertheless, I hope that the terms I used to describe my participants serve the purpose of this study and do the interviewees justice.

1.7   STRUCTURE OF THE BOOK

This book's chapters highlight the different aspects of a feminist woman fan's identity: becoming, being, belonging, representing, and reconciling. Each chapter unravels the complexity, ambivalence, and contradictions between feminism and fandom and later reveals the tactics women develop to overcome them.

The second chapter dealing with my findings, "Becoming a Feminist Fan," reviews the interviewees' biographical narratives, focusing on the routes that led them to identify as fans and feminists. These narratives are accompanied by an exploration of the ways in which the participants expressed and embodied feminism and fandom by taking part in various practices. This chapter introduces feminist women fans' ambivalence regarding the tie between identity and practice regardless of the quantity or quality of their activities. The interviewees claimed that no particular action should be needed in order for them to be entitled to claim fan and feminist identities, but simultaneously felt they were not doing "enough" to be worthy of them. The feelings that are introduced in this chapter foreground the following chapters, which continue to unpack the reasons and mechanisms that contribute to feminist women fans experiencing inner frictions.

After illustrating the paths that lead the interviewees to feminism and fandom, Chap. 3, "Being a Feminist Fan," scrutinizes the ways in which identities such as gender, ethnicity, and age intersect with fandom and feminism. The common thread in the amalgamation of the identities reviewed here is that they are all assumed to be non-existent or a minority in fan and feminist communities, when, in fact, they are actively pushed to the margins and considered illegitimate. Moments of breakage and frictions are framed through the concept of self-categorization in which the participants learned to prioritize the different identities and communities they were associated with, in order to deflect judgment or inner contradictions. This chapter demonstrates the ways in which the fan and feminist identities are challenged, prioritized, or stifled depending on context and time, illustrating moments where certain identities are externalized over others, depending on the situation.

Chapter 4, "Belonging as a Feminist Fan," zooms out and explores feminist women fans' interactions with other members in their community and the ways in which they affect and shape their identities. This chapter primarily focuses on gatekeeping and toxic discourses in science fiction fan communities and their direct impact in the form of the interviewees' feelings of inauthenticity. In this chapter I introduce the concept of conditional belonging, which depicts the liminal state in which feminist women fans exist in fan communities, where they have to prove they deserve to be included. I discuss the two main conditions for belonging to science fiction fandoms: proof of connoisseurship about the object of the fandom and the silencing of their feminist identities/perspectives. The main argument presented in this chapter is that feminist women fans' state of conditional belonging disrupts their ability to perceive themselves as genuine fans and therefore leads to feelings of self-doubt and practices of self-policing.

In Chap. 5, "Representing Women and Feminism in Fandom," I examine how feminist women fans perceive and engage with their favorite content, *Doctor Who* and *Star Wars*, focusing particularly on moments of identification and alienation. The main lens of analysis in Chap. 5 is "representation" and the lively debates on its importance (or unimportance) in popular culture and its contribution to viewers' identities and self-perceptions. The debates on the tie between representation and identification are framed in this chapter through feminist women fans' reading of four women characters: Leia Organa and Rose Tico from *Star Wars* and Martha Jones and the 13th Doctor from *Doctor Who*. The chapter demonstrates the parallels between feminist women fans and the women characters featured in their favorite franchises. Both fans and characters experience continuous belittlement, sexism, racism, and retaliation. Through the ways in which women characters are written, portrayed, and received by the general audience, feminist women fans learn about their own position in the fan community. The chapter also explores the fractures in the feminist woman fan's identity. It demonstrates the difficulty of enjoying content while acknowledging its dismissal and belittlement of its women characters, as well as the viewers who love and promote them.

After revealing the various complications of espousing both fan and feminist identities, I finally review the various tactics that women develop and use to navigate between them. Chapter 6, "Reconciling Feminism and Fandom," includes two clusters of tactics that emerged from the study: "narrative" and "practice." "Narrative tactics" include three justifications and rationalizations that feminist women fans use to allow them to ignore or accept aspects of their fandom that clash with their feminist perspectives. "Practice tactics" reintroduce the fannish practices that were reviewed in Chap. 2. In this context, these practices are redefined as avenues through which women fans practice their feminist identity while pushing the community and the content toward a more equal, inclusive representation of women. The primary purposes for feminist women fans' tactics are as follows: (1) reconciling tensions between fandom and feminism, (2) protecting their identities from being threatened, (3) allowing the enjoyment of fandoms even while criticizing them, and (4) combining feminism and fandom in order to promote equality in the beloved content and fandom community.

Chapter 7, "Finding a Space(ship) of One's Own," marks the conclusion of this book. Here, I tie the findings together and ultimately claim that being a feminist woman fan is hard work, particularly in light of the constant scrutiny and toxicity women experience in their respective communities. Due to ongoing feelings of inadequacy and inauthenticity, women fans constantly have to maneuver between their multiple identities and prove they are "legitimate" in order to alleviate tensions. Thus, in the concluding chapter, I question the importance of producing coherent identities and invite scholars, feminists, and fans alike, to embrace ambivalence and inner contradictions.

The ultimate purpose of this book is not only to offer answers to vital questions but also to open up new queries about the way in which we construct and evaluate identities, especially those of fans and feminists. As I shared earlier, I am still conflicted about some of these questions and have used this book as my first attempt to tackle them and share my resolutions with others. Therefore, I hope that the findings of this book and the engaging accounts it includes will resonate with the readers, provide food for thought, and invite them to ask more questions. Let our journey begin.

References

Abercrombie, N., & Longhurst, B. J. (1998). *Audiences: A sociological theory of performance and imagination*. SAGE Publications Ltd.
Ahmed, S. (2004). Declarations of whiteness: The non-performativity of antiracism. *Borderlands* e-journal, *3*(2). http://www.borderlandsejournal.adelaide.edu.au/vol3no2_2004/ahmed_declarations.htm
Ahmed, S. (2017). *Living a feminist life*. Duke University Press.
Alarcón, N. (1990). The theoretical subject(s) of this bridge called my back and Anglo-American feminism. In G. Anzaldúa (Ed.), *Making face, making soul/haciendo caras: Creative and critical perspectives by women of color* (pp. 356–369). Aunt Lute Foundation.
Ali, S. (2002). Friendship and fandom: Ethnicity, power and gendering readings of the popular. *Discourse: Studies in the Cultural Politics of Education, 23*(2), 153–165.
Alter, B. (2021, February 10). Charisma Carpenter accuses Joss Whedon of creating a toxic work environment. *Vulture*. Retrieved July 2, 2021, from https://www.vulture.com/2021/02/charisma-carpenter-joss-whedon-toxic-work-environment.html
Amos, V., & Parmar, P. (1984). Challenging imperial feminism. *Feminist Review, 17*(1), 3–19.
Anderson, T. (2012). Still kissing their posters goodnight: Female fandom and the politics of popular music. *Journal of Audience & Reception Studies, 9*(2), 239–264.
Ang, I. (2013[1982]). *Watching Dallas: Soap opera and the melodramatic imagination*. Routledge.
Bacon-Smith, C. (1992). *Enterprising women: Television fandom and the creation of popular myth*. University of Pennsylvania Press.
Bailey, C. (1997). Making waves and drawing lines: The politics of defining the vicissitudes of feminism. *Hypatia, 12*(3), 17–28.
Baker, J. (2010). Claiming volition and evading victimhood: Post-feminist obligations for young women. *Feminism & Psychology, 20*(2), 186–204.
Banet-Weiser, S. (2018). *Empowered: Popular feminism and popular misogyny*. Duke University Press.
Banet-Weiser, S., Gill, R., & Rottenberg, C. (2020). Postfeminism, popular feminism and neoliberal feminism? Sarah Banet-Weiser, Rosalind Gill and Catherine Rottenberg in conversation. *Feminist Theory, 21*(1), 3–24.
Banyard, K. (2010). *The equality illusion: The truth about women and men today*. Faber & Faber.

Bargh, J. A., McKenna, K. Y., & Fitzsimons, G. M. (2002). Can you see the real me? Activation and expression of the "true self" on the Internet. *Journal of Social Issues, 58*(1), 33–48.

Bates, L. (2016). *Everyday sexism.* Macmillan.

Bauman, Z. (2004). *Identity: Conversations with Benedetto Vecchi.* Polity Press.

Belam, M. (2018, January 17). Star Wars actors mock fan who recut film to remove women. *The Guardian.* Retrieved April 8, 2019, from https://www.theguardian.com/film/2018/jan/17/star-wars-actors-mock-fan-recut-film-remove-women

Bell, D. (2013). Geek myths: Technologies, masculinities, globalizations. In J. Hearn, M. Blagojević, & K. Harrison (Eds.), *Rethinking transnational men: Beyond, between and within nations* (pp. 92–106). Routledge.

Bennett, A. (2006). Punk's not dead: The continuing significance of punk rock for an older generation of fans. *Sociology, 40*(2), 219–235.

Blay, Z. (2017, July 19). 'Doctor who' backlash exposed the irony of men who don't want women in fandom. *Huffington Post.* Retrieved April 18, 2019, from http://www.huffingtonpost.co.uk/entry/doctor-who-backlash-exposed-the-irony-of-men-who-dont-want-women-in-fandom_us_596f642ce4b0000eb1978720

Bobo, J. (1995). *Black women as cultural readers.* Columbia University Press.

Booth, P., & Kelly, P. (2013). The changing faces of Doctor Who fandom: New fans, new technologies, old practices? *Participations, 10*(1), 56–72.

Bowman, T. (2011). What is fanfiction and why are people saying such nice things about it? *Storyworlds: A Journal of Narrative Studies, 3*, 1–24.

Box office history for Star Wars movies. *The Numbers.* Retrieved December 20, 2017, from https://www.the-numbers.com/movies/franchise/Star-Wars#tab=summary

Boyle, K. (2019). *# MeToo, Weinstein and feminism.* Palgrave Pivot.

Brough, M. M., & Shresthova, S. (2012). Fandom meets activism: Rethinking civic and political participation. *Transformative Works and Cultures, 10*, 1–27.

Brown, J. A. (1997). Comic book fandom and cultural capital. *Popular Culture, 30*(4), 13–31.

Budgeon, S. (2011). *Third-wave feminism and the politics of gender in late modernity.* Springer.

Bury, R. (2005). *Cyberspaces of their own: Female fandoms online.* Peter Lang.

Busse, K. (2005). 'Digital get down': Postmodern boy band slash and the queer female space. In C. Malcolm & J. Nayman (Eds.), *Eroticism in American culture: Essays on the culture and literature of desire* (pp. 104–125). Gdansk University Press.

Busse, K. (2013). Geek hierarchies, boundary policing, and the gendering of the good fan. *Participations, 10*(1), 73–91.

Busse, K. (2015). Fan labor and feminism: Capitalizing on the fannish labor of love. *Cinema Journal, 54*(3), 110–115.

Busse, K., & Gray, J. (2014). Fan cultures and fan communities. In V. Nightingale (Ed.), *The handbook of media audiences* (pp. 425–443). Wiley-Blackwell.

Butler, J. (1990). *Gender trouble and the subversion of identity.* Routledge.

Carter Olson, C. (2016). # BringBackOurGirls: Digital communities supporting real-world change and influencing mainstream media agendas. *Feminist Media Studies, 16*(5), 772–787.

Chess, S., & Shaw, A. (2015). A conspiracy of fishes, or, how we learned to stop worrying about #GamerGate and embrace hegemonic masculinity. *Journal of Broadcasting & Electronic Media, 59*(1), 208–220.

Chichizola, C. (2018, August 21). Star Wars' Kelly Marie Tran opens up about leaving social media after Last Jedi backlash. *Cinema Blend.* Retrieved August 21, 2021, from https://www.cinemablend.com/news/2456089/star-wars-kelly-marie-tran-opens-up-about-leaving-social-media-after-last-jedi-backlash

Chin, B., Punathambekar, A., & Shresthova, S. (2017). Advancing transcultural fandom: A Conversation. In M. A. Scott & S. Scott (Eds.), *The Routledge companion to media fandom* (pp. 298–306). Routledge.

Cho, S., Crenshaw, K. W., & McCall, L. (2013). Toward a field of intersectionality studies: Theory, applications, and praxis. *Signs: Journal of women in culture and society, 38*(4), 785–810.

Click, M. A., & Scott, S. (2018). Introduction. In M. A. Scott & S. Scott (Eds.), *The Routledge companion to media fandom* (pp. 1–7). Routledge.

Cohen, E. L., Atwell Seate, A., Anderson, S. M., & Tindage, M. F. (2017). Sport fans and Sci-Fi fanatics: The social stigma of popular media fandom. *Psychology of Popular Media. Culture, 6*(3). https://doi.org/10.1037/ppm0000095

Cooley, C. H. (1992 [1902]). *Human nature and the social order.* Transaction Publishers.

Crawford, G., & Gosling, V. K. (2004). The myth of the 'Puck Bunny' female fans and men's ice hockey. *Sociology, 38*(3), 477–493.

Crenshaw, K. (1990). Mapping the margins: Intersectionality, identity politics, and violence against women of color. *Stanford Law Review, 43*, 1241–1301.

Davidson, S. (2007). Days of happiness: Female teenager fans of pop groups [in Hebrew]. *Trends in Israeli Society, 45*(1), 121–144.

Davis, A. Y. (2011). *Women, race, & class.* Vintage.

De Kosnik, A. (2013). Interrogating 'free' fan labor. http://spreadablemedia.org/essays/kosnik/index.html#.X4IQvdBKhPZ

De Kosnik, A. & carrington, a. (2019). Fans of color, fandoms of color. *Transformative Works & Cultures, 29*: n.p.

Dean, J. (1998). Feminist solidarity, reflective solidarity: Theorizing connections after identity politics. *Women & Politics, 18*(4), 1–26.

Denzin, N. K., & Lincoln, Y. S. (1998). Introduction. In N. K. Denzin & Y. S. Lincoln (Eds.), *The landscape of qualitative research (Vol. 1)* (pp. 1–34). Sage.

Doctor Who Guide: Ratings Guide. (n.d.). *Doctor Who Guide.* Retrieved December 20, 2017, from https://guide.doctorwhonews.net/info.php?detail=ratings

Dow, B. J. (1996). *Prime time feminism: Television, media culture, and the women's movement since 1970.* University of Pennsylvania Press.

Driscoll, C. (2002). *Girls: Feminine adolescence in popular culture and cultural theory.* Columbia University Press.

Duff, S. (2017, July 16). BBC face furious sexist backlash after announcing Jodie Whittaker as first female Doctor Who. *Mirror.* Retrieved April 18, 2019, from https://www.mirror.co.uk/tv/tv-news/doctor-who-jodie-whittaker-reaction-10811248

Duffett, M. (2013). *Understanding fandom: An introduction to the study of media fan culture.* Bloomsbury Publishing USA.

Dworkin, A. (1987). *Intercourse.* Free Press.

Erickson, R. J. (1995). The importance of authenticity for self and society. *Symbolic Interaction, 18*(2), 121–144.

Ewens, H. (2020). *Fangirls: Scenes from modern music culture.* University of Texas Press.

Exposito, S. (2021, February 15). Male 'Buffy' stars back Charisma Carpenter, other alleging misconduct by Joss Whedon. *Los Angeles Times.* Retrieved July 2, 2021, from   https://www.latimes.com/entertainment-arts/story/2021-02-15/david-boreanaz-buffy-stars-support-charisma-carpenter-joss-whedon-claims

Faludi, S. (2006 [1991]). *Backlash: The undeclared war against American women.* Broadway Books.

Fan, V. (2012). The poetics of addiction: Stardom, "feminized" spectatorship, and Interregional business relations in the Twilight series. *Camera Obscura, 27*(1), 31–67.

Favaro, L., & Gill, R. (2018). Feminism rebranded: Women's magazines online and 'the return of the F-word'. *Revista Dígitos, 4,* 37–66.

Fields, B. J. (2001). Whiteness, racism, and identity. *International Labor and Working-Class History, 60,* 48–56.

Findlen, B. (1995). *Listen up: Voices from the next feminist generation.* Seal Press.

Firestone, S. (1980 [2003]). *The dialectic of sex: The case for feminist revolution.* Macmillan.

Fiske, J. (1992). The cultural economy of fandom. In L. A. Lewis (Ed.), *The adoring audience: Fan culture and popular media* (pp. 30–49). Routledge.

French, M. (1977). *The Women's Room.* Summit Books.

Friedan, B. (1963 [2010]). *The feminine mystique*. WW Norton & Company.
Frith, S. (1996). Music and identity. In S. Hall & P. Du Gay (Eds.), *Questions of cultural identity* (pp. 108–127). Sage.
Garratt, S. (1990). Teenage dream. In S. Frith & A. Goodwin (Eds.), *On record: Rock, pop, and the written word* (pp. 399–409). Routledge.
Gay, R. (2014). *Bad feminist*. Harper Collins.
Genz, S. (2008). "I am not a housewife, but…": Postfeminism and the revival of domesticity. In S. Gill & J. Hollows (Eds.), *Feminism, domesticity and popular culture* (pp. 59–72). Routledge.
Genz, S. (2009). *Postfemininities in popular culture*. Palgrave Macmillan.
Gerrard, Y. (2021). Groupies, fangirls and shippers: The endurance of a gender stereotype. *American Behavioral Scientist*. https://doi.org/10.1177/00027642211042284
Ghai, Y. (2000). *Autonomy and ethnicity: Negotiating competing claims in multi-ethnic states*. Cambridge University Press.
Giddens, A. (1991). *Modernity and self-identity: Self and society in the late modern age*. Stanford University Press.
Gill, R. (2007). Postfeminist media culture: Elements of a sensibility. *European Journal of Cultural Studies, 10*(2), 147–166.
Gill, R., Hamad, H., Kauser, M., Negra, D., & Roshini, N. (2016). Intergenerational feminism and media: A roundtable. *Feminist Media Studies, 16*(4), 726–736.
Gill, R., & Scharff, C. (Eds.). (2011). *New femininities: Postfeminism, neoliberalism and subjectivity*. Springer.
Gillis, S., Howie, G., & Munford, R. (Eds.). (2004). *Third wave feminism*. Palgrave Macmillan.
Goffman, E. (1956). *The presentation of the self in everyday life*. University of Edinburgh Press.
Goffman, E. (1967). *Interaction ritual: Essays on face-to-face interaction*. Pantheon Books.
Goodin, R. E. (1996). Inclusion and exclusion. *European Journal of Sociology/ Archives Européennes de Sociologie, 37*(2), 343–371.
Gray, J. (2003). New audiences, new textualities: Anti-fans and non-fans. *International Journal of Cultural Studies, 6*(1), 64–81.
Green, P. (1979). The feminist consciousness. *The Sociological Quarterly, 20*(3), 359–374.
Grossberg, L. (1992). Is there a fan in the house? The affective sensibility of fandom. In L. A. Lewis (Ed.), *The adoring audience: Fan culture and popular media* (pp. 50–65). Routledge.

Guttmann, G. (2021, March 2). Ray Fisher details racism during Justice League reshoots. *Screen Rant*. Retrieved July 2, 2021, from https://screenrant.com/justice-league-reshoots-ray-fisher-racism-details-wb

Hacking, I. (1999). *The social construction of what?* Harvard University Press.

Hadas, L. (2013). Resisting the romance: 'Shipping' and the discourse of genre uniqueness in Doctor Who fandom. *European Journal of Cultural Studies, 16*(3), 329–343.

Hall, S. (1996). Introduction: Who needs identity? In S. Hall & P. Du Gay (Eds.), *Questions of cultural identity* (pp. 1–17). Sage.

Hall, S. (2017). *The fateful triangle*. Harvard University Press.

Hannell, B. (2020). Fan studies and/as feminist methodology. *Transformative Works and Cultures, 33*. https://doi.org/10.3983/twc.2020.1689

Harrington, C. L., & Bielby, D. D. (2018). Soap fans, revisited. In P. Booth (Ed.), *A Companion to media fandom and fan studies* (pp. 77–90). John Wiley & Sons.

Harrington, C. L., Bielby, D., & Bardo, A. R. (2014). *Aging, media, and culture*. MD Lexington Books.

Harrington, C. L., Bielby, D. D., & Bardo, A. R. (2011). Life course transitions and the future of fandom. *International Journal of Cultural Studies, 14*(6), 567–590.

Harrison, B. (2020). *The empire strikes back*. Bloomsbury.

Hazan, H. (1994). *Old age: Constructions and deconstructions*. Cambridge University Press.

Hesse-Biber, S. N. (2007). The Practice of feminist in-depth interviewing. In S. N. Hesse-Biber & P. L. Leavy (Eds.), *Feminist research practice: A primer* (pp. 111–148). Sage.

Heywood, L., & Drake, J. (Eds.). (1997). *Third wave agenda: Being feminist, doing feminism*. University of Minnesota Press.

Hill Collins, P. (1990). *Black feminist thought: Knowledge, consciousness and the politics of empowerment*. Routledge.

Hill Collins, P. (1993). Black feminist thought in the matrix of domination. In C. Lemert (Ed.), *Social theory: The multicultural and classic readings* (pp. 615–626). Westview.

Hill Collins, P. (1996). What's in a name? Womanism, Black feminism, and beyond. *The Black Scholar, 26*(1), 9–17.

Hill Collins, P., & Bilge, S. (1996). *Intersectionality*. Polity Press.

Hills, M. (2002). *Fan culture*. Routledge.

Hills, M. (2015). The expertise of digital fandom as a 'community of practice' Exploring the narrative universe of Doctor Who. *Convergence, 21*(3), 360–374.

Hills, M. (2017). From fan culture/community to the fan world: Possible pathways and ways of having done fandom. *Palabra Clave, 20*(4), 856–883.

Hobson, J. (2017). Celebrity feminism: More than a gateway. *Signs: Journal of Women in Culture and Society, 42*(4), 999–1007.

Hochman, A. (2019). Racialization: A defense of the concept. *Ethnic and racial studies, 42*(8), 1245–1262.

hooks, b. (1981 [1990]). *Ain't I a woman: Black women and feminism.* Pluto Press.

hooks, b. (2000). *Feminism is for everybody: Passionate politics.* Pluto Press.

Jenkins, H. (1988). Star Trek rerun, reread, rewritten: Fan writing as textual poaching. *Critical Studies in Media Communication, 5*(2), 85–107.

Jenkins, H. (1992). *Textual poachers.* Routledge.

Jenkins, H. (2006). *Fans, bloggers, and gamers: Exploring participatory culture.* New York University Press.

Jenkins, H. (2007). The future of fandom. In J. Gray, C. Sandvoss, & C. L. Harrington (Eds.), *Fandom: Identities and communities in a mediated world* (pp. 357–364). NYU Press.

Jenkins, H. (2018). Fandom, negotiation, and participatory culture. In P. Booth (Ed.), *A Companion to media fandom and fan studies* (pp. 13–26). John Wiley & Sons.

Jenkins, R. (2008). *Rethinking ethnicity.* Sage.

Jenkins, R. (2014). *Social identity.* Routledge.

Jenson, J. (1992). Fandom as Pathology: The consequences of characterization. In L. A. Lewis (Ed.), *The adoring audience: Fan culture and popular media* (pp. 9–29). Routledge.

Jong, E. (1973). *Fear of flying.* Henry Holt and Company.

Jowett, L. (2014). The girls who waited? Female companions and gender in Doctor Who. *Critical Studies in Television, 9*(1), 77–94.

Kalogeropoulos Householder, A. (2019). Lena Dunham, Girls, and the contradictions of fourth wave feminism. In A. Terier-Bienniek (Ed.), *Feminist Theory and Pop Culture* (pp. 21–38). Brill Sense.

Keller, J., & Ringrose, J. (2015). 'But then feminism goes out the window!': Exploring teenage girls' critical response to celebrity feminism. *Celebrity Studies, 6*(1), 132–135.

Kendall, M. (2013, August 14). #SolidarityIsForWhiteWomen: Women of color's issue with digital feminism. *The Guardian.* Retrieved October 6, 2021, from https://www.theguardian.com/commentisfree/2013/aug/14/solidarityis forwhitewomen-hashtag-feminism

Kendall, M. (2021). *Hood feminism: Notes from the women that a movement forgot.* Penguin.

Kozinets, R. V. (2001). Utopian enterprise: Articulating the meanings of Star Trek's culture of consumption. *Journal of Consumer Research, 28*(1), 67–88.

Krachenfels, G. (2017, July 27). Are you a bad feminist for enjoying misogynistic pop culture? *Study Breaks.* Retrieved August 1, 2019, from https://study-breaks.com/news-politics-feminism-pop-culture-media

Kvale, S. (2007). *Doing interviews.* Sage.

Lamerichs, N. (2011). Stranger than fiction: Fan identity in cosplay. *Transformative Works and Cultures, 7*(3). https://doi.org/10.3983/twc.2011.0246

Lamerichs, N. (2018). *Productive fandom.* Amsterdam University Press.

Larsen, K., & Zubernis, L. (2011). *Fandom at the crossroads: Celebration, shame and fan/producer relationships.* Cambridge Scholars Publishing.

Lawler, S. (2014). *Identity: Sociological perspectives.* Polity Press.

Linden, H., & Linden, S. (2016). *Fans and fan cultures: Tourism, consumerism and social media.* Springer.

Looft, R. (2017). #girlgaze: Photography, fourth wave feminism, and social media advocacy. *Continuum, 31*(6), 892–902.

Lopes, P. (2006). Culture and stigma: Popular culture and the case of comic books. *Sociological Forum, 21*(3), 387–414.

Lorde, A. (1984). *Sister outsider.* The Crossing Press.

Lugones, M. (2010). Toward a decolonial feminism. *Hypatia, 25*(4), 742–759.

Mahoney, C. (2020). Is this what a feminist looks like? Curating the feminist self in the neoliberal visual economy of Instagram. *Feminist Media Studies.* https://doi.org/10.1080/14680777.2020.1810732

Mann, S. A., & Huffman, D. J. (2005). The decentering of second wave feminism and the rise of the third wave. *Science & Society, 69*(1), 56–91.

Martin Jr, A. L. (2019). Fandom while black: Misty Copeland, Black Panther, Tyler Perry and the contours of US black fandoms. *International Journal of Cultural Studies, 22*(6), 737–753.

Masters, K. (2021, April 6). Ray Fisher opens up about 'Justice League,' Joss Whedon and Warners: "I don't believe some of these people are fit for leadership." *The Hollywood Reporter.* Retrieved July 2, 2021, from https://www.hollywoodreporter.com/movies/movie-news/ray-fisher-opens-up-about-justice-league-joss-whedon-and-warners-i-dont-believe-some-of-these-people-are-fit-for-leadership-4161658

May, V. (2013). *Connecting self to society: Belonging in a changing world.* Palgrave Macmillan.

Maynard, M. (1994). 'Race', gender and the concept of 'difference' in feminist thought. In H. Afshar & M. Maynard (Eds.), *The dynamics of 'Race' and gender: Some feminist interventions* (pp. 9–26). Taylor and Francis.

McRobbie, A. (1991). *Feminism and youth culture.* Routledge.

McRobbie, A. (2004). Post-feminism and popular culture: Bridget Jones and the new gender regime. *Feminist Media Studies, 4*(3), 255–264.

Mead, G. H. (1972). *Mind, self, and society: From the standpoint of a social behaviorist.* University of Chicago Press.

Melis, A. (2020, November 7). The million dollar question: Is it ok to have a problematic fave? *Geek Girl Authority.* Retrieved July 2, 2021, from https://www.geekgirlauthority.com/the-million-dollar-question-is-it-ok-to-have-a-problematic-fave

Miller, L. (2003). Belonging to country – A philosophical anthropology. *Journal of Australian Studies, 27*(76), 215–223.

Millett, K. (1970). *Sexual politics.* Columbia University Press.

Mittell, J. (2015). *Complex TV: The poetics of contemporary television storytelling.* New York University Press.

Mohanty, C. (1988). Under Western eyes: Feminist scholarship and colonial discourses. *Feminist Review, 30*(1), 61–88.

Moran, C. (2013). *How to be a woman.* Ebury Publishing.

Morimoto, L. (2019a). Physical disability in/and transcultural fandom: Conversations with my spouse. *The Journal of Fandom Studies, 7*(1), 73–78.

Morimoto, L. (Host). (2019b, September 30). Episode 2: Rebecca Williams [Audio podcast episode]. In *It's a thing!.* https://itsathing.net/

Mortensen, T. E. (2018). Anger, fear, and games: The long event of# GamerGate. *Games and Culture, 13*(8), 787–806.

Munford, R., & Waters, M. (Eds.). (2014). *Feminism and popular culture: Investigating the postfeminist mystique: explorations in post-feminism.* I B Tauris.

Nayak, A. (2006). After race: Ethnography, race and post-race theory. *Ethnic and racial studies, 29*(3), 411–430.

Nyberg, A. K. (1995). Comic books and women readers: Trespassers in masculine territory. In S. W. Rollins & P. C. Rollins (Eds.), *Gender in popular culture: Images of men and women in literature, visual media, and material Culture* (pp. 205–224). Ridgemount PR.

Oakley, A. (1985 [1972]). *Sex, gender and society.* Gower Publishing Company.

Oakley, A. (1981). Interviewing women: Contradiction in terms. In H. Roberts (Ed.), *Doing feminist research* (pp. 30–61). Routledge.

Olesen, V. (1988). Feminism and models of qualitative research. In N. K. Denzin & Y. S. Lincoln (Eds.), *The landscape of qualitative research (Vol. 1)* (pp. 300–332). Sage.

Olesen, V. (2005). Early millennial feminist qualitative research: Challenges and contours. In N. K. Denzin & Y. S. Lincoln (Eds.), *The Sage handbook of qualitative research* (pp. 235–278). Sage.

Oluo, I. (2015, March 31). Admit it: Your fave is problematic. *Medium.* Retrieved July 2, 2021, from https://medium.com/matter/admit-it-your-fave-is-problematic-2dfa692f557b

Olufemi, L. (2020). *Feminism, interrupted: Disrupting power.* Pluto Press.

Orme, S. (2016). Femininity and fandom: The dual-stigmatisation of female comic book fans. *Journal of Graphic Novels and Comics, 7*(4), 403–416.

Ortega, M. (2006). Being lovingly, knowingly ignorant: White feminism and women of color. *Hypatia, 21*(3), 56–74.

Pande, R. (2018). *Squee from the margins: Fandom and race.* University of Iowa Press.

Pande, R. (2020). *Fandom, now in color: A collection of Voices*. University of Iowa Press.

Penley, C. (1992). Feminism, psychoanalysis, and popular culture. In L. Grossberg, C. Nelson & P. Treichler (Eds.), *Cultural Studies Now and In the Future* (pp. 479–94). Routledge.

Petersen, A. H. (2011). That teenage feeling: Twilight, fantasy, and feminist readers. *Feminist Media Studies, 12*(1), 51–67.

Petersen, L. N. (2017). 'The Florals': female fans over 50 in the Sherlock fandom. *Transformative works and cultures, 23*, 1941–2258.

Peterson, R. A. (2005). In search of authenticity. *Journal of Management Studies, 42*(5), 1083–1098.

Phillips, A. (2020). *Gamer trouble*. New York University Press.

Phipps, A. (2020). *Me, not you: The trouble with mainstream feminism*. Manchester University Press.

Pugh, M. (2000). *Women and the women's movement in Britain* (2nd ed.). Macmillan Press.

Punch, M. (1988). Politics and ethics in qualitative research. In N. K. Denzin & Y. S. Lincoln (Eds.), *The landscape of qualitative research (Vol. 1)* (pp. 156–184). Sage.

Purkayastha, B. (2005). *Negotiating ethnicity*. Rutgers University Press.

Purvis, J. (2004). Grrrls and women together in the third wave: Embracing the challenges of intergenerational feminism(s). *NWSA Journal, 16*(3), 93–123.

Radway, J. (1984). *Reading the romance*. The University of North Carolina Press.

Rahman, O., Wing-Sun, L., & Cheung, B. H. M. (2012). "Cosplay": Imaginative self and performing identity. *Fashion Theory, 16*(3), 317–341.

Rai, R. (2021). From colonial 'mongoloid' to neoliberal 'northeastern': Theorising 'race', racialization and racism in contemporary India. *Asian Ethnicity*, 1–21.

Ramazanoglu, C., & Holland, J. (2002). *Feminist methodology: Challenges and choices*. Sage.

Reagle, J. (2015). Geek policing: Fake geek girls and contested attention. *International Journal of Communication, 9*: 2862–2880.

Redfern, C., & Aune, K. (2010). *Reclaiming the f word: The new feminist movement*. Zed.

Reed, S. (2021, July 15). I don't trust myself (with loving John Mayer). *InStyle*. Retrieved July 2, 2021, from https://www.instyle.com/celebrity/john-mayer-problematic-fave

Reinhard, C. D. (2018). *Fractured fandoms: Contentious communication in fan communities*. Lexington Books.

Reinharz, S., & Davidman, L. (1992). *Feminist methods in social research*. Oxford University Press.

Rendell, J. (2019). Black (anti) fandom's intersectional politicization of The Walking Dead as a transmedia franchise. *Transformative Works and Cultures, 29*, 1–15.

Riley, M. W., Johnson, M., & Foner, A. (Eds.). (1972). *Aging and society: A sociology of age stratification.* Russell Sage Foundation.

Ringrose, J., & Renold, E. (2016). Teen feminist killjoys?: Mapping girls' affective encounters with femininity, sexuality, and feminism at school. In C. Mitchell & C. Rentschler (Eds.), *Girlhood and the politics of place* (pp. 104–121). Berghahn.

Rivers, N. (2017). *Postfeminism (s) and the arrival of the fourth wave: Turning tides.* Springer.

Rottenberg, C. (2014). The rise of neoliberal feminism. *Cultural Studies, 28*(3), 418–437.

Rubidge, S. (1996). Does authenticity matter? The case for and against authenticity in the performing arts. In P. Campbell (Ed.), *Analysing performance* (pp. 219–233). Manchester University Press.

Salter, A., & Blodgett, B. (2017). *Toxic geek masculinity in media: Sexism, trolling, and identity policing.* Springer.

Salter, M. (2018). From geek masculinity to Gamergate: The technological rationality of online abuse. *Crime, Media, Culture, 14*(2), 247–264.

Sandvoss, C. (2005). *Fans: The mirror of consumption.* Polity Press.

Schwalbe, M. L., & Mason-Schrock, D. (1996). Identity work as group process. *Advances in Group Processes, 13*(113), 47.

Scott, S. (2013). Fangirls in refrigerators: The politics of (in)visibility in comic book culture. *Transformative Works and Cultures, 13.* https://doi.org/10.3983/twc.2013.0460

Scott, S. (2015). *Negotiating identity: Symbolic interactionist approaches to social identity.* John Wiley & Sons.

Scott, S. (2017). Modeling the Marvel everyfan: Agent Coulson and/as transmedia fan culture. *Palabra Clave, 20*(4), 1042–1072.

Scott, S. (2019). *Fake geek girls: Fandom, gender, and the convergence culture industry.* NYU Press.

Sorisio, C. (1997). A tale of two feminisms: Power and victimization in contemporary feminist debate. In L. Heywood & J. Drake (Eds.), *Third wave agenda: Being feminist, doing feminism* (pp. 134–154). University of Minnesota Press.

Sowards, S. K., & Renegar, V. R. (2004). The rhetorical functions of consciousness-raising in third wave feminism. *Communication Studies, 55*(4), 535–552.

Stanfill, M. (2018). The unbearable whiteness of fandom and fan studies. In P. Booth (Ed.), *A Companion to media fandom and fan studies* (pp. 305–318). John Wiley & Sons.

Stein, L. E. (2015). *Millennial fandom: Television audiences in the transmedia age.* University of Iowa Press.

Stryker, S., & Burke, P. J. (2000). The past, present, and future of an identity theory. *Social Psychology Quarterly, 63*(4), 284–297.

Suleri, S. (1992). Woman skin deep: Feminism and the postcolonial condition. *Critical Inquiry, 18*(4), 756–769.

Sweetman, C. (2013). Introduction, feminist solidarity and collective action. *Gender & Development, 21*(2), 217–229.

Thomas, E. E., & Stornaiuolo, A. (2019). Race, storying, and restorying: What can we learn from Black fans? *Transformative Works and Cultures, 29*. https://doi.org/10.3983/twc.2019.1562

Todd, C. (2015). Commentary: GamerGate and resistance to the diversification of gaming culture. *Women's Studies Journal, 29*(1), 64–67.

Tyler, I. (2007). The selfish feminist: Public images of women's liberation. *Australian Feminist Studies, 22*(53), 173–190.

Van de Goor, S. (2015). "You must be new here": Reinforcing the good fan. *Participations, 12*(2), 275–295.

Vary, A. B. (2021, February 10). Charisma Carpenter alleges Joss Whedon 'abused his power' on 'Buffy' and 'Angel': 'Joss was the vampire'. *Screen Rant.* Retrieved July 2, 2021, from https://variety.com/2021/tv/news/charisma-carpenter-joss-whedon-abuse-of-power-allegations-1234904995

Vergès, F. (2021). *A decolonial feminism.* Pluto Press.

Walker, R. (Ed.). (1995). *To be real: Telling the truth and changing the face of feminism.* Anchor.

Walsh, A. (2017, July 6). Why feminism ruined my life. *Topical.* Retrieved August 1, 2019, from https://www.headstuff.org/topical/why-feminism-ruined-my-life

Walter, N. (1999). *The new feminism.* Virago.

Wanzo, R. (2015). African American acafandom and other strangers: New genealogies of fan studies. *Transformative Works and Cultures, 20*(1): n.p.

Ward, R. A. (2010). How old am I? Perceived age in middle and later life. *International Journal of Aging and Human Development, 71*(3), 167–184.

Warner, K. J. (2015). ABC's Scandal and Black women's fandom. In E. Levine (Ed.), *Cupcakes, Pinterest and ladyporn: Feminized popular culture in the early twenty-first century* (pp. 32–50). University of Illinois Press.

Way, L. (2021). Punk is just a state of mind: Exploring what punk means to older punk women. *The Sociological Review, 69*(1), 107–122.

Weiner-Mahfuz, L. (2002). Organizing 101: A mixed-race feminist in movements for social justice. In D. Hernández & B. Rehman (Eds.), *Colonize this!: Young women of color on today's feminism* (pp. 29–39). Seal Press.

Weir, A. (2013). *Identities and freedom: Feminist theory between power and connection.* Oxford University Press.

Whelehan, I. (2007). Forward. In S. Gillis, G. Howie, & R. Munford (Eds.), *Third wave feminism: A critical exploration* (pp. xv–xx). Palgrave Macmillan.

Widmayer, C. J. (2017). The feminist strikes back: Performative mourning in the Twitter response to Carrie Fisher's death. *New Directions in Folklore, 15*(1/2), 50–76.

Williams, R. (2000). *Making identity matter: Identity, society and social interaction.* Sociologypress.

Winch, A. (2015). Feminism, generation and intersectionality. *Soundings, 58,* 8–20.

Winch, A., Littler, J., & Keller, J. (2016). Why "intergenerational feminist media studies"? *Feminist Media Studies, 16*(4), 557–572.

Wirman, H. (2007, September). "I am not a fan, I just play a lot" – If power gamers aren't fans, who are? *DiGRA Conference.* Tokyo, Japan.

Woo, B. (2018). *Getting a life: The social worlds of Geek culture.* McGill-Queen's Press.

Wood, M. (2016). Feminist icon needed: Damsels in distress need not apply. In P. W. Lee (Ed.), *A galaxy here and now: Historical and cultural readings of Star Wars* (pp. 62–83). Mcfarland publishing.

Zakaria, R. (2021). *Against white feminism.* W. W Norton & Company.

Zeisler, A. (2016). *We were feminists once: From riot Grrrl to CoverGirl, the buying and selling of a political movement.* Public Affairs.

CHAPTER 2

Becoming a Feminist Fan

This chapter maps the terrain of feminism and fandom through the lens of biographical narratives. It explores the interviewees' depictions of the ways in which they came to identify and practice feminism and fandom. Drawing on Anthony Giddens' work (1991), I read the participants' biographies as "narratives," meaning constructive, subjective accounts, which are "not wholly fictive" (p. 54), but rather intentionally tailored with the purpose of illustrating a coherent and clear process of becoming feminists and fans. These biographies are mechanisms used to create continuity and harmony between one's identities to avoid being perceived as inauthentic or having inner contradictions (Hall, 1989; Ouellette & Hay, 2008; Ricoeur, 1991; Schwalbe & Mason-Schrock, 1996). Therefore, I read the interviewees' biographical narratives as an active storytelling process in which they carefully chose moments and memories that highlighted an acceptable description of how their identities came to be.

I decided to examine the participants' biographical narratives based on the idea that identity is "produced through the narratives people use to explain and understand their lives" (Lawler, 2014, p. 30). By tailoring their biographical narratives, individuals organize, negotiate, reinforce, and make sense of their identities (De Fina, 2015; Josselson & Lieblich, 1993; Schwalbe & Mason-Schrock, 1996; Yuval-Davis, 2011). Their past reflections inform not only who they were but also how they perceive

N. Yodovich, *Women Negotiating Feminism and Science Fiction Fandom*, Palgrave Fan Studies, https://doi.org/10.1007/978-3-031-04079-5_2

themselves in the present and who they strive to become in the future (Reinhard & Dervin, 2012; Schwalbe & Mason-Schrock, 1996).

In his book, *Fan Cultures* (2002), Matt Hills warns fan scholars against taking fans' accounts at face value. Instead, he urges us to scrutinize and explore incongruence and tensions in their narratives. Following Hills' call, this chapter, too, is dedicated to probing the fractures and coherence in the interviewees' stories, definitions, and perceptions of fandom and feminism and the ways in which they relate to each other. It explores the ebbs and flows of their identities while understanding that they are not constant but ever-changing, ever-evolving constructs.

At the center of this chapter stands the ambivalence feminist women fans feel about their identities. The participants in this study declared that fandom and feminism were self-proclaimed identities that did not require particular behaviors or practices in order to be sustained. Nevertheless, regardless of their statements, the interviewees elaborated on a plethora of practices they took part in to reinforce their identities, even while simultaneously feeling they were not doing "enough" to be "worthy" of them. This contradiction and their feelings of inauthenticity described here are the basis of this research, which I continue to unpack throughout this book.

This chapter has three major goals. First, it describes the routes leading to feminism and fandom and the motivations to proclaim these two identities. Second, it foregrounds the tight bond between identity and practice in which, as the interviewees' accounts reveal, one cannot exist without the other. Following this insight, this chapter's third goal is exploring the interviewees' ambivalence regarding the identity/practice paradigm, which leads them to constantly feel that they can never do enough in order to be accepted as "worthy" of claiming these identities. Before delving into the challenges, gatekeeping, and toxicity that feminist women fans endure, I establish how *they* define and identify as fans and feminists. Simultaneously and gradually, I also expose the initial cracks in feminist women fans' biographical narratives and their uncertainty regarding their ability to pass as "authentic" and legitimate fans and feminists.

I begin this chapter by exploring the paths that led the interviewees to science fiction fandom and the practices they took part in to engage with fandom and solidify their fan identities. Then, I delve into feminist "becoming" stories and the leading arenas that introduced the participants to feminism. Using the interviewees' own words, I also review the practices they engaged in to prove their feminism, similar to the methods they used to solidify their status as fans. After discussing fandom and feminism separately, the last section of this chapter considers fandom and feminism in conjunction and explores the ways in which they differ.

2.1 "Just Like Falling in Love": Becoming a Fan

At the beginning of each interview, I asked the interviewees to share stories about the time they first became fans. This request frequently made the participants reflect on their childhoods. On average, most became fans when they were about eight years old. From their statements, two major pathways leading to fandom were evident: (1) parental exposure or (2) the evolution from casual viewers to fans.

Looking back to their childhoods, several participants reminisced on quality time spent with their parents while consuming science fiction content together:

> My dad is a huge Star Wars fan. I watched the movies when I was wee one. That was well after the prequels came out. I was young, but I watched all the movies. I started with Episode IV because my dad was like, "this is the order they were released." (Daniela,[1] 23, Latina, USA)
>
> I sort of grew up with it. My parents [...] read science fiction and watched Doctor Who. That's how I was introduced to it, watching it with my parents. (Emmy, 42, white, UK)

For Nika, fandom was a multigenerational interest and identity, one that passed from her grandmother, to her mother, to herself:

> I'm a third-generation nerd [...] My grandma's from Mexico, and she was a big fan of the Mexican wrestlers, Lucha Libre. They used to make movies; they were stars in Mexico. They had movies with demons and mummies, horror movies. My grandma was a huge fan of all these things. Any movie that had a monster, she was all about it. She was very atypical for a female at the time [...] By the time I was a little kid, my mom used to take me to movies with her. I was born in 1975, so she took me to see Star Wars when it came out. (Nika, 44, Latina/Chicana, USA)

Historically, fandom has been understood as a pathology, an identity that is developed due to psychological or social deficiencies (Jenson, 1992; Larsen & Zubernis, 2011; Salter & Blodgett, 2017). In contrast to this notion, the narrative told by my participants such as Daniela, Emmy, and Nika demonstrates that fandom is an identity that individuals could be socialized into through bonding familial interactions (Tinson et al., 2017).

---

[1] All interviewees received a pseudonym in order to insure their anonymity.

Here we see examples of occasions where parents actively instilled the appreciation of science fiction and fantasy in their children and encouraged them to become fans.

Through their parents, the participants also learned the "rules" of fandom and of being a "good" fan, such as watching the *Star Wars* films in the "right" order, as Daniela recounted. Elsewhere (2022), I have argued that in many cases in which the interviewees were brought up to become fans by their fathers, they grew to learn that science fiction fandom is not necessarily an arena where they naturally belong. The participants understood that being science fiction fans makes them different from other girls and women. This is also evident in other cases, such as Nika, who was raised into fandom by a succession of geeky women. In her own words, she explains that being interested in science fiction, horror, and fantasy is "atypical for a female."

An alternative, common pathway to fandom was the gradual evolution from a casual viewer into a fan. Anaya's (19, Indian, UK) description of becoming a *Doctor Who* fan illustrates this route:

> I came back from school one day, and I was going through the TV, and I saw one of the re-runs [...] I saw it and thought it was really interesting, "and it's coming every week." I started watching it every week [...] when it stopped airing, I just went online and saw an entire season in two days.

Delmar et al. (2020) asserted that, "When someone identifies him or herself as a fan, he or she transforms consumption into a cognitive-intellectual and socio-emotional adventure" (p. 7). Similarly, the participants described the transition from casual viewer to fan as an emotionally induced process where they felt a unique, deep connection with the cultural content. Some equated the process of becoming a fan to developing a romantic relationship:

> It's almost kind of, you don't choose, it's like you just kind of fall in love, "Oh my gosh, what is happening, I don't understand." Like they say in some groups—"ALL THE FEELS." So true, it's just like, "I have so many feelings right now!" (Ramona, 31, white, Ireland)

The two routes leading to fandom reflect the link between identification and practice. Fandom is created by an action: watching a television series, going to the cinema, reading a book, playing a video game, or listening to music. These practices are then intensified and multiplied as the fan identity becomes more significant to the individual. In their study about identity work, Schwalbe and Mason-Schrock (1996) claimed that when the individual proclaims an identity, "it is necessary to create opportunities for enacting and reaffirming it" (p. 126). Similarly, Scott (2015) argued that identity is not something we have, but "something we do" (p. 9). Indeed, after explicitly identifying as fans, the interviewees took part in countless fannish practices through which they expressed and declared their fan identity. Examples of these practices are explored in the following section.

2.2   Practicing Fandom: A Labor of Love?

Much has been written about the plethora of practices and activities that fans take part in to engage with their favorite content or with one another: from buying merchandise and curating trivia knowledge to cosplaying and writing fan fiction (Bacon-Smith, 1992; Kozinets, 2001; Lamerichs, 2011; Larsen & Zubernis, 2011; Linden & Linden, 2016; Reinhard, 2018; Scott, 2017). These practices are frequently grouped under two main umbrella categories: affirmative and transformative (Hills, 2014; Lamerichs, 2018; Pande, 2020). The first category refers to activities that are "faithful" to the content and the canon[2] and wish to honor it by memorizing details, demonstrating connoisseurship, and developing theories about upcoming storylines. Transformative practices, the second category, are considered more "subversive" in nature, as fans attempt to morph the original text and make it their own, through fan art or fan fiction, for instance. While scholars frequently associate affirmative practices with men and transformative practices with women (Pande, 2020; Salter & Blodgett, 2017; Scott, 2017), the participants in this study engaged in both types of activities.

Indeed, the interviewees were involved in four major types of practices: (1) community-focused practices; (2) consumption; (3) content-producing; and (4) intellectual engagement. Though defined separately, these practices are frequently linked and overlap. Given that researchers have already discussed such fan practices and behaviors, the following section provides a brief overview of these activities espoused by the women I

---

[2] Storylines that are accepted as an official part of the diegesis, unlike fan fiction.

interviewed. This short review serves as the basis for discussing the interviewees' ambivalence about defining and practicing fandom.

Community-focused practices are a curious example of the connection
between identity and practice. The term "fandom" is used to describe the
experience of being a fan, as well as a community of fans (Brough &
Shresthova, 2012; Jenkins, 1992, 2018). Thus, "fandom" inherently con-
ceptualizes fans as social beings who engage with one another through
collective activities. "To be fans," according to Ewens (2020), is to:

> Scream alone together. To go on a collective journey of self-definition. It
> means pulling on threads of your own narrative and doing so with friends
> and strangers who feel like friends. (p. 6)

Community-focused practices played a significant role in the establish-
ment of the participants' identities as fans. Interacting with other fans
provided them with an outlet to affirm and practice their identities.
Community engagement also served as a source of comfort and belonging
(Bourdaa, 2018; Larsen & Zubernis, 2011). In one example, Donna (46,
white, UK) not only stressed the significance of belonging to a fandom
community but also saw it as a significant motivation for becoming a fan:

> When I was in university I got into Star Trek: Next Generation […] I went
> through a breakup, and I felt very alone and confused, didn't have much
> money, and a friend of mine had heard about a Star Trek night on a Saturday
> night and asked me to come with him for his birthday. I kind of walked
> through the door, and it was the first time I experienced walking into a pub
> where everyone is engaging in conversation, and everyone knows every-
> body's name, I'm about to get into the *Cheers* song […] That was 22 years
> ago, I made a lot of friends that I would still call my best friends now. I mar-
> ried my ex-husband and father of my two children, I met him there, and my
> partner I married last month, I also met him there. When I got married last
> month, there were about 50 of the guests from those days.

Similarly, Jessica (32, biracial white-Jamaican, USA) talked about bonding
with her friends over fandom: "This is all I do with my friends. All we do
is *Star Wars, Doctor Who*, video games, that's what my friends are. That's
how we come together." Donna's and Jessica's accounts demonstrate how
fandom serves as a catalyst for creating long-lasting, intimate bonds
between fans, based on shared interests (Baym, 2000; Bourdaa, 2018;
Jenkins, 1992; Zubernis & Larsen, 2018).

The second fannish practice the interviewees discussed was consumerism. Fans are considered "ideal consumers" whose avidness to engage with their fandom results in consistent and dedicated consumption patterns (Cavicchi, 1998; Fiske, 1992; Hills, 2002; Sandvoss, 2005). For instance, many interviewees owned *Star Wars* and *Doctor Who* t-shirts and wore them in public; some even wore them to our interviews. Another interesting example is tattoos. Eve (30, white, UK) and Stephanie (29, white, UK) both have *Doctor Who* tattoos, while Lucia (39, white, Spain) has a gaming-related tattoo. Eve clandestinely tattooed a quote on her ribcage, whereas Stephanie's tattoo was displayed on her arm. Stephanie explained that since the symbol featured in her tattoo is not as identifiable as a Dalek (Doctor Who's arch-nemesis) or the TARDIS (Doctor Who's time machine), it would be recognizable only to people who "have a lot of knowledge of *Doctor Who*." Eve, likewise, took pride in her tattoo, which is also ambiguous to non-fans.

There is a clear connection between identity and practice when it comes to consumption. In her work about visible identities, Alcoff (2005) explained that most social, cultural, and political affiliations are coupled with visible markers, such as specific dress codes, tattoos, or hairstyles. These physical cues have segregative as well as inclusive powers that help us make quick assessments as to who belongs to our group and who does not. Fannish clothing and tattoos are a type of non-verbal, visible practice that serves a performative and social function. Wearing a fan-related t-shirt signals to others that the person identifies as a fan and wants to be acknowledged as such. They also provide an opportunity to prompt interactions with other fans. For instance, the participants shared that when wearing a fannish t-shirt, they watch to see if a passerby recognizes their fandom by smiling or starting a conversation with them. Thus, by performing their fannish identity through t-shirts or tattoos, the participants were able to externalize their identities, prove that they were dedicated fans to fellow community members, and distinguish between fans and non-fans (those who "get" the reference and those who do not).

Even though merchandise consumption is a conventional part of fandom, it is not accessible to all. Growing up in a working-class family, Olivia (40, white, UK) recalled a childhood scarcity of *Star Wars* merchandise. When she was able to provide for herself as an adult, Olivia splurged on *Star Wars* Legos and action figures. Cristina (34, Latina, USA) also referred to the importance of financial resources in another fannish practice, cosplay:

> I think the hierarchies in the fandom really are the people with the money
> and the privilege [...] It's who can make the best cosplay, who can afford to
> buy or produce the best cosplay, the best makeup, the best wigs. Who can
> do it the best. The most accurate. Those are the people who become famous.
> The professional, famous cosplayers. These are all the people with the access
> to be able to afford to do it at that level.

These accounts highlight a side of fandom that is seldom discussed: class
(Geraghty, 2018). Cristina and Olivia call attention to the barriers of
working-class individuals in their pursuit of practicing and engaging with
their fandom. As Cristina's quote exemplifies, a lower income means not
only that fans are unable to engage with their fandom. It also means that
as a by-product of their inability to partake in such practices, they will be
considered lesser fans who are not fully committed to their fandom.

Content-producing, also known in the fan scholarship as transformative
work, is another popular activity among the interviewees. Content-
producing involves fan art (drawing or sculpting characters and symbols
inspired by the object of fandom), fan fiction (writing literature inspired
by the content), and cosplay (creating and wearing costumes resembling
beloved characters), among others (Abercrombie & Longhurst, 1998;
Bacon-Smith, 1992; Brough & Shresthova, 2012; Lamerichs, 2018;
Larsen & Zubernis, 2011; Pande, 2018). Since their childhoods, the
interviewees had taken part in content-producing, such as drawing, writing to fanzines, or creating their own, and playing imaginary games like
pretending to be Princess Leia or one of the Doctor's companions. As they
got older, these practices evolved and developed: from imaginary games to
cosplaying and role-playing games. Tia (34, Black African American,
USA), for instance, recalled how when she was younger, she would "get
the costumes for Halloween [...] I would wear it for six months (laughing). I just ran around the house, pretending I was a ghostbuster." When
she got older, Tia continued dressing up as fictional characters, such as
Marvel's Domino, at various science fiction conventions.

Among the fans who took part in content-producing, three interviewees stood out because they turned these practices into semi-professions.
After reading fanzines in her childhood, Emmy (42, white, UK) began
writing an article series for a *Doctor Who* fanzine in her early teens. In
adulthood, she kept writing books and blogs and taking part in several
audio productions. Lucia (39, white, Spain) runs her own YouTube channel, which has thousands of followers from all over the world. On her

video blogs, she talks about video games, science fiction, and popular culture, and frequently provides a feminist perspective on the content she discusses. Anita (35, white, Italy) created a role-playing game that gained popularity in Italy. She was recently contacted by an American company that asked her to create an international game for them. However, Emmy, Anita, and Lucia do not work exclusively in their fannish professions. They also have "day" jobs. Their practices are sideline hobbies that they have been able to professionalize and sometimes monetize.

The last set of practices, intellectual engagement, expands from curating trivia about fan content to a theoretical analysis of the texts (Abercrombie & Longhurst, 1998; Brown, 1997; Hills, 2002; Reinhard, 2018). My interviewees highly valued these practices and discussed them in depth. For example, Stephanie (29, white, UK) defined fans as individuals who are:

> More interested in the canon. You can watch *Doctor Who* as a regular viewer, in contrast to watching it and understanding all the references, understanding all the details.

In intellectual engagement practices, fans accumulate trivial knowledge related to the object of their fandom such as names, dates, differences between film cuts, and plot details.

Participants recounted devoting their time to watching and reading every piece of content related to their fandom to familiarize themselves with it. Ruby (38, white, UK), for instance, owned a *Star Trek* Encyclopedia, which she "basically memorized." In a different example, Cristina (34, Latina, USA) talked about the importance of being informed about the "behind the scenes" of her favorite films and TV shows thanks to DVD extras:

> I come from an era when you got a DVD, and it came with special features. You put it in and watch everything, every single trailer, every featurette, every "how they did the makeup." You want to know everything about the movies, so when you go back and re-watch the movie or TV show, you have this extra information so that you can see all the hidden layers.

Drawing from Bourdieu, Fiske (1992) explained that knowledge curation produces "cultural capital," providing prestige to fans who demonstrate connoisseurship. Such cultural capital can then be used as part of the fan's performance of his/her identity, especially in order to prove that they are "real" fans who are intellectually engaged with the content (this argument will be expanded in Chap. 4).

Another motivation to curate trivia was using it for exhaustive analysis and theorization, a practice that is also termed "forensic fandom" (Scott, 2017). Here, participants gathered information so they could analyze and interpret the text:

> I want to know the intricate details. I remember the dialogues. I want to talk about the dialogues, "what does it mean?" I want to discuss the dialogues, the characters, how they do things. I want to look at the timeline, try to understand what fits into what. I want to know about the people, what happened to them, their background, that sort of thing. (Samantha, 46, white, UK)

Samantha clarified that not only is it vital for her to expand her knowledge about her favorite content, but also it is imperative to analyze and extract hidden, sub-textual meanings from it. Likewise, Jane (46, white, UK) also explained that she saw fandom as an "intellectual exercise," which provided her with vast universes to explore and analyze. Fans practicing intellectual engagement want to discover hidden meanings, understand the symbolism, and develop theories regarding current plotlines.

Despite having chronicled the influence of fannish practices, the interviewees expressed ambivalence regarding their importance or necessity, arguing that fandom should not require or depend on them. They insisted that fandom should be defined as merely an intellectual, emotional bond with particular content or celebrity. Donna (46, white, UK), for instance, explained that fandom simply means "that you love something, you're fascinated about something." Daniela's (23, Latina, USA) definition shared a similar sentiment: "What makes one a fan is liking the content. It doesn't take much to be a fan."

The narrative presented by the participants regarding their fan identities is, therefore, somewhat inconsistent. On the one hand, they seemed to oppose limiting fan identity to a rigid checklist of practices. On the other hand, they reported a wide variety of practices that they had engaged in over the years. Even though they took part in a variety of activities, they also shared that they felt as if they were not doing enough to qualify as "real" fans:

I'm absolutely a *Doctor Who* fan because I watched it, and I enjoy it, but I think some of the people expect that to be a much deeper commitment to be a fan. (Natalie, 38, white, UK)
      I am not the kind of person who could quote, who could say, "it was this episode, aired on this date." I can remember the stories; I remember the ones that were meaningful to me. I watched back all of them at least twice, if not three times. I think I'm just as much a fan as the people who dress up. (Sheela, 49, Indian-Anglo Saxon, Australia)

I argue that the self-doubt and feelings of inadequacy experienced by women fans result from the external pressures, exposure to toxic discourse, and gatekeeping in fan communities that the participants have internalized. Their awareness and experiences of exclusion, policing, and toxicity have prompted them to advocate for expanding the definition of fandom while simultaneously making them feel as if they are not good enough to merit the title of a fan. This pattern of ambivalence repeated itself when the interviewees reflected on their feminist identities, as the following section reveal.

2.3   FROM FEMINIST MOTHERS TO EMMA WATSON: BECOMING A FEMINIST

In her book, *Feminism, Interrupted*, Olufemi (2020) stated that, "Everybody has a story about how they arrived and keep arriving at radical politics" (p. 1). She continued to argue:

Some of us are politicized by the trauma of our own experiences, by wars waged in our names, by our parents and lovers, by the Internet. It's useful to share the ways we become politicized if only because it helps politicize others. (Ibid.)

Acknowledging the significance of sharing such "becoming" stories, I now discuss the routes that led the interviewees to feminism. Their biographical narratives immediately reveal a significant difference between feminism and fandom. While the participants became fans in their childhoods, most did not identify as feminists until adulthood, at the average age of 20 years old. They described three main arenas that encouraged them to become feminists: (1) the family nucleus, (2) higher education, and (3) popular culture.

Those who were exposed to feminism through their families identified mothers and other relatives, such as grandmothers and aunts, as their feminist inspiration. Camila (33, Latina, Australia), for instance, chronicled being raised as a feminist by a matriarchal family:

> All sides of my family, my mom's side—five sisters plus three brothers and my grandmother, who has a dominant personality. My mom was fairly stubborn, I guess, and straight minded. My dad was brought up by his grandmother and mother, and he has a sister. They already had that influence of "women's opinions matter." So, I grew up with it.

Feminist scholarship frequently depicts the intergenerational passing of feminist thought as a confrontational process in which children reject the mothers' outdated and rigid stances (Bailey, 1997; Budgeon, 2011; Whelehan, 2007; Winch, 2015). In contrast, the participants were inspired by their family members and grateful for their efforts to pass feminism to them:

> She [Jamie's mother] is and was very politically active and very much feminist. I couldn't tell you when I was first introduced to feminism, but I've always been aware of it […] There was politics in our house, and I picked it up. But my mom specifically made sure that I was introduced to novels and stories with strong female characters. She did this whole thing with finding books with characters that had my name, especially if they were strong characters. Feminism was always there. (Jamie, 39, white, UK)

Some interviewees attributed the formation of their feminist identities to the family nucleus but described it as a side effect of their upbringing. For instance, Lucia (39, white, Spain) recounted being raised as a boy due to her parents' disappointment at not having a son. After years of being dressed in boyish clothing and playing football, Lucia noticed she was treated differently during puberty by her peers. When her feminine features became conspicuous, Lucia was no longer included in male-dominated practices and spaces. Understanding that society treats men and women differently made her become a feminist. Similarly, Jessica (32, biracial white-Jamaican, USA) developed a feminist outlook after noticing the different treatment she and her brothers received from their grandparents and mother:

I'm the only female in my generation [...] I remember I figured out that when they would assign us chores, I would be vacuuming or sweeping, or doing the dishes, and the boys got to do the lawn work, which was cool [...] They got to mow the lawn, they got to go play with the animals outside and feed the goats, the cattle. All of the things that I wanted to do. I was like, "why do I have to be stuck inside doing these chores?" My mom explained to me that they do it because they are boys. And I'm like "and? I'm stronger than all of them. I'm faster than all of them. I'll arm wrestle anyone [...] why do they get to do it and I don't?" they said, "it's a boy's thing to do". I was like "no, I'm not cool with this."

Other interviewees identified academia and higher education as the point in their lives when they became feminists. These participants described having subconscious feminist ideas since childhood, which they were later able to articulate, define, and refine thanks to their academic education: "I've never not been a feminist, but I've become a more educated and articulated feminist, far more able to actually understand the problems" (Ally, 39, white, UK). Sheela (49, Indian-Anglo Saxon, Australia) also credited her education with helping her develop her feminist perspective:

It helped me discover more about myself. I think the more you read, the more you educate yourself, the more you figure out who you are and what your place in the universe is.

Here we see that the interviewees' exposure to feminist thought through courses about gender and feminism raised their awareness of gender inequality. Higher education provided them with the language and tools to fight against gender inequality.

The interviewees' eagerness to educate themselves continued after finishing their university degrees. They described how they continued to read feminist academic scholarship and follow feminist activists on social media to keep up with current affairs. Being up to date with feminist discussions was imperative for the interviewees, such as Camila (33, Latina, Australia):

I like to consider myself an informed citizen. I don't like not knowing what's going on. I think being able to understand that structure and how it's been set up and what's going to impact you or your family.

Staying informed meant that the participants could address and take part in current discussions and controversies and fight pushbacks against feminist causes.

The last arena that introduced the interviewees to the feminist movement and catalyzed their feminist identities was popular culture in general and fandom specifically. They talked about the feminist celebrities, iconic fictional characters, or feminist journalists who stirred their feminist imagination:

> I was introduced to the real essence of feminism by Amanda Palmer and Caitlin Moran [...] when Amanda is talking about it while getting undressed and being what she is; there must be something to it. (Courtney, 29, white, Germany)
>
> Princess Leia and Hermione and f****** Erwyn. It was probably... it was a very basic understanding of feminism, but it was like "yo, girls can do this s*** too." (Daniela, 23, Latina, USA)
>
> Maybe the movies I watched? [...] I mean, when we were growing up, having a female character, a female lead character, was a huge thing. I think, probably, having movies that were a little bit less on that annoying damsel in distress thing. I always remember with *Pirates of the Caribbean*, she didn't just wait around, she didn't conform. I remember thinking that was interesting. (Jenny, 31, Chinese, UK)

I argue that exposure to feminist thought through popular culture resembles the process of consciousness-raising (Chesebro et al., 1973; Green, 1979; hooks, 2000). In the traditional consciousness-raising of the 1970s, encounters and open discussions between women revealed a commonality in their experiences, shedding light on collective challenges and struggles beyond the personal. Such discussions motivated women to become feminists and activists. In a similar fashion, Sowards and Renegar (2004) claimed that popular culture content and celebrities also serve as "a vehicle for feminist consciousness-raising for its audiences" (p. 544). Being exposed to fictional and inspiring real-life women, the interviewees began to think more critically about women's roles in society and the lengths they could go to achieve their goals.

The interviewees mentioned not only celebrities and fictional characters as their feminist inspirations but also talked about the significant contribution of fan communities to their feminist identities. Emily (34, white, UK), who grew up in a small, conservative town in Northern Ireland, shared that, "a lot of what I learned about the history of feminism was through fandom." Interacting with other feminist fans online shaped Emily's attitudes regarding women's rights and educated her about the pro-choice movement. I will go back to this point later (Chap. 6) when discussing how women negotiate between feminism and fandom. Some feminist fans do not experience fandom and feminism as a contradiction but as two identities that contribute to each other.

The biographical narratives reviewed in this section emphasize why it is important to share "becoming" stories, as Olufemi (2020) argued. These stories allow us to map the terrain of potentially feminist-catalyzing arenas, which encourage individuals to educate themselves about feminism and gender inequality. Having described the routes that led women to feminism, I now elaborate on the different ways in which they put this identity into practice.

2.4   "BEFORE I DIDN'T CARE, AND NOW IT'S A LOT OF WORK": PRACTICING FEMINISM

Similar to fandom, the interviewees defined feminism primarily as an identity that does not require particular practices in order to be proclaimed. They maintained that one can claim a feminist identity by merely believing in gender equality and were hesitant to tie feminism to specific actions:

> I think someone's a feminist if they recognize the fact that women and men deserve the same opportunities. (Eve, 30, white, UK)
> I'm always kind of reluctant to prescribe specific things and say, 'if you do this, this makes you a feminist'. (Zoe, 32, white, UK)

Nevertheless, I mapped a typology of three primary feminist practices that the interviewees discussed during the interviews: (1) inclusion, (2) public sphere activism, and (3) private sphere activism (everyday feminism).

Inclusion, one of the most repeated terms across the interviews, provides an interesting example of the participants' ambivalence about the relationship between identity and practice. While the second wave of feminism was regarded as largely a community of white women, one of the tenets of the third wave of feminism was inclusion. The concept encapsulates the embrace of diversity and complexity, rejection of ownership of the feminist experience, and engagement with postcolonial, postmodernist, intersectional, and queer theories (Bailey, 1997; Budgeon, 2011; Butler, 1990; Dean, 1998; hooks, 2000; Spivak, 2003). The interviewees described inclusionary feminism as interactions with other women and feminists, which include helping and promoting women, as well as listening to and respecting other women's opinions. They understood feminism as a collective that brings women together in solidarity. For example, Stephanie (29, white, UK) exemplified this approach when discussing her attendance at a feminist academic conference:

> That was all about being body-positive, sex-positive, and inclusive. And... that, to me, that was brilliant. Again, it was like a fandom. We had a basic interest in feminism, and it might be that some people were interested in the historical roots, and others were interested in other issues, but we shared that level of interest.

In a similar fashion, Olivia (40, white, UK) regarded feminism as a "sisterhood, to be supportive of each other."

In alignment with their emphasis on intersectional feminism, many white interviewees addressed their privilege and stressed the importance of supporting marginalized women:

> If you're benefiting from the white privilege system, you should think what you're doing about that, and I think it's the same with feminism. It's also, actually, in post colonialism, with the burkini ban in France, white French feminists said that women shouldn't be allowed to wear the burkini at the beach because they're oppressed by men, and I think... it's just "what logic is that?" (Nina, 25, white, UK)
>
> I try to advocate for trans people in my department [...] I don't have a personal stake here; I just think it's human decency. (Emily, 34, white, UK)

Some interviewees of marginalized ethnicity also used a discourse of inclusion and intersectionality and acknowledged the areas of life in which they were also privileged. Justine (43, Lebanese-Maltese-English, Australia), for instance, explained that despite experiencing barriers due to her ethnicity, she was also university-educated and middle-class, two identities that provide her with social security and inclusion.

Although the interviewees referred to inclusion as a significant feminist value, it was frequently articulated in theoretical, general terms; most did not provide concrete examples of the ways in which they put this important value into practice. For instance, Lily (31, white, UK), a wheelchair user due to an illness, explained that "as a disabled person, I'm not considered as equal to other feminists." She recounted being frequently barred from attending feminist gatherings because they took place in venues that were not wheelchair-friendly. While it is clear that there was a genuine aspiration and eagerness to practice inclusionary feminism, actual steps to ensure this inclusion were frequently absent (this "superficial" inclusion will be unpacked further in the next chapter).

Public and private activism also demonstrate a closer tie between feminist identity and practice. As many scholars have argued, identifying as a feminist not only changes one's perceptions but also motivates action and social activism (Ahmed, 2017; Redfern & Aune, 2010; Sowards & Renegar, 2004; Yoder et al., 2011). Sowards and Renegar (2006) observed that traditional feminist activism used to take place in the public sphere through protests, demonstrations, and partisan movements pushing for change in legislation. Nowadays, they argue, feminist activism can also be found in the private sphere: "For modern feminists, activism need not necessarily be a public or group activity. Powerful forms of activism can be individual and private" (p. 69). Based on Sowards and Renegar's argument, I distinguish between activism in the public and private spheres.

Public sphere activism includes practices designed to promote women and feminism in the public sphere through participating in feminist organizations, communities, and associations. Several interviewees, like Ramona (31, white, Ireland), Wendy (50, white, UK), and Sheela (49, Indian-Anglo Saxon, Australia), were members of feminist organizations and networks. Jessica (32, biracial white-Jamaican, USA) volunteered at a homeless shelter:

> A lot of times, I like to reach out and talk to people in our homeless shelters, especially women who are feeling the need. I usually go to the women's homeless shelter and just talk about different things […] trying to push for and help them realize that, you know, they can do this, they are capable.

In a different example, Gabby (37, Black, USA) talked about her volunteer work in accompanying women who decide to have an abortion:

> Recently there was some kind of pro-life rally or something. A bunch of us gathered together by this women's clinic to kind of like, make sure that the people who are going in are protected.

While describing her activism, Gabby also confessed that she normally shies away from most community engagement activities due to being an introvert. Like Gabby, other interviewees such as Justine (43, Lebanese-Maltese-English, Australia), who called herself "a couch potato feminist," also stated that their feminist work is mainly confined to their private lives. The majority of interviewees felt more confident and keener to engage in activism in the private sphere activism than in the public sphere. Private sphere activism, or "everyday feminism," incorporates feminist practices in one's personal life and immediate social circles. Examples include initiating conversations with loved ones and colleagues about gender and feminism, buying gender-neutral or women-empowering products, consuming popular culture that shares these characteristics, and child-rearing with a feminist agenda. Similar to inclusion, everyday feminism also relates to third wave, postfeminist ideals, which promote individualization, subjectivism, freedom of choice, and agency (Baker, 2010; Genz, 2009; Gill, 2007; McRobbie, 2004; Munford & Waters, 2014; Rottenberg, 2014). These values were articulated by many participants, such as Nina and Anna:

> It's just in my daily life [...] I know I can live on my own without men. I lived on my own. I can do things just like men. I work in a job that mostly men do. (Anna, 27, white, France)
> Being yourself, independent, being true to who you are [...] you should be independent. Even if you have a family, you shouldn't give up on your career [...] also getting an education, mainly because that's the route to independence. (Nina, 25, white, UK)

Many of the participants also mentioned everyday feminism in their definition of the concept. For example, Daria (52, white, Switzerland) explained that feminism means that "you do as you feel without feeling you have to fit into a category, fit to what people think you should be."

Practices of everyday feminism included raising awareness and criticizing wrongdoings in their immediate surroundings. For instance, Angela (55, white, UK), who had served in the military in the past, mentioned speaking up against sexual harassment:

> I had a young woman in my platoon who was sexually assaulted by a bloke. The entire evening he was trying to chat women up. I was a captain, and my major asked me why she was out of sorts, and I told him, and he said: "well, it serves her right for drinking with him." I needed him to get it. He just didn't get it [...] The more I challenged officers my own rank or higher rank, my annual reports got worse, my marks got worse. I quit by then. It's exhausting.

Other interviewees mentioned challenging traditional views of women and femininity, such as Anaya (19, Indian, UK), who shared:

> I pick up on when someone says things like "girls." I look at them like "really?" [...] I don't mind challenging people. I'm not a very aggressive person, but if someone says something... "Actually, no. That's not how it works."

Despite the importance of turning the spotlight on social injustice and gender inequality, the interviewees revealed the downside of being outspoken. Many wished they could "switch off" their feminist awareness and critique, as it took a toll on them emotionally, socially, and professionally. Thinking about the social price she had to pay for her feminist identity, Courtney lamented (29, white, Germany): "Before I didn't see it, I didn't have to, and I didn't care, and now it's a lot of work." When the participants spoke out against misconceptions and social norms, they were called "difficult," "grumpy," and "killjoys," or feared being recognized as such. Anita (35, white, Italy) described the price for going against the tide:

> Being different is difficult, it's terrible [...] If you choose to be different, you fight every day. I try not to judge anybody because fitting in is so much better sometimes. "OK, you made a sexist joke." I don't feel like always standing up and saying, "this isn't right." Sometimes you're just tired.

The participants' accounts echoed arguments made by feminist scholars such as Roxane Gay (2014) and Sara Ahmed, who depict feminists' paradoxical position in society, where "you feel wronged by being perceived as in the wrong just for pointing out something is wrong" (Ahmed, 2017, p. 38). Feminist women fans' self-policing due to fear of ostracization will be explored further in the following chapters.

In parallel to fandom, the interviewees were reluctant to tie feminist identity to a particular set of practices. Simultaneously, they reported feeling guilty for not being active enough. While studying contemporary forms of feminist activism, Sowards and Renegar (2006) argued that young feminists experience "blame for not doing enough" (p. 71). They explained that contemporary feminist activists feel guilty when comparing their actions to traditional forms of activism such as protests and campaigns undertaken by their predecessors. Despite being active and promoting feminism in various arenas, the interviewees felt they were not "good" feminists.

Even those who engaged in both private and public activism felt inadequate. For example, after sharing stories about standing up against sexual assaults in the army and volunteering in a women's organization, Angela (55, white, UK) said she felt ashamed about not being a "good enough" feminist:

> I have my everyday feminism. But there are those, and we need them, who are campaigning, who are more... more livid. I go along in my life, and I have a wife, being a *Doctor Who* fan, doing police work, bringing awareness, and so my feminism comes along with me, but it's not... I don't campaign for it, I don't work towards it, I don't write about it. Other people are really working for it, promoting feminism all the time, that's their life, that's their role.

Like Angela, many participants placed themselves on the lower levels of an imagined feminist ladder. In this hierarchy, there were those who "deserved" to be accepted as feminists and those who did not. Most of the participants identified themselves with the latter group.

2.5   Conclusions: Feminist Versus Fan Labor

This chapter described the paths that led women into fandom and feminism and explored the complex relationship between identity and practice. The interviewees' biographical narratives established that once the "fan" and "feminist" identities were adopted, they were reinforced and performed through practice. This process, however, was met with ambivalence by the participants. On the one hand, taking part in activities revolving around their fandom or the promotion of gender equality provided feminist women fans with a sense of accomplishment and fulfillment. The interviewees emphasized their eagerness to turn feminism and fandom into a significant part of their identities and demonstrate their dedication through action. On the other hand, being active in fandom and feminism often felt like an obligation rather than a right. Thus, the interviews reflected the inner contradictions among the participants, who talked about not putting much emphasis on their practices, while at the same time expressing guilt for not doing "enough" to be entitled to their claimed identities.

While the participants expressed the same ambivalence toward fandom and feminism when discussing the connection between identity and practice, some significant differences between fandom and feminism also emerged. First, fandom was a lifelong identity, one that the interviewees had embraced since childhood, while feminism was the more recent of the two, as it was developed during their adulthood. Second, and more importantly, the interviewees were more motivated to take part in countless fannish practices. In contrast, when discussing feminism, the participants focused on values and perceptions and took part in fewer feminist activities compared to those related to fandom. I argue that they were more eager to take part in fannish practices than feminist ones because, ultimately, they found fandom more fun and satisfying than feminism. Feminism, in contrast, was "tiring" and felt like an uphill battle. It required a strong sense of moral obligation and invited criticism and ostracism from their social surroundings. Since feminist practices, especially public sphere activism, were regarded as very demanding, the interviewees hesitated to participate in them. I suggest that because the interviewees identified as both fans and feminists, they were more inclined to engage with everyday feminism instead of public sphere activism and used their fandom as a platform to develop and express their feminist identities.

To conclude, this chapter sheds light on the feelings of conflict, guilt, and inauthenticity that accompany feminist women fans. It reveals that feminist women fans sometimes find practicing their identities an arduous duty despite them being necessary and potentially enjoyable for them. As the following chapters reveal, the interviewees' expressions of guilt were due not only to an insufficient quantity or quality of their fannish and feminist practices but also to external pressures, deriving from their engagement in communities that frequently police and marginalize them.

References

Abercrombie, N., & Longhurst, B. J. (1998). *Audiences: A sociological theory of performance and imagination*. SAGE Publications Ltd.

Ahmed, S. (2017). *Living a feminist life*. Duke University Press.

Alcoff, L. M. (2005). *Visible identities: Race, gender, and the self*. Oxford University Press.

Bacon-Smith, C. (1992). *Enterprising women: Television fandom and the creation of popular myth*. University of Pennsylvania Press.

Bailey, C. (1997). Making waves and drawing lines: The politics of defining the vicissitudes of feminism. *Hypatia, 12*(3), 17–28.

Baker, J. (2010). Claiming volition and evading victimhood: Post-feminist obligations for young women. *Feminism & Psychology, 20*(2), 186–204.

Baym, N. K. (2000). *Tune in, log on: Soaps, fandom, and online community*. Sage.

Bourdaa, M. (2018). "May we meet again": Social bonds, activities, and identities in #clexa fandom. In P. Booth (Ed.), *A Companion to media fandom and fan studies* (pp. 385–400). John Wiley & Sons.

Brough, M. M., & Shresthova, S. (2012). Fandom meets activism: Rethinking civic and political participation. *Transformative Works and Cultures, 10*, 1–27.

Brown, J. A. (1997). Comic book fandom and cultural capital. *Popular Culture, 30*(4), 13–31.

Budgeon, S. (2011). *Third-wave feminism and the politics of gender in late modernity*. Springer.

Butler, J. (1990). *Gender trouble and the subversion of identity*. Routledge.

Cavicchi, D. (1998). *Tramps like us: Music and meaning among Springsteen fans*. Oxford University Press.

Chesebro, J. W., Cragan, J. F., & McCullough, P. (1973). The small group technique of the radical revolutionary: A synthetic study of consciousness raising. *Communications Monographs, 40*(2), 136–146.

De Fina, A. (2015). Narrative and identities. In A. De Fina & A. Georgakopoulou (Eds.), *The handbook of narrative analysis* (pp. 351–368). John Wiley & Sons.

Dean, J. (1998). Feminist solidarity, reflective solidarity: Theorizing connections after identity politics. *Women & Politics, 18*(4), 1–26.

Delmar, J. L., Plaza, J. F., & Sánchez Martín, M. (2020). An approach to defining the identity of a media fan. *Palabra Clave, 23*(2), 1–19.

Ewens, H. (2020). *Fangirls: Scenes from modern music culture*. University of Texas Press.

Fiske, J. (1992). The cultural economy of fandom. In L. A. Lewis (Ed.), *The adoring audience: Fan culture and popular media* (pp. 30–49). Routledge.

Gay, R. (2014). *Bad feminist*. Harper Collins.

Genz, S. (2009). *Postfemininities in popular culture*. Palgrave Macmillan.

Geraghty, L. (2018). Class, capital, and collecting in media fandom. In M. A. Scott & S. Scott (Eds.), *The Routledge companion to media fandom* (pp. 212–220). Routledge.

Gill, R. (2007). Postfeminist media culture: Elements of a sensibility. *European Journal of Cultural Studies, 10*(2), 147–166.

Green, P. (1979). The feminist consciousness. *The Sociological Quarterly, 20*(3), 359–374.

Hall, S. (1989). Ethnicity: Identity and difference. *Radical America, 23*(4), 9–20.

Hills, M. (2002). *Fan culture*. Routledge.

2 BECOMING A FEMINIST FAN   67

Hills, M. (2014). From Dalek half balls to Daft Punk helmets: Mimetic fandom and the crafting of replicas. *Transformative Works and Cultures, 16*, 1–20.

hooks, b. (2000). *Feminism is for everybody: Passionate politics*. Pluto Press.

Jenkins, H. (1992). *Textual poachers*. Routledge.

Jenkins, H. (2018). Fandom, negotiation, and participatory culture. In P. Booth (Ed.), *A Companion to media fandom and fan studies* (pp. 13–26). John Wiley & Sons.

Jenson, J. (1992). Fandom as pathology: The consequences of characterization. In L. A. Lewis (Ed.), *The adoring audience: Fan culture and popular media* (pp. 9–29). Routledge.

Josselson, R., & Lieblich, A. (1993). *The narrative study of lives*. Sage.

Kozinets, R. V. (2001). Utopian enterprise: Articulating the meanings of Star Trek's culture of consumption. *Journal of Consumer Research, 28*(1), 67–88.

Lamerichs, N. (2011). Stranger than fiction: Fan identity in cosplay. *Transformative Works and Cultures, 7*(3). https://doi.org/10.3983/twc.2011.0246

Lamerichs, N. (2018). *Productive fandom*. Amsterdam University Press.

Larsen, K., & Zubernis, L. (2011). *Fandom at the crossroads: Celebration, shame and fan/producer relationships*. Cambridge Scholars Publishing.

Lawler, S. (2014). *Identity: Sociological perspectives*. Polity Press.

Linden, H., & Linden, S. (2016). *Fans and fan cultures: Tourism, consumerism and social media*. Springer.

McRobbie, A. (2004). Post-feminism and popular culture. *Feminist media studies, 4*(3), 255–264.

Munford, R., & Waters, M. (Eds.). (2014). *Feminism and popular culture: Investigating the postfeminist mystique: Explorations in post-feminism*. I B Tauris.

Olufemi, L. (2020). *Feminism, interrupted: Disrupting power*. Pluto Press.

Ouellette, L., & Hay, J. (2008). *Better living through reality TV*. Blackwell.

Pande, R. (2018). *Squee from the margins: Fandom and race*. University of Iowa Press.

Pande, R. (2020). *Fandom, now in color: A collection of Voices*. University of Iowa Press.

Redfern, C., & Aune, K. (2010). *Reclaiming the f word: The new feminist movement*. Zed.

Reinhard, C. D. (2018). *Fractured fandoms: Contentious communication in fan communities*. Lexington Books.

Reinhard, C. D., & Dervin, B. (2012). Comparing situated sense-making processes in virtual worlds: Application of Dervin's sense-making methodology to media reception situations. *Convergence, 18*(1), 27–48.

Ricoeur, P. (1991). Narrative identity. *Philosophy Today, 35*(1), 73–81.

Rottenberg, C. (2014). The rise of neoliberal feminism. *Cultural Studies, 28*(3), 418–437.

Salter, A., & Blodgett, B. (2017). *Toxic geek masculinity in media: Sexism, trolling, and identity policing*. Springer.

Sandvoss, C. (2005). *Fans: The mirror of consumption*. Polity Press.

Schwalbe, M. L., & Mason-Schrock, D. (1996). Identity work as group process. *Advances in Group Processes, 13*(113), 47.

Scott, S. (2015). *Negotiating identity: Symbolic interactionist approaches to social identity*. John Wiley & Sons.

Scott, S. (2017). Modeling the Marvel everyfan: Agent Coulson and/as transmedia fan culture. *Palabra Clave, 20*(4), 1042–1072.

Sowards, S. K., & Renegar, V. R. (2004). The rhetorical functions of consciousness-raising in third wave feminism. *Communication Studies, 55*(4), 535–552.

Sowards, S. K., & Renegar, V. R. (2006). Reconceptualizing rhetorical activism in contemporary feminist contexts. *The Howard Journal of Communications, 17*(1), 57–74.

Spivak, G. C. (2003). Can the subaltern speak? *Die Philosophin, 14*(27), 42–58.

Tinson, J., Sinclair, G., & Kolyperas, D. (2017). Sport fandom and parenthood. *European Sport Management Quarterly, 17*(3), 370–391.

Whelehan, I. (2007). Forward. In S. Gillis, G. Howie, & R. Munford (Eds.), *Third wave feminism: A critical exploration* (pp. xv–xx). Palgrave Macmillan.

Winch, A. (2015). Feminism, generation and intersectionality. *Soundings, 58*, 8–20.

Yoder, J. D., Tobias, A., & Snell, A. F. (2011). When declaring "I am a feminist" matters: Labeling is linked to activism. *Sex Roles, 64*(1–2), 9–18.

Yodovich, N. (2022). Like father, like daughter: The intergenerational passing of Doctor Who and Star Wars fandoms in the familial context. In: B. Kies & Connor, M. (Eds.), Fandom, the next generation (pp. 57–67). Iowa University Press.

Yuval-Davis, N. (2011). *The politics of belonging: Intersectional contestations*. Sage.

Zubernis, L., & Larsen, K. (2018). Make space for us! Fandom in the real world. In P. Booth (Ed.), *A Companion to media fandom and fan studies* (pp. 145–160). John Wiley & Sons.

CHAPTER 3

Being a Feminist Fan

The previous chapter illustrated the paths that lead women to become feminists and fans and detailed the struggles and hesitations that some participants experienced on their road to proclaiming these identities. Chapter 2, however, did not probe into women's additional social identities that might contribute or hinder their process of identifying as fans and feminists. Therefore, this chapter delves deeper into the ways in which identities and social categories such as gender, ethnicity, and age intersect with fandom and feminism, focusing particularly on the moments in which they clash.

After expanding on the use of biographical narratives as a mechanism of clarifying one's identity in Chap. 2, this chapter examines the breaks in one's self-categorization. Self-categorization is an active process in which the individual makes sense of her identity and its components (Krane & Barber, 2005; Lawler, 2014; Turner & Reynolds, 2011). Through this process, the individual learns the norms and values attached to each identity she proclaims by observing how others who belong to the same category behave (ibid.). The question that arises here is as follows: what happens when the individual faces contradictions between the different identities she holds? These contradictions could be reflected in conflicts between the norms and values embedded in the different identities or the internalization that specific social categories are regarded as incompatible with each other.

N. Yodovich, *Women Negotiating Feminism and Science Fiction Fandom*, Palgrave Fan Studies, https://doi.org/10.1007/978-3-031-04079-5_3

69

Self-categorization is understood here as a product of context and time. As Shaw (2011) argued, "People work within contexts in which particular identities are articulated [...] inhibiting a certain identity categories can shift one's relationship with another category" (p. 30). Chapter 2 examined the formation of identity over time, highlighting the important events that shaped feminist women fans' identities, such as puberty or going to college. This chapter adds another layer to the unpacking of the fan and feminist identities by highlighting the ways in which different social contexts affect individuals' development and the management of their identities.

The linchpin of this chapter is the conflicts that arise during self-categorization processes, which lead to feelings of inner tension and contradictions. Examples include discord between identities such as gender and fandom, ethnicity and fandom/feminism, and age and fandom. The primary goal of this chapter is to explore the conflicts involved in espousing such identities together and to determine why they are regarded as being in conflict with one another at all. By doing so, this chapter helps expand fan studies beyond white and young subjects and promotes critical reflection on whiteness in feminism and fandom.

I begin this chapter by sharing the accounts of feminist women of marginalized ethnicities and their difficulty in relating to a movement that frequently disregards them. Then, I focus on the intersection of fandom with gender, ethnicity, and age and the various ways women feel like they are not suitable to identify as science fiction fans.[1] The examination of the amalgamation of various social identities, of course, invites the use of an intersectionality lens (Alarcón, 1990; Crenshaw, 1990; Hill Collins & Bilge, 2016). Through intersectionality we not only recognize the multifaceted nature of our identities, but also learn how such identities contribute to our privilege or disenfranchisement. Therefore, in this chapter intersectionality is expressed through the layered and multiple discriminations and stigma the interviewees in this study experienced.

---

[1] Like much of the rest of this book, the conflicts and challenges presented here are based on the interviewees' accounts. As a result, other possible identity intersections, such as feminism and age, are not discussed here because the interviewees did not regard them as incompatible, unlike the examples cited here.

3.1   "I CAN'T STAND HERE WITH YOU, BECAUSE YOU DON'T SEE ME": MARRYING FEMINISM AND MARGINALIZED ETHNICITIES

The interviewees' "becoming" stories that were chronicled in Chap. 2 included accounts in which feminist consciousness was developed through conflicts, especially with the participants' family members. Nevertheless, in most cases, their decision to embrace feminism was relatively effortless and definitive. This, however, was not the case for the interviewees who identified with a marginalized ethnicity.

Participants such as Gabby (37, Black, USA) shared that espousing a feminist identity was a process that was filled with doubt and inner conflict:

I was hesitant to… not so much hesitant to use the term, but again, with the different intersections of being a Black woman, it was kind of like, "is this feminism? Does it represent me as well?" kind of thing.

Like Gabby, other feminists of marginalized ethnicities questioned whether feminism was a movement that included them and fought for them:

I do feel left out. When you say it's 100 years for voting, for who? My dad was born before we had the right to vote. I'm very confused about that, too. It's not 100 years for me. Women of color are completely left out of this equation. It's frustrating […] You don't see me, so I can't stand here with you because you don't see me. (Tia, 34, Black African American, USA)

I sort of feel more invisible in terms of my culture. Also, because I pass for white very easily. It was really easy for that to be invisible, whereas I did become more vocal about my cultural background and really naming it and claiming it a lot more. (Sheela, 49, Indian-Anglo Saxon, Australia)

The main concern that interviewees such as Gabby, Tia, and Sheela raised is that the current structure and articulation of mainstream feminism do not foreground race and ethnicity. Traditionally, the points of reference for many strands of feminism are white, middle-class, heterosexual cisgender women. As a result, the feminist movement is often blind to the particular challenges confronting women who are not part of these social categories (Ahmed, 2004, 2017; Carby, 1982; Hill Collins, 1996; hooks, 1990, 2000; Joseph, 1981; Kendall, 2020; Ortega, 2006; Phipps, 2020; Vergès, 2021; Wing, 2000; Zakaria, 2021). Phipps (2020) articulated the prevalent white feminism consciousness when stating that "White feminists are 'everything.' We speak for other groups rather than letting them speak for themselves. We think of ourselves as experts and saviors" (p. 62). Concordantly, hooks (2000) claimed, "Foregrounding gender meant that white women could take center stage, could claim the movement as theirs, even as they called on all women to join" (p. 56). Thus, this kind of movement, which prioritizes white, middle-class women, simply cannot be an intellectual home and a safe haven for women of marginalized ethnicities.

Acknowledging the ubiquity of whiteness in its thought and members made certain interviewees feel like outsiders to the feminist movement. As Ortega (2006) described, "White feminists stand as the guardians of the doors of feminism, while women of color are those who remain homeless" (pp. 70–71). Gabby (37, Black, USA), for instance, provided an interesting example of the alienation she experienced during the Women's March in the USA:

> I guess, maybe two years ago or so, going to the Women's March and just seeing… thinking, "yeah, I'm a woman, of course, I'm going to participate in this." My husband's with me, and we're going around and just noticing that… seeing everybody in their pink hats and stuff, and I'm not quite sure that that's the exact group that I fit in. Looking around at the crowd and there's actually not a lot of people who looked like me: "Oh, this is a little bit strange." I know that we are here for equal rights for everyone, then why does the crowd not represent what I'm envisioning?

While Gabby's feelings of marginalization were implied and inferred based on the majority of the Women's March participants, other interviewees also experienced explicit pushback in feminist discussions and spaces:

> I have definitely experienced multiple times of being talked over by white women, especially because usually, if I'm speaking out, it's to point out maybe a blind spot in social justice spaces and I think that results in discomfort for them, so they shut me down. (Daniela, 23, Latina, USA)

As Carby (1982) argued, white feminists see themselves as oppressed while failing to acknowledge that they also serve as oppressors of women of marginalized ethnicities. Therefore, Nash (2018) explained that Black feminists' role is to incite and encourage intersectional thought and highlight one's privilege or lack thereof. However, speaking up about racial discrimination could potentially come with the price of becoming "precisely what the field imagines them to be—relentless, demanding" (pp. 34–38). Perhaps Nash's argument could be expanded to other women of marginalized ethnicities, like Daniela, for whom speaking up in white spaces meant being talked over, dismissed, and shut down.

Understanding that feminism, as it stands today, does not fully encompass women of marginalized ethnicities urged certain interviewees to choose between their identities and prioritize their battles. Are they fighting for women and risking becoming invisible in a movement that white women govern? Or, are they fighting for the members of their ethnic community and risking being marginalized in their own communities due to their gender? This predicament was poignantly articulated by Jessica (32, biracial White-Jamaican, USA), who shared: "My grandma would tell me, 'you were always more upset about the boy/girl thing than you were about the black/white thing.'" She then continued:

> Sometimes it feels like I need to be more about feminism, and sometimes I feel like I need to be more about my rights as a person of color. It's really sad that a lot of times, they are seen as separate [...] I don't think I've really realized that myself, but yeah, it feels like I either have to be a person of color or a woman. They want you to choose almost. Society tries to push you to choose, "which one you're going to go for today?"-"I guess the one that is suffering the most today."

In a different example, Jenny (31, Chinese, UK) declared that she chose the battle against racism over misogyny:

> At present, racism seems to be something that is so... I'm an Asian woman, but cognitively, I know that I'm an Asian woman rather than a woman who is also Asian [...] I feel like it's so mainstream now [...] it's easier for people to accept that something is a gender problem than for people to accept it's a race problem.

Like Jessica, Jenny expressed feeling pressured to "choose a side," between her gender and ethnic background. To her, as well as to other participants who identified with a marginalized ethnicity, feminism and race-based activism simply could not coexist together. Given that feminism has gained more visibility and acceptance in the public sphere than racial discrimination, Jenny decided to prioritize the latter.

When prioritizing their identities, the participants took part in what Wemyss (2006) recognized as "hierarchies of belonging." This concept refers to the ways in which individuals organize and prioritize the different components of their identities. As established here, being a feminist and a woman of a marginalized identity creates an imbalance in which the two identities compete for priority. Therefore, feminist women of marginalized ethnicities are forced to create a hierarchy of their identities and their communities and decide which identity to emphasize or prioritize to resolve the tension. Such hierarchies of belonging were evident in Jessica's and Jenny's discussions on the ways in which they decide to prioritize feminism and ethnicity.

The reports from Jenny and Jessica also reflect the importance of context in identity management and self-categorization (Kraus, 2013). As these participants described, the identities or communities they sided with were decided upon based on current events or the social and cultural climate. In Jenny's case, because she felt that feminism is generally embraced in popular discourse and is no longer frowned upon, fighting racism appeared more urgent. Jenny is an immigrant in the UK, where she is considered a minority. When she visits her home country, Singapore, she is no longer considered a minority. In that context, her priorities shift: "In Singapore, because of my position in society, I think I would have to argue more about women's issues, and I have." In parallel, Jessica explained that she gives preference to her gender or ethnicity based on whoever is "suffering the most" that day.

In other cases, the interviewees turned to womanism to reconcile their unease with the current state of the feminist movement and community:

> When I found out about womanism, I was like, "this makes sense where I intersect" [...] I can respect, like, my Blackness and still be a feminist. I don't have to pick one or the other. I can have both because both of them are who I am. (Tia, 34, Black African American, USA)
> There was womanism. As I've gotten older, it's just like, "yes, I am a feminist whether or not I relate to what every other feminist says." I had to find my own community within that community. (Gabby, 37, Black, USA)

Womanism, coined by Alice Walker (1983), offers an alternative to feminism for women of marginalized ethnicities, especially Black women. While feminism's focal point of critique is the patriarchy, womanism "offers a distance from the 'enemy,' in this case, white people in general and white women in particular, yet still raises the issue of gender" (Hill Collins, 1996, p. 11). Based on the understanding that "women" and "men" are umbrella terms that should not be understood as homogeneous, womanism clearly distinguishes between white men and women and Black men and women. Womanism regards Black men not as Black women's enemies but as their allies and comrades in fighting against racism and gender-based oppression. Therefore, womanism provided an intellectual home for women such as Tia and Gabby, who were keen to develop a nuanced critical social standpoint on gender inequality without compromising their ethnic identity.

In the previous chapter, most of the interviewees talked about inclusion as one of the main pillars of feminism. Nevertheless, the experiences of women of marginalized ethnicities demonstrate that discussions about inclusion usually lack real meaning and intent. For instance, Daniela (23, Latina, USA) highlighted the superficial engagement with diversity and inclusion in many feminist circles:

> Susan B Anthony is still today heralded as a feminist icon when she was violently racist. I think a lot of how people understand feminism is this very surface-level movement of like "yay, equality!" without any real nuance or depth to that understanding.

Indeed, hooks (2000) commented poignantly on feminism's failure to acknowledge its own contribution to racism, noting that: "It must have felt so awesome to have white women evoke sisterhood in a world where they had mainly experienced white women as exploiters and oppressors" (p. 56). Ahmed (2004) continued to develop the theme of the responsibility of white feminists, arguing that by presenting themselves as inclusionary, "anti-racism becomes a matter of generating a positive white identity, an identity that makes the white subject feel good about itself" (p. 6).

Even though espousing an intersectional perspective has been a major talking point of feminism for many years now (Byrne, 2015; Hill Collins & Bilge, 2016; McCall, 2005; Nash, 2018; Salem, 2013), despite the white interviewees' focus on engaging in practices of inclusion, the accounts of feminists of marginalized ethnicities prove that there is still severe inequality in the feminist community and theory. The interviewees' real-life experiences demonstrate that women still feel that feminism and the fight against racism do not necessarily go hand in hand. These feelings of incompatibility in their self-categorization accompanied the interviewees in their negotiation of the fan identity, as the following sections will reveal.

The intersection between feminism and ethnicity reveals the self-categorization processes that white women and women of marginalized ethnicities go through. Many white feminists see themselves and others primarily through the lens of gender. Feminists of marginalized ethnicities, however, incorporate their ethnicity into their self-categorization, which adds tension to their self-categorizations and self-perceptions. Understanding that feminism and their ethnicity do not necessarily go hand in hand, women of marginalized ethnicities are often left with the feeling that their identities cannot be whole as they are. They must choose between their gender and their ethnicity. Moving on to fandom, I reveal how gender, ethnicity, and age can all hinder women's self-categorization processes.

3.2   "Into these boys' things": Marrying Fandom and Gender

After "falling in love" with popular culture texts, such as the *Ghostbusters*, *The NeverEnding Story*, *Doctor Who*, and *Star Wars*, as described in Chap. 2, the interviewees quickly internalized that their geeky interests were considered "unconventional" for girls and women.

When reflecting on their childhoods, the interviewees reminisced about growing up as "one of the boys" and enjoying what they regarded as traditionally masculine practices:

> I self-identify as a geek, the girl who was into science fiction, and that's part of how I viewed myself [...] I identified myself as being into these "boys' things" (laughs). (Jane, 46, white, UK)
> I was the geeky kid. The other girls were into pop music. I was the girl who didn't fit in with the girls most of the time, the only girl in chess club. (Bernie, 50, white, UK)

In addition to indicating the fans' awareness about the prominence of men in science fiction fandom and other "geeky" communities, these quotes also suggest a sense of "specialness" that sometimes accompanies women fans of science fiction (Yodovich, 2016). The interviewees saw their interests in "boys' things" as a reflection of their rebellion against gender norms and a demonstration of their nonconformity. "For girls," Bucholtz (1999) explains, "nerd identity […] offers an alternative to the pressures of hegemonic femininity" (p. 214). Bucholtz claims that associating oneself with identities that are traditionally male-dominated means that girls and women gain power over the performance of their gender. Unlike those who so-called succumb to gender norms, nerdy and geeky girls are not required to be "cute" or "attractive," according to Bucholtz. They are free to experiment with their looks and hobbies. Thus, for many women fans, prioritizing traditional masculine interests over feminine ones is regarded as a symbol of their individualism and agency.

Feelings of specialness and uniqueness were, nevertheless, accompanied by ridicule and stigma. Women fans of science fiction were regarded as an anomalous minority "invading" fandom for the "wrong" reasons. Such women fans encountered various stereotypes and tropes that were used against them, such as the "girlfriend," "fangirl," and "fake geek girl" (Busse, 2013; Cote, 2020; Gerrard, 2021; Orme, 2016; Salter & Blodgett, 2017).

Based on the assertion that women are not genuinely interested in science fiction, the interviewees reported being frequently referred to as men fans' girlfriends. Jamie (39, white, UK), for example, recalled: "When I'm with my husband in conventions, or even in social events, it's presumed that he is the fan and I'm just kind of there." In another example, Anita (35, white, Italy) discussed the disregard of women in role-playing communities:

> There's this expression, "the GM's girlfriend".[2] The GM's girlfriend is always the girlfriend that comes along, plays, and ruins the game because she doesn't know how to play. So I made myself a t-shirt, "I'm no GM's girlfriend." Everybody was staring at me, surprised I came because I love it. I am here alone.

Anita's experiences in the role-playing community are parallel to those of women who play video games, where women are assumed to be interested in video games only because of their boyfriends (Condis, 2018; Cote, 2020). Due to their minimal experience in gaming, these girlfriends are considered unskilled and hazardous to include in multiplayer games as they might compromise the team's chances of winning (Bryce & Rutter, 2005; Cote, 2020). Understanding that she might be belittled or excluded

[2] Gamemaster is the organizer and moderator of a role-playing group.

from the games due to her presumed lack of experience made Anita create a t-shirt that tackled and shattered this stereotypical misconception explicitly.

The "girlfriend" trope reflects the suspicious reception of women who are interested in science fiction and other geeky content. It is as if women cannot be interested in science fiction unless their partners are fans or looking for a new geeky romantic partner. Isabel (26, white, Spain) rejected this assumption and argued: "They think I'm faking it to get a guy [...] to get attention. Why would I want your attention in the first place?" The idea of women looking for a date in fandom conventions has been discussed in Bacon-Smith's seminal work, *Enterprising Women* (1992), as well as in studies on other male-dominated arenas such as ice hockey fandom (Crawford & Gosling, 2004), football fandom (Jones, 2008), and skater communities (Currie et al., 2006). In all of these arenas, the perception is the same: women's interest in presumably masculine hobbies is inauthentic and is driven only by romantic associations with men, whose interest in the medium is for the "right" reasons.

Women fans are not only assumed to be interested in science fiction because of their real-life romantic relationships, but also accused of fawning over fictional characters and handsome actors. A ubiquitous stereotype in fan communities is the "fangirl" trope, which represents a rabid, hysterical, obsessive fan whose primary attraction to popular culture content is the good looks of the actors featured in them (Driscoll, 2002; Hadas, 2013; Larsen & Zubernis, 2011; O'Day, 2013; Reinhard, 2018). The fangirl is usually prone to diverge from the canon, "ship[3]" random couples, and write fan fiction about them (Hadas, 2013; Salter & Blodgett, 2017). The fangirl is, therefore, interested in the "wrong" things for the "wrong" reasons (Busse, 2013). Her inappropriate enthusiasm for good-looking actors distracts her from appreciating the intellectual depth of the content and limits her ability to analyze it. Much like the "girlfriend" trope, the "fangirl" stereotype is used to belittle women fans' legitimacy and authenticity: "you're just a fangirl, and you're only into it because the guys are hot" (Emily, 34, white, UK). In a different example, Jenny (31, Chinese, UK) remembered being scolded for talking about her fandom openly and enthusiastically:

---

[3] Short for "relationship." Shipping means rooting for a couple in a popular culture content.

I remember once when I was 14, I got a comment from my friend's parents. My friend's mom told her, "why is your friend so boy-crazy?" That was also one of the reasons why I didn't really talk about it.

Women are frequently sanctioned for expressing their sexuality and sexual attractions openly and unashamedly, and it is no different in fandom. Women fans' sexual interests turn them into a target for mockery and dismissal, as emotionally or sexually induced motivations to pursue fandom are considered irrational, superficial, and illegitimate. The automatic assumption that the fangirl is drawn to pop culture content because of a sexual or romantic attraction also fails to acknowledge the wide array of motivations leading women to become fans, as well as the diverse spectrum of women's sexuality. Ramona (31, white, Ireland) articulated this idea when reflecting on the fangirl trope:

> I am asexual so I don't know… It doesn't annoy me but it's something I can't really relate to that much. I sometimes get crushes, but it's very rare. So, when people go on about that [the assumption she is interested in *Doctor Who* because she is attracted to the Doctor], I'm like, "shut up."

The "fake geek girl" is another prominent trope in science fiction fandom (Orme, 2016; Reagle, 2015; Reinhard, 2018; Salter & Blodgett, 2017; Simon, 2011). Following up on the fangirl trope, this stigma of the fake geek girl persecutes women in particular who attempt to join the fan community in order to find a romantic partner or to simply feel desirable. In his paper about fake geek girls, Reagle (2015) explored men fans' suspicion of women who show interest in their "geeky" hobbies. He cited journalist John Peacock's article about fake geek girls, in which he called them the "6 of 9" women. Inspired by the *Star Trek* character called Seven of Nine, Peacock claimed that women who are a "6" in the real world (on a 1–10 scale, vis-à-vis their physical appearance) join male-dominated fandoms to become a "9." According to Peacock, taking advantage of the traditional notion that men fans are lonely and sexually deprived, women parade in sexy costumes at fan conventions in order to feel desirable in such male-dominated spaces (Peacock in Reagle, 2015). Given the supposition that the fake geek girl is feigning interest in science fiction in order to be fawned over by legions of men fans, the authenticity of her identity as a fan is questioned or completely dismissed (Orme, 2016; Reagle, 2015; Simon, 2011).

The prominent stereotypical perceptions of women fans teach women about their second-class citizens in science fiction fandom. It reveals to them that their legitimacy and authenticity are always questioned. In contrast to feminists of marginalized ethnicities, women fans do not necessarily find that their gender contradicts their fandom. The tensions that they report here are not due to a conflict of interests or values. Instead, the challenge that arises in women fans' self-categorization is the perception that the science fiction fan is an identity that men primarily espouse (or "should" primarily espouse). However, I acknowledge that women are not a uniform entity. Therefore, the following sections examine the intersections of fandom and gender with ethnicity and age by focusing on women fans of marginalized ethnicities and older women fans.

3.3   "I'M TOLD IT'S A WHITE THING": MARRYING FANDOM AND ETHNICITY

When Tia (34, Black African American, USA) described the process of becoming a fan, she explained that fandom initially appeared antithetical to her ethnic background:

> I'm Black, and I grew up in a Black family around Black people, so, in my culture experience, it was seen as the thing that white people like to do.

Tia's claim was not unique to her. Most of the interviewees who identified with a marginalized ethnicity such as Jenny (31, Chinese, UK) or Daniela (23, Latina, USA) echoed these sentiments.

In light of the established fandom scholarship and mainstream media, it is unsurprising that many assume that people of marginalized ethnicities do not identify as fans or rarely participate in such communities. Fiske (1992), for instance, notably acknowledged his inability to find what he called, nonwhite fans, for his seminal study. Similarly, some works only briefly acknowledged ethnicity, while others primarily included white participants (Hellekson & Busse, 2006; Larsen & Zubernis, 2011; Orme, 2016). Whiteness, by the same token, is often accepted as a given and is rarely scrutinized analytically. It is unmarked, unarticulated, and unnamed in fan communities as well as in fan studies (Pande, 2018; Stanfill, 2011; Wanzo, 2015; Warner, 2015; Woo, 2018).

Recently, fan studies scholars have tried to demonstrate that fans of marginalized ethnicities are not absent or non-existent but rather pushed out and silenced. Martin (2019), for instance, who interviewed Black fans, revealed that his participants usually do not attend big opening nights for most *Marvel* movies because they feel alienated in such white-dominated hotspots. By merely "existing," Pande (2018) asserts, fans of marginalized ethnicity are perceived as an uninvited disruption of the social norm in fan communities. Understanding their marginalized, unwanted position in many fandoms, Black fans "choose to exist despite their invisibility and exclusion from mainstream fan spaces" (Warner, 2015, p. 35).

Indeed, fandom, particularly that of science fiction, is fixtured as a "white thing," so much so that certain people of marginalized identities refrain from approaching it and openly claiming this identity:

> It was always funny to me because my dad is a huge Trekkie, but he doesn't tell people. I used to record Next Generation because he had to work when it was airing. So, I would record it for him, and he would sit there in his room when he got home and watched it, like, religiously. "You are a huge nerd, and you're not letting anybody know." There's this level of secrecy with it. It wasn't something you're supposed to be open about. (Tia, 34, Black African American, USA)

The secrecy that Tia's father adopted perhaps indicates that being a science fiction fan is perceived as crossing into foreign, hostile terrain. It is a territory in which Black people feel alienated and therefore one that they should not gravitate toward in the first place.

In some cases, being interested in a "white" hobby meant that Tia (34, Black African American, USA) and other women fans of marginalized ethnicities found it even more difficult to locate a community where they fully belonged:

> At school, it was just weird because it was weird, and at home, it was weird because it's what white people did. It was difficult to navigate. I understand to some degree why my family didn't get it. It was frustrating at school that other kids… I'm told it's a white thing, so they should at least get it, but you don't get it.

As Tia's account indicates, proclaiming an identity that attracts its own stigma, such as science fiction fandom, is even more complicated for those who already have other social burdens. As Wanzo (2015) stated, the only ones who are allowed to be openly fannish and out and about in fan communities are white individuals. She explained that by situating themselves as an "opposition to normative practices of consumption" (Wanzo, 2015, n.p.), white fans have proudly monopolized the position of the "other" in media engagement. Unlike communities that have been "othered," such as marginalized ethnicities, white fans can choose to distance themselves from mainstream audiences and maintain a position of power. Fans of marginalized ethnicities do not have the luxury of parading their otherness without being sanctioned.

In contrast to Tia's experience, Nika (44, Latina/Chicana, USA) found comfort in the amalgamation of her stigmatized identities. She formed a community with others who also experienced alienation. She described how fandom and other geeky interests were a refuge to her, as well as to other outcast teenagers in her school:

> In middle school, I met some kids who wanted to play D&D, and I learned to play. It was the scrawny, pale kids who everyone thought were hillbillies. The Asian kid who everybody thought their family was gangsters. It was a bunch of reject kids who played Dungeons and Dragons.

Nika's example demonstrates once again that self-categorization is contextualized. Tia, as well as her father, understood that fandom and other geeky interests were not accepted by their immediate social surroundings. Tia's fannish pursuits were also discouraged by individuals from outside her community, such as her classmates. Therefore, she felt like an outsider in all of her social circles. In contrast, fandom and ethnicity converged remarkably well for Nika. They helped her find common ground with her schoolmates who were also looked down upon due to their ethnic background or class.

While women fans of marginalized ethnicities were well aware of how their ethnicity was interlaced with their fan identity, white women rarely acknowledged aspects of their identities that facilitated their acceptance as fans. As I will demonstrate later in the next chapter, most white women's accounts centered on gender-based exclusion in fan communities. Whiteness, on the other hand, was not a topic of discussion with such participants. It was not a category that the participants thought to scrutinize or unpack in relation to fandom. As Woo (2018) noted, "Privilege is so unremarkable to its holders that it becomes invisible" (p. 251).

Anita (35, white, Italy) was one of the only white participants who briefly addressed the privilege of whiteness:

I am probably more privileged in some way because I am white, I am straight, I have a lot of things. I don't have to live in an environment where every day I have to be challenged. That challenge is there for me to grab it or not, do it or not do it, it's up to me.

"Admitting to being white," Vergès (2021) declared, is "admitting that privileges have historically been granted to this color" (p. 26). Indeed, when reflecting on her ethnicity, Anita was aware of the various invisible ways in which she was free from context-based self-categorization restrictions. Unlike women of marginalized ethnicities, she acknowledged that she could easily blend in with the crowd. She could often choose when to tackle conflicts or discrimination or take part in spaces that might be hostile toward her. Others, such as women fans of a marginalized ethnicity, do not get to enjoy this social advantage.

In fandom, much like in feminism, ethnicity becomes an "issue" or an obstacle in one's self-categorization process when one is not white. Even though many white interviewees felt like second-class citizens in fandom because of their gender, they were free of other kinds of discrimination due to the color of their skin. Such a "free pass" was taken for granted, so much so that many participants did not even acknowledge their other privileges beyond their gender. Another almost "invisible" social category that certain participants did not consider was age. However, as the next section details, ageism targets women who are considered "too old" to be fans.

3.4   "They're not making it for us": Marrying Fandom and Age

The previous sections highlighted the contextuality of self-categorization and how, in some social settings, proclaiming particular identities simultaneously becomes challenging. This section addresses the cumulative effects of context and time constraints on self-categorization. Here, I review the life course of the fan identity (Harrington et al., 2011, 2014) and the ostracization that occurs when a woman is considered "too old" to continue identifying as a fan. In contrast to ethnicity, which automatically hinders individuals from identifying as fans or feminists, so-called older age is a social category that we are not born with but are "granted" later in life. As individuals age or are regarded as old, what was once acceptable or unquestioned could become anomalous and odd.

While it is difficult to determine the exact age at which one turns from simply a "fan" to being an "old fan," it appears to be relatively early in one's lifespan. For example, in her book about music fandoms, *Fangirls*, Ewens (2020) rightfully stressed that research on older women fans is scarce. As she urged scholars and journalists to highlight this sector in fan communities, she provided examples of "old" women who were *in their 30s*. By the same token, Emily (34, white, UK), who was younger than the average age of this study's pool of interviewees, situated herself "on the older end" of the fandom age scale.

Age is an interesting prism through which to explore fan identities because it exemplifies the subjective context in which fandom is embedded. In her study on singlehood and time, Lahad (2017) highlighted how the same biological age is constructed differently based on one's marital status. While 30-year-olds are on the threshold of becoming "old maids" when they are single, they could also be considered "young mothers" when married with children. Comparably, women in their late 20s could be categorized as young professionals in the workforce but thought of as too old for certain leisure hobbies, such as fandom.

Justine (43, Lebanese-Maltese-English, Australia), for example, received feedback from her surroundings that science fiction fandom is childish and unsuitable for people her age:

> People are accepting if you talk about it in a nostalgic framework. But it's not ok to, like, be excited at my forties when The Force Awakens came out. People are like, "whatever, it's just a movie, it's make-believe, and it's silly."

A similar sentiment echoed through Donna's interview (46, white, UK) when she talked about the latest *Star Wars* trilogy: "You know what, they're not making it for us, it's for the next generation, we have to just kind of let it go." Fandom, therefore, is perceived as belonging to one's childhood and youth. Once becoming an adult, it is an identity that is expected to be shaken off and bequeathed to the next generation of younger people. As both interviewees indicate, it is acceptable to feel nostalgic about beloved content from one's childhood but frowned upon to actively engage with the same content as an adult. Similarly, Bennett (2006) and Way (2021), who studied older punk fans, described how such individuals are frequently perceived as those who refuse to grow up or stubbornly cling to their youth.

"Older" participants reported being explicitly pushed to the margins and feeling like outsiders in fan communities. Jane (46, white, UK), for instance, explained that she feels old when she listens to podcasts created by younger fans:

> They say things like, "we're not going to go back too much into the history of fandom, so we're not going to talk about *Buffy the Vampire Slayer*." I thought that it means that they're not going to talk about *Sherlock Holmes*, but the 90s is ancient. It's strange (laughs). They had an episode about intergenerational interactions in fan fiction, and their old persons were in their late twenties.

This example establishes again the subjective context of age and identity, where people in their 20s are considered old, and the history of fandom begins in the 1990s. In a community in which individuals have such a short expiration date, getting older becomes a disruptive factor in one's self-categorization process.

The fan activity that reflected the exclusion of older women fans the most was merchandise consumption, especially the consumption of fannish fashion. "Older" interviewees expressed their frustration when browsing through the shelves of stores and not finding clothes that were manufactured for them:

> I do like clothes, and I do like fashion, and I like expressing fandom in a way that is not just the stereotypical nerd, a nice item you'd like to own anyway. I can go to the supermarket and buy men's t-shirts, I can even go to the Disney store, they have a great Rey [Star Wars' first onscreen woman protagonist] jacket, but it's for girls. If they did it in my size, I would buy it. (Ally, 39, white, UK)

Santo (2017) reviewed Disney's consumer product teams: infants and children, boys and geeks, girls and tweens, and adults. This categorization, as Santo claimed, not only is gendered (geekdom is only for boys) but also connotes the perception that "geekiness" or fannish behaviors expire in adulthood. Thus, as some of the participants indicated, "older" women fans are not the consumers that manufacturers envision. Similar discrimination occurs with football teams' merchandise, another arena that women, especially those who are "older," are not expected to inhabit (Sveinson et al., 2019). When shirts do not come in sizes that fit women in football fandoms, they are forced to purchase large-sized t-shirts that were originally manufactured for young boys. Understanding that manufacturers ignore a potential market hints that perhaps this sector, older women, is not the kind of audience that some franchises would like to associate with their brand.

The lack of merchandise for older women, who are, as a result, deprived of a common form of expressing their fandom, could lead to the false conclusion that older women are not interested in science fiction. In his study on older punk fans, Bennett (2006), as an example, recounted that he struggled to find older women to interview. Way (2021), who specifically targeted older women in her research, did not encounter such a challenge. Neither did I. Older women fans might be easy to ignore or overlook, but they do exist. The same is true for fans of marginalized ethnicities. As other scholars point out, there is a correlation between aging and invisibility, especially for women in spaces that are considered male-dominated (Bennett et al., 2019; Chess, 2020; Hall Jamieson, 1995).

According to Reinhard (2018), older individuals, particularly older women, seem idiosyncratic in fandom communities. As the interviewees explained, men have more leeway as they grow old in fan communities, whereas older women are expected to "retire" from fandom:

> I think it's more accepted for guys my age to admit to being a fan of *Star Wars* or Captain America or whatever, than it is for a woman my age or older. (Justine, 43, Lebanese-Maltese-English, Australia)

In a different example, women fans such as Lucy (41, white, UK) shared that they feel awkward going to movie premieres:

> I know that men my age can go [to a movie premiere] on their own and can go as a group, and it's fine, but women my age, you're only there if you're someone's mom.

Internalizing that being a so-called older fan is inappropriate made the interviewees such as Lucy refrain from attending fannish spaces where she might be ridiculed or treated as an outsider.

To explain the misconception that women stop identifying as fans when they get older, Ewens (2020) speculated that perhaps older women fans are difficult to find because they have less time to be active fans. In my study, however, "older" interviewees reported an increase in their fannish engagement compared to one or two decades earlier. Angela (55, white,

UK), the oldest participant in the research, started attending conventions and dabbling with cosplaying for the first time only after reaching her 50s. As she explained it, now that her children were older and she had achieved financial stability, she had more time and money to invest in *Doctor Who* conventions, merchandise, and cosplay. Petersen (2017) reported similar findings in her study on *Sherlock Holmes*' women fans who are over 50. Therefore, while the common wisdom is that fandom requires spare time, scholars should be mindful of how free time fluctuates through one's lifespan.

The case of the self-categorization of older women fans requires us to understand that age is subjective. It is not the objective biological entity that we commonly tend to envision. Age is a subjective construct that affects the ways in which we perceive our identity and are then represented to others. As longtime fan favorites such as *Star Wars* and *Doctor Who* continue to develop and expand, their fandoms will continue to vary in terms of their age. While indeed, for some interviewees, moments such as parenthood or developing a career put their fandom on hold, these fannish interests spiked again later in life. Therefore, fandom should be regarded not as linear but as an identity embodied and practiced differently at different moments in time.

3.5   CONCLUSIONS: IDENTITIES IN CRISIS

Mercer (1990) notably argued, "Identity only becomes an issue when it is in crisis" (p. 43). This statement is certainly true for the identities discussed in this chapter. As the findings provided here demonstrate, self-categorization can be an effortless, subconscious process for those equipped with privileged identities. For others, self-categorization is an onerous procedure that frequently invites awareness of the fragility of one's identity that occurs in moments of conflict and discord.

To further unpack self-categorization, this chapter identifies the ways in which the fan and feminist identities are challenged, prioritized, or stifled depending on context and time. The findings of this chapter reveal that many feminist women fans do not, or cannot, perceive their identities as a whole. Instead, their identities are constantly fractured and in need of maintenance and navigation. Due to the social categories they were born into, and others they have chosen to proclaim, the interviewees experienced continuous turmoil. The intersection of gender, ethnicity, and age demonstrated the layered challenges and stigma facing those who proclaim these identities in conjunction. Facing the complexity of their identities made women create a hierarchy for them, in which they were forced to prefer one over the other. The prioritization processes and the rationales the interviewees constructed for them highlight the sad truth that the participants experienced these identities as almost inherently contradictory.

The common thread between the various intersections of identities reviewed here is that they are all assumed, to some extent, to be non-existent or a minority. In reality, these social groups exist, but are pushed to the margins and considered illegitimate. Internalizing the notion that espousing feminism and fandom is not suitable for their identities caused some women to feel conflicted about the legitimacy and coherence of their identities and refrain from disclosing them.

This chapter highlights the feminist woman fan and the internal processes she goes through when self-categorizing her identity. However, when discussing such procedures, it is impossible to separate the individual from other social players who come into contact with her. Such interactions play a significant role in shaping one's identity, which can potentially include practices of gatekeeping and toxicity. While such social encounters were hinted at in this chapter, they will be discussed more fully in the next chapter. Chapter 4 continues to unpack the challenges facing women feminist fans of science fiction by examining their interactions with other fans, their experiences of exclusion, and what I call their conditional belonging status.

REFERENCES

Ahmed, S. (2004). Declarations of whiteness: The non-performativity of anti-racism. *Borderlands e-journal, 3*(2) http://www.borderlandsejournal.adelaide.edu.au/vol3no2_2004/ahmed_declarations.htm
Ahmed, S. (2017). *Living a feminist life.* Duke University Press.
Alarcón, N. (1990). Chicana feminism: In the tracks of 'the'native woman. *Cultural Studies, 4*(3), 248–256.
Bacon-Smith, C. (1992). *Enterprising women: Television fandom and the creation of popular myth.* University of Pennsylvania Press.
Bennett, A. (2006). Punk's not dead: The continuing significance of punk rock for an older generation of fans. *Sociology, 40*(2), 219–235.
Bennett, D., Hennekam, S., Macarthur, S., Hope, C., & Goh, T. (2019). Hiding gender: How female composers manage gender identity. *Journal of Vocational Behavior, 113*, 20–32.

Bryce, J., & Rutter, J. (2005). Gendered gaming in gendered space. In J. Raessens & J. Goldstein (Eds.), *Handbook of computer game studies* (pp. 301–310). MIT Press.

Bucholtz, M. (1999). "Why be normal?": Language and identity practices in a community of nerd girls. *Language in Society, 28*(2), 203–223.

Busse, K. (2013). Geek hierarchies, boundary policing, and the gendering of the good fan. *Participations, 10*(1), 73–91.

Byrne, B. (2015). Rethinking intersectionality and whiteness at the borders of citizenship. *Sociological Research Online, 20*(3), 178–189.

Carby, H. V. (1982). White woman listen! Black feminism and the boundaries of sisterhood. In *The Empire Strikes Back: Race and Racism in 70's Britain* (pp. 212–235). Routledge.

Chess, S. (2020). *Play like a feminist.* MIT Press.

Condis, M. (2018). *Gaming masculinity: Trolls, fake geeks, and the gendered battle for online culture.* University of Iowa Press.

Cote, A. C. (2020). *Gaming sexism: Gender and identity in the era of casual video games.* NYU Press.

Crawford, G., & Gosling, V. K. (2004). The myth of the 'Puck Bunny' female fans and men's ice hockey. *Sociology, 38*(3), 477–493.

Crenshaw, K. (1990). Mapping the margins: Intersectionality, identity politics, and violence against women of color. *Stanford Law Review, 43*, 1241–1301.

Currie, D. H., Kelly, D. M., & Pomerantz, S. (2006). 'The geeks shall inherit the earth': Girls' agency, subjectivity and empowerment. *Journal of Youth Studies, 9*(4), 419–436.

Driscoll, C. (2002). *Girls: Feminine adolescence in popular culture and cultural theory.* Columbia University Press.

Ewens, H. (2020). *Fangirls: Scenes from modern music culture.* University of Texas Press.

Fiske, J. (1992). The cultural economy of fandom. In L. A. Lewis (Ed.), *The adoring audience: Fan culture and popular media* (pp. 30–49). Routledge.

Gerrard, Y. (2021). Groupies, fangirls and shippers: The endurance of a gender stereotype. *American Behavioral Scientist.* https://doi.org/10.1177/00027642211042284

Hadas, L. (2013). Resisting the romance: 'Shipping' and the discourse of genre uniqueness in Doctor Who fandom. *European Journal of Cultural Studies, 16*(3), 329–343.

Hall Jamieson, K. (1995). *Beyond the double bind: Women and leadership.* Oxford University Press on Demand.

Harrington, C. L., Bielby, D., & Bardo, A. R. (2014). *Aging, media, and culture.* MD Lexington Books.

Harrington, C. L., Bielby, D. D., & Bardo, A. R. (2011). Life course transitions and the future of fandom. *International Journal of Cultural Studies, 14*(6), 567–590.

Hellekson, K., & Busse, K. (Eds.). (2006). *Fan fiction and fan communities in the age of the internet: new essays.* McFarland.

Hill Collins, P. (1996). What's in a name? Womanism, Black feminism, and beyond. *The Black Scholar, 26*(1), 9–17.

Hill Collins, P., & Bilge, S. (2016). *Intersectionality.* Polity Press.

hooks, b. (1981 [1990]). *Ain't I a woman: Black women and feminism.* Pluto Press.

hooks, b. (2000). *Feminism is for everybody: Passionate politics.* Pluto Press.

Jones, K. W. (2008). Female fandom: Identity, sexism, and men's professional football in England. *Sociology of Sport Journal, 25*(4), 516–537.

Joseph, G. (1981). The incompatible menage a` trois: Marxism, feminism, and racism. In L. Sargent (Ed.), *Women and revolution* (pp. 91–108). South End Press.

Kendall, M. (2020). *Hood feminism: Notes from the women white feminists forgot.* Viking Press.

Krane, V., & Barber, H. (2005). Identity tensions in lesbian intercollegiate coaches. *Research Quarterly for Exercise and Sport, 76*(1), 67–81.

Kraus, W. (2013). A quest for a third space: Heterotopic self-positioning and narrative identity. In C. Holler & M. Klepper (Eds.), *Rethinking narrative identity: Persona and perspective* (pp. 69–84). John Benjamins Publishing Co.

Lahad, K. (2017). *A table for one: A critical reading of singlehood, gender and time.* University of Manchester, UK; Manchester University Press.

Larsen, K., & Zubernis, L. (2011). *Fandom at the crossroads: Celebration, shame and fan/producer relationships.* Cambridge Scholars Publishing.

Lawler, S. (2014). *Identity: Sociological perspectives.* Polity Press.

Martin, A. L., Jr. (2019). Fandom while black: Misty Copeland, Black panther, Tyler Perry and the contours of US black fandoms. *International Journal of Cultural Studies, 22*(6), 737–753.

McCall, L. (2005). The complexity of intersectionality. *Signs: Journal of Women in Culture and Society, 30*(3), 1771–1800.

Mercer, K. (1990). Welcome to the jungle: Identity and diversity in postmodern politics. In J. Rutherford (Ed.), *Identity, community, culture, difference* (pp. 43–71). Lawrence and Wishart.

Nash, J. C. (2018). *Black feminism reimagined after intersectionality.* Duke University Press.

O'Day, W. (2013). Social spaces: British fandom to the present. In G. I. Leitch, D. E. Palumbo, & C. W. Sullivan III (Eds.), *Doctor Who in time and space: Essays on themes, characters, history and fandom 1963–2010* (pp. 25–43). McFarland & Company Inc.

Orme, S. (2016). Femininity and fandom: The dual-stigmatisation of female comic book fans. *Journal of Graphic Novels and Comics, 7*(4), 403–416.

Ortega, M. (2006). Being lovingly, knowingly ignorant: White feminism and women of color. *Hypatia, 21*(3), 56–74.

Pande, R. (2018). *Squee from the margins: Fandom and race.* University of Iowa Press.

Petersen, L. N. (2017). The florals: Female fans over 50 in the Sherlock fandom. *Transformative works and cultures, 23.* https://doi.org/10.3983/twc.2017.0956

Phipps, A. (2020). *Me, not you: The trouble with mainstream feminism.* Manchester University Press.

Reagle, J. (2015). Geek policing: Fake geek girls and contested attention. *International Journal of Communication, 9,* 2862–2880.

Reinhard, C. D. (2018). *Fractured fandoms: Contentious communication in fan communities.* Lexington Books.

Salem, S. (2013). Feminist critique and Islamic feminism: The question of intersectionality. *The Postcolonialist, 1*(1), 1–8.

Salter, A., & Blodgett, B. (2017). *Toxic geek masculinity in media: Sexism, trolling, and identity policing.* Springer.

Santo, A. (2017). Fans and merchandise. In M. A. Scott & S. Scott (Eds.), *The Routledge companion to media fandom* (pp. 329–336). Routledge.

Shaw, A. (2011). Do you identify as a gamer? Gender, race, sexuality, and gamer identity. *New Media & Society, 14*(1), 28–44.

Simon, L. (2011). *Geek girls unite: How fangirls, bookworms, indie chicks, and other misfits are taking over the world.* Harper Collins Publication.

Stanfill, M. (2011). Doing fandom, (mis)doing whiteness: Heteronormativity, racialization, and the discursive construction of fandom| Stanfill| Transformative Works and Cultures. *Transformative Works & Cultures, 8.* https://doi.org/10.3983/twc.2011.0256

Sveinson, K., Hoeber, L., & Toffoletti, K. (2019). "If people are wearing pink stuff they're probably not real fans": Exploring women's perceptions of sport fan clothing. *Sport Management Review, 22*(5), 736–747.

Turner, J. C., & Reynolds, K. J. (2011). Self-categorization theory. *Handbook of Theories in Social Psychology, 2*(1), 399–417.

Vergès, F. (2021). *A decolonial feminism.* Pluto Press.

Walker, A. (1983). *In search of our mothers' gardens.* Harcourt, Brace Jovanovich.

Wanzo, R. (2015). African American acafandom and other strangers: New genealogies of fan studies. *Transformative Works and Cultures, 20*(1), n.p..

Warner, K. J. (2015). ABC's Scandal and Black women's fandom. In E. Levine (Ed.), *Cupcakes, Pinterest and ladyporn: Feminized popular culture in the early twenty-first century* (pp. 32–50). University of Illinois Press.

Way, L. (2021). Punk is just a state of mind: Exploring what punk means to older punk women. *The Sociological Review, 69*(1), 107–122.

Wemyss, G. (2006). The power to tolerate: contests over Britishness and belonging in East London. *Patterns of Prejudice, 40*(3), 215–236.

Wing, A. K. (2000). *Global critical race feminism: An international reader.* New York University Press.

Woo, B. (2018). *Getting a life: The social worlds of Geek culture.* McGill-Queen's Press.

Yodovich, N. (2016). "A little costumed girl at a sci-fi convention": Boundary work as a main destigmatization strategy among women fans. *Women's Studies in Communication, 39*(3), 289–307.

Zakaria, R. (2021). *Against white feminism.* W. W. Norton & Company.

CHAPTER 4

Belonging as a Feminist Fan

The identification and self-categorization processes depicted so far in this book have focused primarily on the feminist woman fan as an individual, excluding an in-depth critical reflection on her social surroundings and social interactions. However, as Alcoff (2005) maintains, "The other gives content to our self, and also affirms that our self-estimation is real and not just imagined" (p. 116). Therefore, it is impossible to disregard other social players, especially when exploring the ways in which we construct our identities and social worlds (DeNora, 1999). Therefore, in this chapter I focus primarily on feminist women fans' interactions with other members in their fan communities and the ways in which these social relationships affect and shape their identities. In this manner, the experiences of exclusion that were briefly touched upon in Chap. 3 will now be fully fleshed out.

To discuss these experiences of exclusion and their impact on the interviewees' perceptions about their identities, I turn to the seminal works of Mead (1972) and Cooley (1992). Both scholars emphasize the importance of the social surroundings in the formation of one's identity. Mead contended that the self is a social product. He argued that people develop their identity to the fullest only when considering how others see them. However, when Mead discussed the "other," he referred to a "generalized other" rather than a specific person/s. The generalized other includes the

© The Author(s), under exclusive license to Springer Nature   93
Switzerland AG 2022
N. Yodovich, *Women Negotiating Feminism and Science Fiction Fandom*, Palgrave Fan Studies,
https://doi.org/10.1007/978-3-031-04079-5_4

attitudes and perceptions of members of society about the individual. "Only by taking the attitude of the generalized other toward himself, in one or another of these ways, can he think at all," Mead asserted (1972, p. 156). According to Mead, people are never free from the influence of the generalized other. They can fully grasp their own identity only through the perceptions of others. In parallel to Mead's theory, Cooley (1992) developed the concept of the "looking-glass self" to explain how individuals learn about themselves through society's attitudes toward them. According to Cooley, our sense of self and ability to perceive our identities as authentic and coherent are contingent on how we imagine ourselves through the eyes of others. Mead's and Cooley's theories are helpful in thinking and theorizing about the experiences of women fans who are in constant need of affirmation from other members of their community while frequently experiencing policing and exclusion.

Given that Mead and Cooley neglected to discuss gender, ethnicity, or age in their work, I am conscious of their blind spots. My goal is to expand their theories and demonstrate how such social categories are crucial to their scholarship. I illustrate how young white men, who are accepted as synonymous with science fiction fans, function as women fans' generalized other. Men fans (or, more specifically, white men) are regarded as the majority in the community and dictate the rules of inclusion in it. Thus, women of various backgrounds and age groups evaluate their identities and their "right" to be affiliated with the fandom by observing themselves through the eyes of a hostile generalized other. Exposure to men fans' scrutiny and ridicule led the interviewees to doubt their own identities.

The importance of the "other" in women fans' perceptions of their identities is also encapsulated in the concept I developed, conditional belonging (Yodovich, 2020a). I define conditional belonging as a social, liminal state in which individuals are required to demonstrate conformity to the community they wish to join. During their conditional belonging, individuals' access to the community's goods is restricted, and they are not allowed to challenge the collective's hegemonic values and norms. In the qualification process, these individuals are initially suspected to be inauthentic. They are treated as second-class members by founders or veteran members until their allegiance to and compatibility with the community are proven. In some cases, conditional belonging is not a mandatory process for every individual. Some people who appear to be a "natural" fit, thanks to their ethnicity, gender, age, or other social categories, will be automatically considered members. Others will go through the process of conditional belonging, which might conclude with their inclusion through their demonstrated alignment with the community's values and cultural identity, or their exclusion and rejection because the community does not regard them as legitimate members.

This chapter makes several theoretical and empirical contributions to the existing knowledge on fandom. First, it implements the seminal works of Mead and Cooley to elucidate the ways in which the generalized "fan community" shapes the ways in which feminist women fans perceive themselves. By doing so, it expands helpful but incomplete theories by considering the intersection of different social categories. Second, my conceptualization of conditional belonging provides a useful tool to explore the fragile position of feminist women fans in science fiction fan communities. Here, I argue that feminist women fans' state of conditional belonging disrupts their ability to see themselves as genuine fans and leads to feelings of self-doubt and practices of self-policing. This chapter, therefore, tackles the impact of gatekeeping and toxic discourse in science fiction fandoms on feminist women fans' feelings, leading to their feelings of inauthenticity. In underscoring the importance of belonging to one's self-perception (Jenkins, 2014; May, 2013; Yuval-Davis, 2011), this chapter demonstrates how gatekeeping and rigid definitions of "real" fans damage feminist women fans' self-perceptions.

This chapter's structure is as follows. First, I unpack the gatekeeping practices targeted at women in general, women fans of marginalized ethnicities, and older women, more specifically. Then, I discuss feminist women fans' particular state of conditional belonging in science fiction communities. I examine two main conditions for belonging to science fiction fandoms: proof of connoisseurship about the object of the fandom and the silencing of feminist identities and perspectives. I begin by exploring the pushback against women fans and the historical processes that serve men fans' motivation for their exclusion.

4.1   "How dare they?! With their breasts?!": Gatekeeping of Women Fans

The previous chapter reviewed women fans' internalization of the prevalence of men fans in science fiction fandoms. Nevertheless, the interviewees acknowledged the gradual visibility of women in fan communities in recent years:

> The thing with *Doctor Who* was that something about the new series had a lot of women coming out of the woodwork, "yes, I'm a *Doctor Who* fan." (Emmy, 42, white, UK)

Earlier on, when you were geeky about something, people mistreated you. It was mostly boys; geeks were mostly boys. Now more girls are coming in, the general public doesn't think it's so weird. (Anaya, 19, Indian, UK)

In her analysis of *Star Wars: The Empire Strikes Back (Episode V)*, Harrison (2020) reviewed the dedicated participation of women during the film's release. For instance, she explained that women waited in line for hours to watch the new *Star Wars* installment, just as much as men. They also responded more positively than men to the movie during test screenings. What surprised Harrison in her study was the blasé media coverage of women's engagement with the franchise. In a similar manner, older participants also reflected on the "unremarkableness" of being a woman fan when they were younger:

> I think because there were less channels, we've had like four channels, people kind of watched the same thing a lot more, and we've played with each other's toys [...] I feel like nowadays girls and women are targeted as being fans of stuff, where it used to be "oh, you're a girl, and you like that stuff, that's kind of cool," now it's like "oh, you're not a real fan." (Lucy, 41, white, UK)

Regardless of the numerical participation of women in science fiction communities throughout the decades and their reception, women today seem to encounter severe gatekeeping practices due to their gender. As Lucy claimed:

> Just being female is enough to get a black mark. It doesn't matter how much you know, just the fact of coming in as female, automatically it's like— "take a step back," because you can never be a true fan, you came with the wrong biology for that.

Researchers and participants alike explain that men have been protective of their fandoms in recent decades because fandom and geekdom have finally become socially accepted after years of marginalization and stigma. The shift of men fans of science fiction from marginalized individuals to individuals who exclude others is well documented in fan studies. Scholarly depictions of the traditional stigma stamped on men fans of science fiction traditionally refer to the infamous 1986 *Saturday Night Life* skit featuring *Star Trek*'s star, William Shatner (Bury, 2018; Jenkins, 1992; Pearson, 2010; Woo, 2018). The scene featured men who were presented as socially awkward, physically unattractive individuals who obsess over minor details in the series. Baffled by their obsession, the popular *Star Trek* star asked the fans if they had ever kissed a woman and urged them to "get a life." This skit has become a staple of the demeaning, emasculating stereotypes attributed to men fans, which have haunted them since then.

Indeed, the traditional narrative in many fan communities is that men fans have historically been mocked for not adjusting to gender norms and hegemonic masculinity, which values such as physical strength, confidence, and interest in sports and athletics (Wilson, 2018). Due to their assumed undesirable traits (poor hygiene, lack of social skills, virginity, and inability to communicate with women) and disproportionate enthusiasm for the "wrong" things, men fans were chastised by non-fans, women and men alike (Gray, 2003; Lopes, 2006; Nyberg, 1995;Orme, 2016 ; Salter & Blodgett, 2017 ; Wilson, 2018).

However, since the 2000s, and thanks to the evolvement of digital media (another "geeky" interest), a new type of masculinity has broken into the mainstream: geek masculinity (Orme, 2016; Salter & Blodgett, 2017; Wilson, 2018). Famous geeky men, such as Mark Zuckerberg (founder of Facebook), Elon Musk (founder of Tesla and SpaceX), or Evan Spiegel (founder of Snapchat), were able to translate geeky interests in science and technology into social and economic capital, which brought them immense financial success and popularity with the opposite sex. In another example, the newfound popularity of geekdom and fandom was placed front and center in television series such as *The Big Bang Theory* (2007–2019), *Silicon Valley* (2014–2019), and *The IT Crowd* (2006–2013), which centered on geeky men. After years of scorn and castigation, this stigma has faded as fandom and geekdom became more mainstream.

After finally being accepted by society and the media, men fans were able to enforce strict boundaries on their communities to prevent the penetration of those they regarded as one of their main taunters: women. The so-called flocking of women to science fiction fandoms overwhelmed some of the veteran men fans, who were uninterested in letting women join their all-boys club:

> They have been told probably since their childhood that this [being a fan] makes them uncool and unattractive to women, and suddenly women try to take over. "How dare they?! With their breasts?!" They think it's their space, and it's now taken over by women. (Zoe, 34, white, UK)

As Zoe explained, some men fans have gone through years and possibly decades of being looked down upon by certain women. They were rarely regarded as potential romantic partners and frequently mocked for their offbeat interests. Now that science fiction has become more mainstream, and men fans are finally recognized as a major financial force by the media, women are not invited to reap the rewards of years of overcoming stigma. Jessica compassionately described this process:

> I've always been a firm believer that sometimes you run into the meanest people in the fandoms because the rest of the world beat them down for so long. That's how they respond. (Jessica, 32, biracial white-Jamaican, USA)

Banet-Weiser (2018) described the pushback against the "invasion" of women into geeky hobbies and professions in her book, *Empowered: Popular Feminism and Popular Misogyny*. She explained that because the popularity of geek masculinity is so recent, it is still fragile and in constant need of maintenance. Therefore, geeky men cannot allow women access to their "club" because it might weaken their already unstable position in the hierarchy of masculinities. Salter (2018) presented a similar commentary when they asserted that geeky masculinity "contains a contradictory construction" (p. 250). On the one hand, men geeks and fans are outsiders in general society, making them inferior to others. On the other hand, they have garnered enough power to marginalize others by providing them limited access to their communities.

Women's interest in traditionally male-oriented mediums may seem like "gender deviance that requires correction" (Cote, 2017, p. 139). These corrective measures lead to the stereotypical tropes that were reviewed in the previous chapter, such as "fake geek girl," the "fangirl," or the "girlfriend." Having gained power and control over their communities, men fans can now turn the stigma from which they suffered on to others and use it to legitimize the newcomers' ostracism (Salter, 2018; Salter & Blodgett, 2017; Scott, 2019). Based on Goffman's (1963) seminal work on stigma, such tropes are used against women fans as an excuse to disqualify them "from full social acceptance" (p. 4). It is the first step taken in setting the boundaries between "us" and "them" (Link & Phelan, 2001), between men fans, who were there "first" (presumably), and the women "newcomers," who do not deserve to be involved.

The stigma against women fans is also frequently accompanied by verbal and sexual harassment (Cote, 2017; Salter, 2018). As Tia described (34, Black African American, USA):

> When it comes to being a female, there is this notion that you don't know as much, which is annoying. There is this notion that when we're in cosplay, especially if it looks sexy, that all of a sudden, we are like "heeeey." Please don't talk to me. There is this level of sexism that is toxic and really frustrating. I want to enjoy something. I don't want to hear you trying to tell me what you want to do to me or that character.

Here Tia addresses the unwanted attention such as catcalling or groping that is given to women cosplayers. These kinds of behaviors are not exclusive to conventions. They also occur on online platforms. In a different example, Emily (34, white, UK) explained that she would keep her gender a secret on traditionally male-dominated websites, such as Reddit, because "the second they know you're a woman, they creep at you." Thus, by enforcing a regime of stigma and sexism, some men fans are able to chase women out of their communities.

As fandom becomes more acceptable, Pande (2018) asks us to ponder "*which* fans are considered the most 'valued'" (p. 319, emphasis in the original). As this section indicates, women as a whole are considered second-class citizens in many science fiction fandoms. Nevertheless, following up on the previous chapters of this book, I acknowledge the cumulative challenges and barriers that are embedded in the experiences of women whose identities intersect with other marginalized social categories. Thus, the following sections delve deeper into the particular obstacles that confront women of marginalized ethnicities and older women as they engage with the members of their fan communities.

4.2   "Can you move over?": Gatekeeping of Women Fans of Marginalized Ethnicities

"Nonwhite fans," Pande (2018) explained, "interrupt normative operations" in fandom (p. 6). Against the backdrop of the invisible, taken-for-granted whiteness of the assumed majority of its members, fans of marginalized ethnicities stand out as "space invaders" (Puwar, 2004). They are seen as an uninvited nuisance whose goal is to disrupt the social status quo:

Sci fi fandom is considered a white thing, a straight cis thing. Because of that, because that visibility is so tied to whiteness and patriarchy, these privileged folks feel forceful entitlement to these spaces. With that, recent adjustments that were made in the entertainment industry, that entitlement turned into a really aggressive self-defense. (Daniela, 23, Latina, USA)

Daniela's comment highlights the lack of openness toward those who are not white, cis, abled men in many science fiction fan communities. Anyone who attempts to stretch the borders of such communities is sanctioned and rejected. To address the intersection between the dominance of patriarchy and whiteness in fandoms, this section illuminates the experiences of women fans of marginalized ethnicities in white-dominated, male-dominated fan communities.

One of the leading fan spaces in which women fans of marginalized ethnicities encounter racism and exclusion is conventions, particularly when taking part in cosplaying:

I tend to cosplay in a group, so you have multiple characters from the same fandom. Usually, people stop you and be like, "hey, can we get a picture of ya'll?" But then there's been a couple occasions where they want to take pictures of just one person or two other people from the same group instead of the whole group. We will all pose, and then they'll ask me to step out [...] I was the only person of color. I was cosplaying at the time as a character from *Zelda*, I forgot her name. She's a pirate, so she has a tan. I was cosplaying with the whole group, and I've been asked to step out because I'm not the color of that character. I'm not a white person (laughing) [...] We were posing, and... one of the girls in the front taking the picture was like, "I'm sorry, can you move over? I don't want you in this picture." And I'm like... you can tell that it hurt my feelings, probably on my face. And she was like, "no, no, your cosplay is great, you're great, I just really love this character so much, and I just want a standalone." I'm like, "yeah, you could just crop it" [...] she knew she put her foot in her mouth. When I thought about it, she tried to make it better, but still, she asked me to stay out of the picture so she could take it without me. You obviously don't think something about me is that great. (Jessica, 32, biracial white-Jamaican, USA)

Jessica being asked explicitly to step out of a group photo exemplifies racism in fandom in various ways. First, Jessica notes the difficulty of finding characters to dress up as, due to the lack of characters of marginalized ethnicities in science fiction and video games. Given the scarcity of women characters with a similar complexion as Jessica's, her optimal cosplay choice was dressing up as a character with a tan instead. However, when she did so, other fans criticized her, disapproving of her cosplaying outside her ethnicity. Second, Jessica recounts being frequently singled out and asked not to participate in group photos. She interpreted her exclusion from the group by other fans as an act of implicit racism. As she stated: "You obviously don't think something about me is that great."

While Jessica was rejected at conventions due to her ethnic background, Tia reported being objectified:

> When I was Domino[1] people wanted to reach for my hair, and I was like "nooo." I put too much time and energy in this thing. It doesn't mean you get to touch anything. (Tia, 34, Black African American, USA)

Tia's particular sexist and racist harassment in science fiction conventions could be considered an example of "misogynoir." The term, which was coined and developed by Bailey and Trudy. (2018), depicts the intersection between misogyny, sexism, and racism directed toward Black women. Dash (2019), noting white people's fascination with Black hair, states, "Black hair is seen as alluring yet threatening [...] it symbolizes a distant other world detachment, and the perceived lower 'racial' status" (p. 34). Thus, the touching of Black women's hair is a racist-induced objectifying practice, where their bodies are considered public property and a form of entertainment (Dash, 2019; Orey & Zhang, 2019). While Tia finally found a character to dress up as, who shared the same ethnicity as her, she was still vulnerable to racist and sexist behaviors from fellow fans.

The sexualization of women fans of marginalized ethnicities also seeps into other geeky arenas. Aside from being a science fiction fan, Daniela (23, Latina, USA) was also a devoted D&D (*Dungeons and Dragons*) player. On one occasion, Daniela visited a tabletop games store and joined a group of men in a game of D&D:

> One of the male players, presumably because of the way I look, decided he wanted to use this role playing experience to act out a rape fantasy onto my character. I was like, "I'm going to leave." I have not played D&D in a store since then.

[1] A character played by a Black actress in Deadpool 2.

The previous chapter introduced the common misconception wherein women who inhabit geeky and fannish places are considered potential romantic partners for men fans. While men fans are commonly recognized as those with an authentic and legitimate interest in the content, women often function as men's "plus one." The lack of respect and appreciation of women fans in a community that is accepted as male-dominated quickly turns them into targets of sexism and harassment (Bacon-Smith, 1992; Reagle, 2015; Ruberg et al., 2019). Daniela's upsetting account is an extreme example of the violent racism and sexism that it denotes. The male player who interacted with Daniela did not choose to act out any random sexual fantasy, but a particular one that placed Daniela in a weak, inferior position against his powers. As Bhattacharyya (2002) and Lundström (2006) explained, Latina women are frequently seen through a postcolonial lens through which they are incorrectly regarded as overtly sexual beings. Such perceptions of Latina women lead to the degrading treatment they often receive from some men, as was the case in Daniela's account.

The experiences that were reviewed here revealed how racism and sexism are intersected and embedded in fan communities. Women of marginalized ethnicities are discriminated against twice in fan communities: once for their gender and second for their ethnicity. Such an amalgamation of social categories not only is an obstacle in their self-categorization process (see Chap. 3), but also puts them in actual jeopardy of being abused and harassed.

4.3   "SOMEONE'S MOM": GATEKEEPING OF OLDER WOMEN FANS

Following up on the intersection of gender and fandom with ethnicity, this section adds a different dimension, age. The last chapter revealed the particular self-categorization process that "older" women fans go through. After being somewhat included in their younger years, "older" women fans faced another obstacle to their inclusion in fandom: their age. Nika (44, Latina/Chicana, USA) articulated the process of gradually becoming an outsider in the fandom she was a part of for decades:

> It's interesting because there are lots of women who grew up with *Star Wars*, so many of us, and there's all these dudes out there who are convinced

that it's just them. Dudes who all identify with Han Solo, who think we don't have a place in the fandom.

Lucy (41, white, UK) asserted that the main reason that "older" women are discounted in science fiction communities is because they no longer serve as "eye candy" or potential romantic partners:

> When you're young, and you're female, especially if you're slim and pretty, people, I mean, men, they will make some amount of space for you [...] even if you're not going to sleep with them, they think you might one day [...] as women, we reach, probably even mid to late 20s, when you either become invisible or you're treated like a hostile... like you don't belong there.

Having once worked in a comic-book shop, Lucy now feels like an outsider when walking into one. This feeling also accompanies her when she frequents fan conventions:

> When we get to conventions, I'm really aware of it as well. There's the moms. You're so irrelevant or invisible, you're just not part of it.

Lucy also noted the poignant transition from being addressed as "someone's girlfriend" to being referred to as "someone's mom." While the first offered limited access to the fan community, the latter completely eliminated the women's chances of being accepted. Nevertheless, both terms, "someone's girlfriend" and "someone's mother," strip women of their agency as fans and pigeonhole them in a relational position with men. Their presence in fandom is never of their own volition but based on their association with someone else, usually a man, who is the "real" fan.

Nika (44, Latina/Chicana, USA), however, also reported a new sense of liberation that emerged with age, now that her fan identity was no longer evaluated based on her looks:

> I'm older now. I used to be more attractive, younger woman. Imagine a more attractive young woman in a situation where you're like, "that's Chris Claremont!" and like, every fucking idiot around you, "did you know he invented Wolverine?"—"No, I had no idea, I'm only with a Wolverine backpack" (sarcastic tone).

Nika's account demonstrates the pressure that is put on geeky women's appearance. To be included, they should be young and pretty, but not too pretty, because attractive women are not expected to be geeks (Reagle, 2015; Yodovich & Kim, 2021). Nevertheless, getting older is a double-edged sword. Older women fans are less pressured to fit into the rigid beauty standards in fan communities. However, instead of having their appearance constantly scrutinized, older women fans become invisible.

So far, I have shed light on the various identity intersections that result in the multilayered marginalization and exclusion of women fans. In the second half of this book, I focus on the conditions that fan groups dictate to feminist women fans who want to be included. The two conditions include a demonstration of connoisseurship about the object of the fandom and the silencing of one's feminist inclinations. The following sections reveal how feminist women fans navigate the two conditions and their impact on their self-perceptions.

4.4   CONDITIONAL BELONGING: PROOF OF CONNOISSEURSHIP

In many of the interviews, the participants opened with what seemed like an apology for what they saw as a lack of fluency about the object of their fandom:

> I am not familiar with the entire universe of *Doctor Who* and *Star Wars*. If you're asking about minor characters, I'm not going to be able to answer. I don't remember everything that's going on in those universes […] last night when I thought about the interview; I thought to myself, 'I should look up Wikipedia,' because sometimes… most of the time… when being a fan comes up, you always need to…I always feel like I need to prove myself. I don't know if it's connected to being female, I don't know, maybe. I kinda think it is. (Anita, 35, white, Italy)
> I was really nervous before our conversation, and I was thinking why I am so nervous, it's not an exam. Then I realized that, in a way, I question myself if I'm enough of a fan (nervous laugh). And then I realized it's part of the problem, that I feel like I have to prove it to you. (Isabel, 26, white, Spain)

The worry that the interview might include an impromptu pop quiz demonstrates how the scrutiny of their knowledge was engrained in the women's experience as science fiction fans.

According to the interviewees, connoisseurship is one of the primary indicators of being a "real" fan. It is one of the leading conditions for belonging to the community. Emily (34, UK) provided an interesting example of the distinction between authentic and non-authentic fans while discussing *Doctor Who* fans' use of the discourse "We" and "Not We." In part of an episode from 1982, a tribe used "We" and "Not We" to distinguish between themselves and the rest of the world. *Doctor Who* fans adopted the terms to create a boundary between "real" and "fake" fans, who were not allowed or deserved to be part of the "we" (Hills, 2015; Reinhard, 2018). This segmentation is inherent in the processes of belonging (Goodin, 1996; Hall, 1996; Jenkins, 2014; May, 2013). The collective always defines itself and what "we" have in common as opposed to those who do not belong and cannot be part of the community (ibid.).

To prove that they belonged as legitimate members of their fan communities, women fans frequently had to demonstrate connoisseurship about their favorite franchises: from remembering esoteric details to being fluent in the canon. For instance, many interviewees recollected being "grilled" by other fans:

> Even the simplest question like, "who is your favorite Doctor?" could explode in your face: "ok… what just happened?!" If you don't know something, someone would say, "how can you not know this?! Are you sure you're a real fan?!" (Jenny, 31, Chinese, UK)

It appears that due to the ever-growing popularity of franchises such as *Doctor Who* and *Star Wars*, some men fans take advantage of transmedia culture to enforce rigid rules of inclusion and exclusion in the fandom community (Van de Goor, 2015). Merely watching the movies or the series is not enough; the fan must be familiar with and remember every storytelling platform involved in the diegesis.

Participants also had to indicate that their interpretations of the diegesis aligned with the hegemonic reading. For instance, Ally (39, white, UK) encountered men who talked about "*my Star Wars*" when dismissing narratives and analyses that were not to their liking. In another example, participants reported clashing with other men fans when the first woman Doctor in *Doctor Who* was announced (Yodovich, 2020b). Women fans, who supported the new casting, referred to plotlines that proved that the Doctor could switch gender. Their justifications were dismissed by certain men who argued that such arguments were not fully validated by the canon.

The interviewees were ambivalent about the use of connoisseurship as an admission ticket into the fan community. On the one hand, they were eager to pass the tests and be considered legitimate fans. On the other, they questioned why connoisseurship was chosen to begin with as the primary indicator of a fan's authenticity:

> You see that kind of thing happening, "how long is a freaking star destroyer?" I don't care about this stupid trivia [...] It should be fun, and people who turn it into a test or exam are missing the point. (Ally, 39, white, UK)
>
> Why do we need to be divisive? "I'm a better fan than you are because I know more than you do. I declare that you are not a fan, you must remove yourself from the fandom immediately, surrender all your fandom items" (mocking tone). (Cristina, 34, Latina, USA)

Writing about music fandom, Ewens (2020) raised similar questions and suggested that for some men, "it's about the technicality of the music [...] they've made that more important than how you feel about it [...] they've made it like a bus timetable" (p. 90). In other words, the focus on connoisseurship potentially compromises or discredits the fan's emotional engagement and turns fandom into an intellectual chore.

In her paper about transmedia fan culture, Scott (2017) argued that the emphasis on knowledge in fandom is designed "to structurally support stereotypically masculinized modes of fan engagement such as the collection, critical analysis, and curation of narrative data" (p. 1057). The prioritization of such expertise in transmedia culture, an interest that is already synonymous with men fans, automatically places women fans in an inferior position. Including a stereotypically masculine practice as a sign of authenticity positioned men at the hierarchical apex and women, and any traditional so-called feminine fannish practice, at the bottom (Busse, 2015). For instance, when evaluating her fan identity, Natalie (38, white, UK) automatically saw herself as a lesser fan than the men she knew:

> I have often felt that I was inadequately fannish. In my head, I connect that to being a girl. There's a correlation there. I am aware I am not as obsessive about going back and watching all the catalog of *Doctor Who*, I'm aware I haven't read as many *Star Wars* spinoff books [...] I have noticed a correlation that amongst my friends, it's the men who go further, they go deeper (laughs). I sometimes feel like my lack of knowledge is a weakness. I'm a little bit sensitive to that.

Reinhard (2018) explained the processes leading to segmentation and hierarchies in fandom. Those who consider themselves "real" fans are self-appointed authorities within the community and dictate the rules that everyone must follow. These "codes of behavior" are internalized, practiced, and preserved, until "individuals [...] unconsciously perpetuate the system of structures in place and reinforce notions of proper behavior and practice" (Van de Goor, 2015, p. 280). Thus, I argue that because men fans perceive themselves as those who inhabited their communities "first," they have the authority to design fandom's "ideal type," which everyone else has to follow. Jessica (32, biracial white-Jamaican, USA) articulated this process quite well:

> I think part of it is that this has been their sanctuary. When you have somebody in a sanctuary, they are very, very aware of what that means, what that sanctuary looks like. If they're letting you into that sanctuary, they want you to respect every detail and know everything. Just like you would in a church. This is a sanctuary to them, it's almost like religion. If you don't know everything about it, you're not studying enough, you're not religious enough. Because it has become their sanctuary, they've regressed into it a little bit. I understand it's a safe and comforting thing for them, but at the same time, it closes them off. I think that that closure, taking yourself away from everything, and not letting other people into sanctuary actually ends up making that toxic behavior.

Utilizing Cooley's concept of the looking-glass self, I argue that women fans judge themselves harshly because they internalize how their male peers in fan communities see them. Women fans assess their authenticity according to values set by their generalized other and feel that they could never measure up to their standards. The participants have been exposed to scrutiny so often that they no longer need to experience it to feel ashamed or apologetic. They instinctively feel the urgency to defend themselves and the level of their fluency in their beloved content, even in unthreatening conversations, as in the case of the interviews I conducted.

4.5   Conditional Belonging: The Silencing
of Feminism

In addition to having to prove they were connoisseurs of their object of fandom, the interviewees also identified another condition of their belonging and inclusion in fan communities: the silencing of their feminist identities and critiques.

The participants revealed that to prevent being excluded and attacked, they learned to avoid discussing feminism, gender, or the interpersonal relationships between the characters in the object of their fandom. Wendy (50, white, UK), for instance, recollected how she was regularly shut down when trying to talk about the women characters in *Doctor Who* and their role on the show:

> I wanted to talk about Sarah Jane and Ace, and everyone else wanted to talk about the Doctor. They were quite a sexist bunch, as well. I tried to introduce basic concepts of gender equality at times, and they just never heard it before, never thought about it before. It was all about the Doctor.

Similarly, Ally (39, white, UK) shared that she learned to adjust her comments to the talking points that men find interesting, explaining: "I refrain myself from talking about stuff that I want to talk about."

Quite often, feminism is considered one of science fiction fandoms' strongest foes. According to some men fans, feminism is a threat to traditional conventions that have been ingrained in the favorite content for years and decades (Scott, 2019; Yodovich, 2020b; Yodovich & Kim, 2021). As Ahmed (2017) cleverly articulated, feminists are seen as "killjoys" when they comment on sexism, misogyny, racism, ableism, transphobia, and other wrongdoings in society. Thus, when feminist fans ask for better representation and diversity in franchises, their calls are read as threats to the status quo, the intrusion of PC (political correctness) culture, or simply an attempt to "ruin the fun" in fandom. In the eyes of some men, these so-called threats to the social and cultural fabric in fandom turn feminists into an enemy that must be chastised and pushed away.

Feminist women fans' awareness of the hostile reactions that they might encounter leads them, once again, to self-censorship:

> I read about the Gamergate stuff that came out. I'm thinking, "Yeah... You might reach a few people who are like-minded, but you might also attract a

lot of trolls." I don't really need that in my life, to be honest. (Sheela, 49, biracial Indian-Anglo Saxon, Australia)

In this comment, Sheela referenced one of the most momentous controversies in recent years, Gamergate, which occurred in 2014. During Gamergate, women involved in the gaming industry, such as developers, gamers, and critics, experienced a barrage of abrasive comments online, as well as doxing (the sharing of private information) and explicit threats to their lives (Chess & Shaw, 2015; Mortensen, 2018; Salter, 2018; Todd, 2015). As the aftermath of Gamergate continues to linger on and permeate other male-dominated geeky arenas, many feminist women fans choose to stay under the radar.

Only one interviewee, Jessica (32, biracial white-Jamaican, USA), bravely dived into toxic online discussions in the hopes of building bridges between both sides of the conflict. As she explained:

I wanted the backlash because I think the backlash is necessary to open people's eyes. The thing is, you are what you're making fun of right now. If you've ever been hurt or even been called a name or ever been looked down upon because you like *Star Wars*, how are you any different? You are becoming the enemies of our fandom. Why would you do that? Yes, I'm ashamed of you. I want you to backlash at me, so I can hopefully help you see that you're hurting us.

Jessica was an exception to the norm, as most interviewees preferred to lurk in online discussions on *Star Wars* and *Doctor Who*. Others, such as Emily (34, white, UK), described that they would choose whether to talk explicitly about feminism and fandom based on their "audience." For instance, Emily shared: "I won't mention feminism on Reddit. I'll be more critical in female-dominated space, such as Tumblr."

To refrain from being attacked due to their feminist identities, the participants partook in what Goffman (1961) termed "audience segregation" and "role segregation." In the first tactic, individuals expose different parts of their identities based on the people with whom they interact. Much like Emily's example above, several interviewees chose to share their feminist perspectives only with other feminists while staying mum in conversations with anti-feminist fans. In "role segregation" one chooses to accentuate a specific identity over the other, for instance, silencing one's feminist identity and emphasizing one's fan identity.

During my interview with Emmy (42, white, UK) she demonstrated how she engages in role segregation when interacting with men. Emmy, who had decades of experience with the *Doctor Who* fan community, called her tactics the "Sansa" and the "Arya," based on two women characters in the series, *Game of Thrones*:

> You had to put up with a lot of men stuff, fully aware that I was supporting the patriarchy by being quiet. With Game of Thrones, there's two models of feminism: you got the Aria, and you got the Sansa. You got the woman who outwardly rejects the patriarchy, learns sword fighting, and becomes an assassin, but you also got the woman who is conventionally feminine and plays by society rules and winds up as queen of the North. I've done both in my time, but I felt that time that I was being Sansa, the woman who doesn't say "this is bulls***." Now I also put up with bulls***, but I keep suggesting female guests [in conventions], I'll write articles about women in *Doctor Who*, but at the same time I'll bite my tongue and let you say, "women don't like *Doctor Who*."

Emmy's experience demonstrates that role segregation is an effective tactic that also comes with a price. The "Sansa" tactic prioritizes fandom over feminism and denotes that to be included and accepted, a woman must play down her feminist identity. Therefore, even though the "Sansa" tactic eased Emmy's entrance into the fandom community, it erased her feminist identity when she conformed to male fans' impositions. The "Arya" approach, in contrast, prioritizes feminism over fandom and challenges men's control over the fandom. This tactic is also risky, as it puts the feminist fan in danger of being attacked.

The Goffmanian tactics presented here exemplify how feminism and fandom become conflicted in male-dominated communities, leading feminist women fans to choose between them. Undoubtedly, masking the stigmatized or undesired trait spares the feminist woman fan from scrutiny and exclusion, but also leads her to feeling inauthentic.

4.6   Conclusions: Belonging in Crisis

To tie the discussion about gatekeeping and conditional belonging in white, young men-dominated science fiction fandoms, I argue that two contrasting processes have occurred. On the one hand, the borders of fandoms have been opened up, where marginalized individuals of all sorts of backgrounds are more visible and vocal in various fandoms. On the other hand, this shift has attracted strong pushback, as some men fans feel threatened and motivated to maintain the status quo in fan communities. Being confronted with the hostile scrutiny of their identities by men fans, women fans internalized that they are not "good enough" or "real" fans, as per Mead's (1972) and Cooley's (1992) theories. Women fans have grown so accustomed to being judged and marginalized that they automatically assumed their identities would be scrutinized. Despite distancing themselves from provocations and retaliation, having experienced them in the past, or observed others who underwent scrutiny or harassment, feminist women fans were haunted by feelings of self-doubt and insecurity that pushed them to the fringes of fan communities.

Self-censorship and self-policing were among the most common ways feminist women fans maneuvered in male-dominated fan communities. Nevertheless, such tactics came with the price of the participants feeling untrue to themselves. While their ethnicity or feminist identities were essential to their self-categorization in other contexts, such identities were regarded as an obstacle to their inclusion in the context of fandom. No matter which identity was downplayed, this practice resulted in a feeling of inauthenticity. Thus, for most feminist women fans, interactions with other fans did not create the feeling of intimacy and togetherness often associated with belonging to a community (May, 2013; Miller, 2003; Yuval-Davis, 2011). The opposite was true. Feminist women fans' state of conditional belonging was a source of angst and alienation.

The feminist women fans' constant state of alertness, wherein every sentence they write or say is carefully chosen, provides a poignant insight into belonging. If women have to adjust or censor themselves to be included in science fiction fandoms, do they actually belong? The interviewees were not explicitly, bluntly excluded from discussions, but they were aware that if they wanted to be part of the conversation, they had to accommodate the men fans' interests and values. Consequently, women fans were denied the right to articulate and define fandom's rules of conduct. Not being able to take an active part in the communities' production of meaning and values is yet another element demonstrating partial inclusion and conditional belonging (Shotter, 1993). If women fans cannot discuss their passions and interests out of fear of being subjected to mockery, stigma, or harassment, they might be included, but they do not belong.

REFERENCES

Ahmed, S. (2017). *Living a feminist life.* Duke University Press.

Alcoff, L. M. (2005). *Visible identities: Race, gender, and the self.* Oxford University Press.

Bacon-Smith, C. (1992). *Enterprising women: Television fandom and the creation of popular myth.* University of Pennsylvania Press.

Bailey, M., & Trudy. (2018). On misogynoir: Citation, erasure, and plagiarism. *Feminist Media Studies, 18*(4), 762–768.

Banet-Weiser, S. (2018). *Empowered: Popular feminism and popular misogyny.* Duke University Press.

Bhattacharyya, G. (2002). *Sexuality and society.* Routledge.

Bury, R. (2018). "We're Not There": Fans, Fan Studies, and the Participatory Continuum. In M.A Click & S. Scott (Eds.), *Routledge Compation to Media Fandom* (pp. 123-131). Routledge.

Busse, K. (2015). Fan labor and feminism: Capitalizing on the fannish labor of love. *Cinema Journal, 54*(3), 110–115.

Chess, S., & Shaw, A. (2015). A conspiracy of fishes, or, how we learned to stop worrying about #GamerGate and embrace hegemonic masculinity. *Journal of Broadcasting & Electronic Media, 59*(1), 208–220.

Cooley, C. H. (1992 [1902]). *Human nature and the social order.* Transaction Publishers.

Cote, A. C. (2017). "I can defend myself" Women's strategies for coping with harassment while gaming online. *Games and Culture, 12*(2), 136–155.

Dash, P. (2019). Black hair culture, politics and change. *International Journal of Inclusive Education, 10*(1), 27–37.

DeNora, T. (1999). Music as a technology of the self. *Poetics, 27*(1), 31–56.

Ewens, H. (2020). *Fangirls: Scenes from modern music culture.* University of Texas Press.

Goffman, E. (1961). *Encounters: Two studies in the sociology of interaction.* Bobbs-Merrill Company.

Goffman, I. (1963). *Stigma: Notes on the management of spoiled identity.* Simon and Schuster.

Goodin, R. E. (1996). Inclusion and exclusion. *European Journal of Sociology/ Archives Européennes de Sociologie, 37*(2), 343–371.

Gray, J. (2003). New audiences, new textualities: Anti-fans and non-fans. *International Journal of Cultural Studies, 6*(1), 64–81.

Hall, S. (1996). Introduction: Who needs identity? In S. Hall & P. Du Gay (Eds.), *Questions of cultural identity* (pp. 1–17). Sage.

Harrison, B. (2020). *The empire strikes back.* Bloomsbury.

Hills, M. (2015). The expertise of digital fandom as a 'community of practice' Exploring the narrative universe of Doctor Who. *Convergence, 21*(3), 360–374.

Jenkins, H. (1992). *Textual poachers.* Routledge.

Jenkins, R. (2014). *Social identity.* Routledge.

Link, B. G., & Phelan, J. C. (2001). Conceptualizing stigma. *Annual Review of Sociology, 27*(1), 363–385.

Lopes, P. (2006). Culture and stigma: Popular culture and the case of comic books. *Sociological Forum, 21*(3), 387–414.

Lundström, C. (2006). 'Okay, but we are not whores you know' Latina girls navigating the boundaries of gender and ethnicity in Sweden. *Young, 14*(3), 203–218.

May, V. (2013). *Connecting self to society: Belonging in a changing world.* Palgrave Macmillan.

Mead, G. H. (1972). *Mind, self, and society: From the standpoint of a social behaviorist.* University of Chicago Press.

Miller, L. (2003). Belonging to country – A philosophical anthropology. *Journal of Australian Studies, 27*(76), 215–223.

Mortensen, T. E. (2018). Anger, fear, and games: The long event of# GamerGate. *Games and Culture, 13*(8), 787–806.

Nyberg, A. K. (1995). Comic books and women readers: Trespassers in masculine territory. In S. W. Rollins & P. C. Rollins (Eds.), *Gender in popular culture: Images of men and women in literature, visual media, and material Culture* (pp. 205–224). Ridgemount PR.

Orey, B. D. A., & Zhang, Y. (2019). Melanated millennials and the politics of black hair. *Social Science Quarterly, 100*(6), 2458–2476.

Orme, S. (2016). Femininity and fandom: the dual-stigmatisation of female comic book fans. *Journal of Graphic Novels and Comics, 7*(4), 403–416.

Pande, R. (2018). *Squee from the margins: Fandom and race.* University of Iowa Press.

Pearson, R. (2010). Fandom in the digital era. *Popular Communication, 8*(1), 84–95.

Puwar, N. (2004). *Space invaders: Race, gender and bodies out of place.* Berg.

Reagle, J. (2015). Geek policing: Fake geek girls and contested attention. *International Journal of Communication, 9,* 2862–2880.

Reinhard, C. D. (2018). *Fractured fandoms: Contentious communication in fan communities.* Lexington Books.

Ruberg, B., Cullen, A. L., & Brewster, K. (2019). Nothing but a "titty streamer": Legitimacy, labor, and the debate over women's breasts in video game live streaming. *Critical Studies in Media Communication, 36*(5), 466–481.

Salter, A., & Blodgett, B. (2017). *Toxic geek masculinity in media: Sexism, trolling, and identity policing.* Springer.

Salter, M. (2018). From geek masculinity to Gamergate: The technological rationality of online abuse. *Crime, Media, Culture, 14*(2), 247–264.

Scott, S. (2017). Modeling the Marvel everyfan: Agent Coulson and/as transmedia fan culture. *Palabra Clave, 20*(4), 1042–1072.

Scott, S. (2019). *Fake geek girls: Fandom, gender, and the convergence culture industry*. NYU Press.

Shotter, J. (1993). *Cultural politics of everyday life: Social constructionism, rhetoric and knowing of the third kind*. University of Toronto Press.

Todd, C. (2015). Commentary: GamerGate and resistance to the diversification of gaming culture. *Women's Studies Journal, 29*(1), 64–67.

Van de Goor, S. (2015). "You must be new here": Reinforcing the good fan. *Participations, 12*(2), 275–295.

Wilson, K. (2018). Red pillers, sad puppies, and gamergaters: The state of male privilege in internet fan communities. In P. Booth (Ed.), *A Companion to media fandom and fan studies* (pp. 431–446). John Wiley & Sons.

Woo, B. (2018). *Getting a life: The social worlds of Geek culture*. McGill-Queen's Press.

Yodovich, N. (2020a). Defining conditional belonging: The case of female science fiction fans. *Sociology, 55*(5), 871–887.

Yodovich, N. (2020b). "Finally, we get to play the doctor": feminist female fans' reactions to the first female Doctor Who. *Feminist Media Studies, 20*(8), 1243–1258.

Yodovich, N., & Kim, J. (2021). Exploring the Feminization of Backseat Gaming Through Girlfriend Reviews YouTube Channel. *Games and Culture*, https://doi.org/10.1177/15554120211056124

Yuval-Davis, N. (2011). *The politics of belonging: Intersectional contestations*. Sage.

CHAPTER 5

Representing Women and Feminism in Fandom

One of the main goals guiding this research is exploring the tensions between fandom and feminism and the ways in which women navigate them. The fractions that have been scrutinized so far in this book are internal, within the feminist women fans' self-categorization processes, and external, between the feminist women fans and other members of their community. In this chapter, I highlight another aspect of fandom that is a potential terrain of friction for feminist women: the object of the fandom itself or, in the case of this study, *Star Wars* and *Doctor Who*. By examining how feminist women fans perceive and engage with their favorite content, the current chapter explores moments of identification and fascination with the object of their fandom, as well as times of alienation and frustration.

As scholars previously noted, fans frequently identify with the object of their fandom, aspire to resemble their favorite characters, and articulate their political and social stances through fannish debates (Jenkins, 1992; Kligler-Vilenchik, 2015; Reinhard, 2018; Sandvoss, 2005). Sandvoss (2005), for instance, maintained that fans make sense of their fandoms in relation to themselves. In other words, fans are subconsciously attracted to elements in the content that they recognize in themselves or, alternatively, project their identities, perspectives, and interpretations onto the object of their fandom. Shaw (2015) asserted that popular media not only

N. Yodovich, *Women Negotiating Feminism and Science Fiction Fandom*, Palgrave Fan Studies, https://doi.org/10.1007/978-3-031-04079-5_5

taps into who we are in a particular moment but also provides new possibilities of who we can be and how we can live. As she argued, "Media texts provide us with source material for what might be possible, how identities might be constructed, and what worlds we might live in" (p. 3). Nevertheless, Shaw claimed that the ways in which we understand identification with media engagement should be more complex and should not be regarded as a binary state. Identification is not a linear, consistent experience either, but one that fluctuates through time and draws attention to different elements of the fan and character's identities.

Identification with popular culture content can become more challenging when the characters featured in it do not represent the viewers' identities. Lack of representation leads to a lack of identification, which might end with a lack of engagement (Cicci, 2017; Thomas, 2019; Wanzo, 2015). This kind of symbolic annihilation makes marginalized viewers apathetic about or frustrated with such content (ibid.). Thomas (2019) cleverly called the lack of representation an "imagination gap" (pp. 6–7). According to Thomas, such an imagination gap occurs when children cannot find book characters of the same ethnicity as theirs or when characters are reimagined as white in film adaptations, despite diegetic indications that they could be read as dark-skinned (Dubrofsky & Ryalls, 2014; Thomas & Stornaiuolo, 2019; Toliver, 2018). Imagination gaps are also evident when characters of marginalized backgrounds are pigeonholed as the white protagonist's second fiddle. Other times, such characters are simply non-existent in the content. In addition, Thomas explained that characters who represent marginalized ethnicities are scarce or poorly written not only because the audience that consumes the content is presumed to be white but also because it is assumed that white audiences would not connect with them.

The rarity of a diverse cadre of characters in mainstream media in general and science fiction and fantasy content in particular has become more scrutinized in recent years. Currently, there are lively discussions on representation and the reasons why it should, or should not, matter (Fürsich, 2010; Gray, 2015; hooks, 1992, 2019; Lapointe, 2020; Pande, 2018; Pande & Moitra, 2020; Phillips, 2018; Sobande, 2020). Such debates have been ongoing in recent decades, motivated by the desire to undo the structural inequality in society by bringing marginalized voices into the center stage of mainstream media. The focus on representation, therefore, is motivated by the idea that through unpacking whose stories are told, by whom, and from what standpoint, we can reveal and challenge the power imbalance in society, which permeates into our cultural worlds.

According to Hall (1993), representation is not an objective, accurate reflection of society but an outcome of an active, selective process in which ideas and narratives are chosen in order to shape the ways in which we perceive our social world. Hall describes popular culture as an arena,

> Where we discover and play with the identification of ourselves, where we are imagined, where we are represented, not only to the audiences out there who do not get the message, but to ourselves for the first time. (p. 114)

The understanding that what we see onscreen can then shape the ways we envision ourselves and others leads to the motivation to promote the representation of marginalized individuals in mainstream media, from films and television to video games and comic books (Fürsich, 2010; Howard & Jackson II, 2013; Phillips, 2018; Thomas, 2019; Wanzo, 2009, 2020). Creating a space for more diversity and visibility in popular culture is regarded as a catalyst for actual change in society at large (Martin, 2019; Phillips, 2018; Wanzo, 2009). A well-known example of the impact of a positive representation in popular culture is the "Scully Effect" (Geena Davis Institute on Gender in Media, n.d.). The Scully Effect refers to the surge of young women who registered for STEM degrees in American universities after watching the portrayal of a woman scientist, Dana Scully, in the successful science fiction series, *The X-Files* (1993–2002, 2016–2018). In a different example, the Wakanda salute that was featured in the first Black superhero-led film, *Black Panther* (2018), was embraced and replicated by audiences. In recent years the salute has been used in sports matches and other public events to signify Black excellence and the coming together of the global African diaspora (Alemoru, 2018; Phillipson, 2020).

On the other hand, scholars (Banet-Weiser, 2018; Phillips, 2018; Sobande, 2020) warn against an exaggerated emphasis on representation in popular culture as it distracts from activism that should take place in the "real" world, in areas such as politics or the workforce. Those who are weary of representation-focused activism argue that introducing a marginalized character into a successful franchise has become the end goal and has stopped being part of a larger social project to achieve equality in society. According to this perspective, representation for the sake of representation is devoid of meaning. The representation of marginalized individuals can also be harmful when it depicts them inaccurately or stereotypically (Besana et al., 2019; Brown, 2013; hall, 1997; hooks, 1992, 2019;

Nadkarni & Sivarajan, 2020; Tyree, 2013). Therefore, Sobande (2020), for instance, suggests casting a critical eye on representation to determine how it reflects or relates to other power structures in society. In light of the contrasting views in this debate, I explore how feminist women perceive and are affected by representation in the context of their fandoms.

The debate on women feminist fans' engagement with the object of their fandom is therefore framed through the discourse on representation. This examination aims to answer questions such as the following: what is the significance of the representation of gender, ethnicity, and age in *Star Wars* and *Doctor Who* for the identities of feminist women fans and their perception of themselves? What makes a particular character portrayal a "good" or positive representation, according to the participants? And most importantly, how do feminist women fans manage the backlash aimed at characters who represent marginalized communities? Through the discussion on representation, this chapter also demonstrates the parallels between feminist women fans and the women characters featured in their favorite franchises. As I will soon describe, both the fans and characters experience continuous belittlement, sexism, racism, and retaliation. Through the ways in which women characters are written, portrayed, and received by the general audience, feminist women fans learn about their own position in the fan community.

I discuss representation and identification through feminist women fans' reading of four women characters: Leia Organa and Rose Tico from *Star Wars* and Martha Jones and the 13th Doctor from *Doctor Who*. Even though the interviewees mentioned a plethora of other characters from these fandoms (as well as other fandoms), I chose these characters because they best embody the feminist women fans' complex relationship with the object of their fandom. These characters exemplify the participants' urge to find positive role models to identify with and be inspired by, and their disappointment when such characters are misused, stereotyped, or purposefully written to cater to men. This analysis also explores how feminist women fans negotiate their disappointment and the backlash and uproar that was targeted against some of these fictional characters.

Each character highlights different moments of fractures and challenges that feminist women fans experience when engaging with their fandoms. By focusing on Leia, I depict the participants' conflicted approach to sexualized characters, as well as the older interviewees' reception of the depiction of aging women onscreen. When discussing Martha Jones and Rose Tico, I review the identification of the fans of marginalized ethnicities with characters of similar backgrounds and the importance of representation. At the same time, I unpack the participants' emotional turmoil due to the backlash the two characters received and their reactions to the poor way Martha and Rose were written. Lastly, I examine feminist women fans' attitudes toward the first woman protagonist in their beloved franchise, as well as the ways in which they managed the pushback she received as well.

5.1   Princess Leia/Slave Leia/General Organa: When Sexism Meets Ageism

Leia Organa (1977–1983, 2015–2019), played by the late Carrie Fisher, is undoubtedly one of the most beloved characters in the *Star Wars* franchise. Many of the *Star Wars* fans participating in this study identified Princess Leia as the primary source of attraction to the franchise, calling her their childhood's feminist icon:

> Pretty much my all-time hero (laughs). She [Leia] was incredibly important to me growing up [...] she was pretty much the only character that had agency, that was actually doing things, she had a political role. (Jamie, 39, white, UK)
>
> When I was seven, I went to see Snow White and then the week after I saw *Star Wars* and I thought that if I could be a princess, I'd like to be Princess Leia because she always argued with everybody. (Samantha, 46, white, UK)

In another example, Ally (39, white, UK) reminisced about the first time she saw a Leia action figure before watching the films. She described it as a profound moment that awakened her interest in inspiring women characters:

> When I was five or six [...], I have a distinct memory of playing at a friend's house with Star Wars toys and stuff, and the figure of Leia had a helmet. It was a particular moment when I took the helmet off, and it was a girl. It blew my mind to a point where I remember it very vividly. It was a whole thing where I thought Princess Leia could do anything the boys can do.

These interview excerpts convey the overwhelming, lasting impression Leia left on the participants in their childhoods and her significant role in their biographical narratives. Each fan provided a striking, almost picturesque account of her first encounter with Leia and the enduring impact this pivotal, formative moment had on the rest of their life. According to the interviewees, Leia was a catalyst to becoming fans of *Star Wars* and feminists and shaped the women they had become. The interviewees frequently stressed how unique Leia was in the science fiction genre. She pioneered the portrayal of women characters who refused to be victims and insisted on being the heroes. Since she was called "princess" and taken captive in the first minutes of the film, the interviewees were primed to think that Leia would simply serve as yet another damsel in distress and a prize to be won by the heroic men sent to save her. But Leia surpassed their expectations. She was feisty, charismatic, witty, and a brave leader who needed no saving:

> Leia in 1977 being a leader of a rebel force... I try to rack my brains if there was a female general in any movie [...] She's presented straight away as a hero, and she remains the hero in every single movie. There's no question, nobody questions that she's a leader. She's a princess, she's a senator, she's a rebel leader, she's leading the military, she's making strategies, she's picking up guns. (Justine, 43, Lebanese-Maltese-English, Australia)

Despite crowning Leia as their feminist icon, many feminist fans were critical of *Star Wars* for its historical scarcity of female characters. Lucia (39, white, Spain), for instance, sardonically commented that, based on *Star Wars'* storyline, "there are no other women in the galaxy" but Leia. The scarcity of women characters led Isabel (26, white, Spain) to assert that she "wouldn't consider *Star Wars* movies feminist. Even if they have Princess Leia, who is a feminist icon, the movies are not feminist." Indeed, the first trilogy of *Star Wars*, which includes a plethora of human and non-human characters, features just four women with a speaking role (some with only one line of dialogue), an issue that attracted feminist critiques (Bowman, 2005; Harrison, 2020; Wood, 2016). Furthermore, the participants argued that *Star Wars* was not a feminist franchise due to the ways in which the women characters were written over the years, especially when their role was diminished to playing a sex object or a love interest. The case of "Slave Leia" served as an exemplar of this kind of sexist, objectifying writing to many of the interviewees.

Leia became a sex symbol after a few short scenes from *Episode VI: Return of the Jedi* (1983). *Return of the Jedi* opens after Leia and Han Solo are captured by Jabba the Hutt, Han's foe. While Han is frozen in carbonite, Leia is enslaved by Jabba. Her iconic, fully covering white dress is replaced with a minimal golden bikini. She is also shackled to Jabba by the neck, who yanks it when aggravated, thereby choking and pulling her closer to his body. Later, Leia breaks free by strangling Jabba with these chains.

The interviewees' readings of the controversial, provocative "Slave Leia" scenes were divided. Some participants found them a triumphant feminist moment and emphasized that Leia killed Jabba with the very shackles used to sexualize her:

> All the men who drool over the Slave Leia costume tend to forget that she strangled the bastard [...] I think it's not a weakness. In fact, it's a moment of strength: the one who put her in that position is killed by her with the actual chains, I mean, talk about metaphor. (Samantha, 46, white, UK)

These participants were excited to see Leia reveal her sexy side, especially after previously donning a white, virginal long gown:

> She could be in robes and f****** fighting and pew-pewing and all of that, and she could be in her f****** slave bikini and choking toxic masculinity out with the very chain that they tried to enslave her with. I think that is the most powerful message of the power of feminism. (Cristina, 34, Latina, USA)

Feminist fans, such as Samantha and Cristina, found symbolism in Leia's bikini and chains, reading Jabba's demise as Leia taking down the patriarchy by using its own instruments. Being dressed in a bikini did not compromise any of Leia's skills or abilities. If anything, it demonstrated that a woman could be strong and sexy at the same time.

In contrast, other interviewees condemned the skimpy bikini and degrading chains:

> Brilliant, she gets to save the day in a bikini, and everyone gets to talk about how hot she is until the rest of time. For me, watching it, personally, it felt completely out of sync with the rest of the way Leia's portrayed. It's just the question of why does the female character have to be put in that position at some point in order for her to be an actual protagonist. (Olivia, 40, white, UK)
>
> She's got chains on her! It's not empowering to be chained up by someone and being made to wear clothes you don't want to wear, even if you end up killing them with chains. That's not what empowering is. Choice is empowering, and her choice was taken away from her in that scene. (Nina, 25, white, UK)

The participants who argued against the Slave Leia scenes were critical because even though both Han Solo and Leia were held hostage, only Leia was dressed in minimal clothing. They reckoned that Leia was sexualized because she was the only woman in an ensemble of men.

The interviewees' reactions to the scenes were also informed by what they had learned about Carrie Fisher's experiences during filming. Some participants declined to support a scene that had made Fisher feel pressure to lose weight and feel uncomfortable:

> I don't think it's her choice, it's the director's choice to actually portray her like that. When you look at all the puzzle pieces of this scene, the actress didn't want to do it, she pretty much starved herself to do it, she was uncomfortable with the objectification [...] For me, there is not one aspect of this that leads to empowerment. If Jabba had been like, "you're not allowed to wear this bikini," and f****** Carrie Fisher was like, "in this scene, I want to take off everything," I would be like, "ok, go off." (Daniela, 23, Latina, USA)

Daniela's comment emphasizes that the critique of the scenes is not against the character or the actress but against the men pulling the strings backstage: the writers, directors, and producers. The feminist fans I interviewed accused George Lucas (the creator of *Star Wars*) and his team of betraying Leia and Fisher. They felt that this depiction of Leia tainted a beloved character who inspired them to become fans and feminists. The participants argued that George Lucas used his women characters as "wish fulfillment" (Natalie, 38, white, UK), as they embodied his and other men's fantasies.

Feminist women fans also expanded their critique to the men viewers who enjoyed the sexualization of an enslaved woman:

> Young, creepy, old dudes, creepy fans, hanging around wanting girls to be Slave Leia. "What's your fantasy?"—"Slave Leia." They didn't get that that's what powerful men reduce women to. Some gross dude, "what's your fantasy for your girlfriend to dress up as?"—"oh, Slave Leia." So basically, you're identifying yourself as Jabba, with no sense of irony whatsoever. She wasn't interested in Jabba. She wouldn't be interested in you. (Lucy 41, white, UK)

Since 1983, Slave Leia has become a global sex symbol among teenage heterosexual boys and men. Participants such as Daria (52, white,

Switzerland) suggested that the motivation to sexualize Leia was based on the assumption that the majority of *Star Wars'* fan base is cishet men: "Of course it was sexualized because it's a male audience watching it mainly." The interviewees lamented that a relatively short scene in which a woman is enslaved and bullied is read as a sexual fantasy and is still so prominent and referenced in popular culture:

> The thing that I found harder wasn't the film, because it was very brief, but wider cultural aspects outside the Star Wars fandom. It became the way that Leia was represented, every teenage boy's fantasy. I found that part more depressing than a relatively short part of the film. I feel like the film let her down. (Jamie, 39, white, UK)
> I think for some people, this caused a disruption because, for some people, it was all about Carrie Fisher in a bikini [...] she's a very strong character, but the thing she is remembered for was the bikini. (Bernie, 50, white, UK)

Slave Leia is a textbook exemplar of Mulvey's conceptualization of "the male gaze" (1975). The male gaze is a perspective taken by men viewers, creators, and characters, which turns women characters into an erotic spectacle and deprives them of agency and control over their bodies and representation. Scenes that are written to pander to the heterosexual male gaze fail to acknowledge other audience members' existence. Leia's portrayal as a sexy slave demonstrated the disregard of women viewers and symbolized to the interviewees that *Star Wars* was created *by* men *for* men. The interviewees internalized this perspective so much so that some of them conceded to Leia's sexualization, understanding that the producers had to tailor the content to heterosexual young men without considering other viewers.

Women fans' frustration with the portrayal of Leia lingered on in her final appearance in the third trilogy. After more than 30 years, Carrie Fisher reprised her role in the new *Star Wars* trilogy. In *Episode VII:The Force Awakens* (2015) and *Episode VIII:The Last Jedi* (2017), Leia is a middle-aged woman, a general, and the mother of the new villain, Kylo Ren. Since one of the last depictions of Fisher until her reprisal was the slave costume, the response of fans and media to the older Carrie Fisher was harsh. Fisher was closely scrutinized, and audiences were eager to discuss whether she had "aged well." The overall response amongst fan communities and media outlets was that she had not (Said-Moorhouse,

2015; Tonic, 2015). Fellow actors, Harrison Ford and Mark Hamill, who also returned to the franchise decades later, did not receive the same criticism or scrutiny.

While there was no apparent difference between the interviewees in the reading of Slave Leia, the older participants were distinctly more conscious of the ageist reception of Leia and Carrie Fisher. Older women fans, especially mothers such as Sharon (39, white, UK) and Lucy (41, white, UK), shared their grief over the close inspection of Carrie Fisher's looks and the plethora of remarks about her "looking old." Lucy further lamented that after being a heroine in her own right, Leia's role in the franchise had become limited to being "someone's mom." Growing older and no longer being able to serve as eye candy, the character of Leia was reduced to her relationship to men.

Following up on Shaw's (2015) approach to the fluctuations of identification with media culture, it appears that some women fans identified with Leia the most when they both had grown "older." Ageist comments targeted against Carrie Fisher and the older Leia hit a sensitive nerve among older participants, who also experienced pressure to try to hold on to their individuality and sense of worth as they were suddenly deemed "too old" to be members of fan communities (Chap. 4). Therefore, older interviewees were keen to discuss the portrayal of older Leia, while younger ones were more preoccupied with other facets of her characterization throughout the years.

The interviewees' reading of Leia foregrounds the complex attitudes of feminist women fans to the ways in which women are represented in science fiction. Regardless of the intensity of their identification, the participants' responses to Leia were intertwined with their views of themselves in the context of the *Star Wars* fandom. Such a symbiosis between fans and characters followed the interviewees' reception of later characters, Martha Jones (*Doctor Who*) and Rose Tico (*Star Wars*).

5.2   Rose Tico and Martha Jones: When Sexism Meets Racism

When probing Tia (34, Black African American, USA) on the reasons why science fiction fandom is perceived as primarily appealing to white audiences, she explained that lack of representation is the primary reason:

They (her family) would consider mainstream science fiction as white-centered. So, if you don't dig a little deeper, you don't find Octavia Butler. You don't know unless you go looking for it. So, there is a disconnect that they can't relate to it.

Like scholars such as Wanzo (2015) and Thomas (2019), Tia claimed that the main reason individuals of marginalized ethnicities do not engage with science fiction is that they do not see themselves represented in mainstream content and, therefore, cannot connect with it. Thus, when *Doctor Who* featured its first Black companion after more than 40 years since the series' debut, the casting was considered a meaningful step forward for its fans of marginalized ethnicities.

Unfortunately, Martha Jones was not well received by the *Doctor Who* fandom or the participants, regardless of their ethnicity. Martha joined the series after the 10th Doctor and his former companion, Rose Tyler, separated ways. The profound emotional connection between the two reached a poignant conclusion when Martha was introduced to the series, setting her up as an unsatisfying replacement to the beloved Rose. As Jessica (32, biracial white-Jamaican, USA) said: "Coming right after Rose Tyler, no one is going to love you (laughing)." Martha was a physician and a capable woman in her own right. Nevertheless, she decided to leave her established life behind and follow the Doctor's time and space travels. Soon thereafter, Martha fell in love with the Doctor, but her feelings were not reciprocated. The fact that Martha changed from an independent woman to a companion whose main motivation was romantic love disappointed the interviewees:

> She was a doctor, so she was quite independent, and then she started moping over the Doctor all the time, and I thought that was a real shame. I thought it was a real waste of what could have been a great opportunity. (Natalie, 38, white, UK)
>
> The writing kind of just made her this companion, a follower, a lovesick puppy. (Jessica, 32, biracial white-Jamaican, USA)

The interviewees' main concern was that the first Black character who was introduced to the show as a well-rounded individual was quickly reduced to the role of the unloved woman.

In parallel to the writing of Leia, the participants found Martha's story arc the result of men writers who did not know or were uninterested in writing compelling women characters of marginalized ethnicities:

> I was a bit annoyed that Martha had to be so in love with him as well. Why did we have to have all this nonsense? That was unnecessary. The Martha stuff was a bit… it was written obviously by a man, shall we say? (Wendy, 50, white, UK)
> The Martha dynamic was that she's supposed to be a medical student but what she mostly does is wander around whining because the Doctor doesn't love her. I'm very surprised that people who identify as feminists have not picked up on it more. (Zoe, 34, white, UK)

According to Zoe, the writing of Martha is a red flag to its feminist viewers, as it demonstrates that the women commonly featured in *Doctor Who* are not as well developed and explored as the character of the Doctor. Instead, they are pigeonholed in the roles of the companion, the sidekick, or the love interest.

The reception of Martha by the interviewees of marginalized ethnicities was complex, as they were upset but also nonchalant about her storyline:

> I kind of had mixed feelings about it. It was like, again, seeing somebody onscreen who I can relate to, and it's like, well, I don't think we're going to have that kind of portrayal where you're falling in love with someone who looks like her […] I think it's just unfortunate how I'm conditioned to look at stories and things like that […] It sucks. It's not something that makes me happy. It makes me sad to think about it. It's one of those things that you get used to. You get desensitized to it. I'm not going to get excited about it because it's not going to go there. (Gabby, 37, Black, USA)

Unpacking Gabby's statement about Martha leads to interesting yet saddening insights. Gabby, whose identification with Martha is apparent, poignantly accepts that Martha or "someone who looks like her" is not considered worthy of reciprocated romantic love. In her examination of the portrayal of Black characters in science fiction and fantasy Thomas (2019) discussed the lack of presentation of Black characters as love interests. She provided the example of the TV series *Merlin* (2008–2012), in which a Black actress portrays the character of Guinevere Pendragon (or Gwen in short). Viewers continuously questioned why the fair-skinned

King Arthur would fall in love with Black Gwen and deemed the relationship unbelievable. In light of such claims, Thomas asserted:

> Why is it easier to believe in talking dragons than in Black princesses and queens? It is because the dark fantastic cycle in our collective imagination makes it difficult to suspend our disbelief that a Black girl can live happily ever after. (2019, p. 102)

Thomas' use of *Merlin* is helpful here because it demonstrates recent efforts to diversify traditional, white-centered science fiction and fantasy staple diegeses. In such narratives, where fictional beings such as dragons are more common than Black characters, let alone leading characters, it is almost inconceivable, among some viewers, to imagine a Black woman leading the storyline and being loved. Drawing from Thomas' work, it is understandable why interviewees such as Gabby simply conceded to Martha experiencing heartbreak. It is so uncommon for women of marginalized ethnicities to experience a happy and healthy romantic relationship in mainstream media that viewers simply become "desensitized" to storylines where they get their hearts broken.

In contrast to Gabby, Tia was less tranquil in her reaction to the way Martha was written in the series:

> When they first brought in Martha on *Doctor Who* and the way they wrote her character, I was like, "I might actually be done." You did not do her justice [...] she was a Black woman who is a doctor, that is great, good job. But then, instead of actually allowing her to grow, they kind of put her in this "rebound girlfriend" mode [...] The episode where he didn't have his memory, and she was basically working as the help, I wanted to throw my remote at the screen. I'm like, "you really put her... you really did this and didn't even make the Doctor aware enough to actually address it." You're expecting me to believe this 100-year-old man doesn't understand what is happening. I was frustrated. There were no people of color when you wrote that. (Tia, 34, Black African American, USA)

Like Wendy before her, Tia addressed the lack of diversity in the series' writing room when Martha was created. Interestingly, while Wendy focused on the writers' gender, Tia referred to their ethnicity, demonstrating once again that white feminists traditionally observe the world through the prism of gender without necessarily adding a second lens of ethnicity.

Martha was considered a case of a misguided representation, which offered minor improvement or inspiration to its viewers. The interviewees embraced the inclusion of a new Black woman character, but her mere existence was not enough for them. Martha was ultimately a one-dimensional character, who was a clear second fiddle to the leading white protagonist.[1] This kind of poor writing of women of marginalized ethnicities is also prominent in the next case I examine, Rose Tico from *Star Wars*.

Rose Tico, who was first introduced in *Episode VIII:The Last Jedi* (2017), is arguably one of the most controversial *Star Wars* characters in recent years. Played by actress Kelly Marie Tran (of Vietnamese descent), Rose is a mechanic who sides with the Resistance. She plays a significant part in the storyline in her first movie appearance as she collaborates with Finn, a Black ex-stormtrooper, to disable the First Order's hyperspace tracker. Unfortunately, both the character Tico and the actress Tran were met with an almost unprecedented backlash and venomous online attacks, so much so that Tran closed her social media accounts (Chichizola, 2018; El Mahmoud, 2019).

While the interviewees were primarily disappointed with the way Martha was written, they were quite satisfied with Rose's storyline in *The Last Jedi*. It was the pushback against Rose and Tran that upset the participants:

> When we had Rose, that turned my stomach to this day. I'm so mad about that entire situation. I literally posted that I was ashamed of my fandom because of how they were treating this girl, who was essentially me. I'm looking at me on the screen. She's fangirling, I fangirl all the time. That's all she's doing. And they're just tearing her to shreds and just being mean and rude [...] I've never been so upset and livid. It was so wrong what happened to her. She is one of my favorite characters for that reason. (Jessica, 32, bira-cial white-Jamaican, USA)

Jessica's remark on the heated reactions against Rose demonstrates her identification with the character. Shaw (2015), for instance, emphasized the difference between identifying *with* and identifying *as*, when exploring consumers' identification with characters in popular culture (p. 69). Even though Jessica does not share the same ethnic background as Rose, she

---

[1] The interviewees also addressed the redemption of Martha when she reprised her role later on in the show. Due to the scope of this chapter, I will not cover their reading of those episodes.

identified with her experiences as a marginalized woman trying to find her place in a fandom with strict terms of inclusion. Because of her identification, Jessica took the attacks on the character and the actress personally. She found them a marker of the racism that is also targeted at fans like her in the *Star Wars* fan community.

After receiving severe pushback during the release of *The Last Jedi*, Rose's role was minimized in the following cinematic installment, *Episode IX: The Rise of Skywalker*. From playing a significant part in the storyline in the *Last Jedi*, Rose's screen-time was reduced almost to that of an extra, with only a few scenes and lines of dialogue. The interviewees interpreted this "creative" decision as an attempt to pacify the angry (white) viewers who passionately expressed their hatred of Rose:

> It was hard for me to comprehend. She was just trying to do her job. White people want to see white people. In the end, well, she's a minority in the movie, and you're giving her c*** for this. It just doesn't make sense. It's life reflecting life again. For a whole continent, they were super excited to finally see an Asian person in the movie, let alone a woman. I didn't get it. Must have been tough for her. (Camila, 33, Latina, Australia)

As Camila indicated the primary motivation behind the backlash against Rose and Tran was blunt racism. Some of the white fans of the franchise were against the inclusion of Rose because it appeared to be motivated by so-called political correctness considerations that they argued ended up compromising the film's diegetic and artistic quality. This retaliation led to Rose being almost entirely written out of the franchise.

According to the participants, the "downgrade" of Rose's role in the trilogy's last installment was yet another shoddy execution of the representation of marginalized ethnicities:

> I think, to me, characters like Finn and Rose Tico, they scream tokenism, and the treatment of the characters in the movies screams tokenism [...] If you're going to make a song and dance and introduce these cool characters that people have been asking for, do them justice and give them development and a story. Otherwise, what's the point? To quote Yoda, "do or do not, there is no try" (laughing). There is no point in creating these half-developed, underdeveloped characters as characters that people are meant to identify with. Otherwise, just have them in the background. It doesn't serve them well. It doesn't serve the franchise well. (Justine, 43, Lebanese-Maltese-English, Australia)

> Then, Rose suddenly has only two lines of dialogue. I understand that
> there wasn't much of a place for her, but they could have done it better. You
> can't give us a character who seems important, and then she's like "bye."
> (Nika, 44, Latina/Chicana, USA)

As Justine says, the inclusion of Rose felt like tokenism and a cheap trick
to appear as if the *Star Wars* franchise was committed to equal and diverse
representation in its content. As in Martha's case, casting a woman of a
marginalized ethnicity is not enough and should not be considered as
such. Characters like Martha or Rose deserve to lead their own stories and
portray fully fleshed-out women.

The discussion about Martha and Rose also reveals the symbiotic relationship between fans and characters. When these characters were first
introduced into the franchises, women fans of marginalized ethnicities
finally felt seen and acknowledged. The fans' excitement was quickly
replaced by anguish, as these characters, especially Rose, faced vigorous
racist attacks. The interviewees felt personally attacked and offended when
Rose and Martha were received with animosity and belittlement. Their
attitudes toward the two characters were even more complicated because
they were not necessarily pleased with them either. Therefore, they had to
deal with their own disappointment while advocating for them at the same
time. Such negotiation was also needed when the first woman was cast in
the role of the Doctor, as the following section reveals.

5.3   THE 13TH DOCTOR: WHEN CHANGE
MEETS BACKLASH

Since 2017, and for the first time since the series' inception in 1963, the
13th incarnation of the Doctor has been embodied by a woman. While
some hailed the promotion of a woman to its forefront, others argued that
Doctor Who's creative team had succumbed to the pressure of "political
correctness" (Powell & Spencer, 2017; Szalai, 2017).

In answer to the backlash against the gender change, the interviewees
argued that women were merely starting to get their fair share in an arena
that traditionally discriminates in favor of (white) men:

> Obviously, men are feeling so threatened by it, but all we are doing is asking
> for the same: to see ourselves on the screen the same way they have seen
> themselves on screen for their entire lives. Why can't we just have a little

corner of the industry? What's so wrong with a little corner of a franchise that has someone that looks like us, right? (Sheela, 49, Indian-Anglo Saxon, Australia)

When Jodie got the part, I said, "you know what, there are an awful lot of people in this world who get film roles solely on the basis of their gender and their race, but guess what? They're white dudes!" Those are the ones that get jobs based solely on their ethnicity and their sex. (Donna, 46, white, UK)

The participants pointed out the double standards in the entertainment industry where the casting of white men is seldomly questioned. In contrast, the casting of women and other marginalized identities is automatically considered a decision that is detached from artistic or creative motivations but is made to pander to so-called social justice warriors.

Ultimately, the interviewees and the media embraced the 13th Doctor (Hooton, 2018; Mangan, 2018). The majority of the participants felt reassured by the relative positive reception of the new Doctor and regarded it as their own personal triumph:

She seems to have become in a very short time a beloved Doctor, and it's such a huge relief to not have to battle the 'I don't hate women, but …" crowd anymore. She's won the battle for us. (Samantha, 46, white, UK)

Exploring feminist women fans' defense of casting a woman as the Doctor reveals that the controversy signified more than a simple dispute over a television series. Knowing how popular culture has impacted them, feminist women fans were elated by the possibility that younger generations would grow up with inspiring women characters. Feminist women fans felt seen by *Doctor Who*'s creative team as their pleas for a woman Doctor were finally heard and addressed. Therefore, the backlash felt like a personal attack against them, the loyal women audience who were consistently disregarded by the show's creators and men fans alike (Jowett, 2014; Walter, 2017).

Despite their general embrace of the 13th Doctor, several interviewees asserted that the creators played it safe by casting a white woman for the role:

I didn't even let myself get excited about who they're going to pick. They're picking a white woman. That's what's going to happen. That is what would make the most sense. (Tia, 34, Black African American, USA)

> I am pragmatic enough to know that you can't go straight from a white man to a Black woman. (Sheela, 49, Indian-Anglo Saxon, Australia)

Knowing how rare it is for women of marginalized ethnicities to lead science fiction franchises, the participants did not allow themselves to fantasize about a *Doctor who* looked like them. Even though they were disappointed by the assumption of whiteness, they acknowledged that switching from a white man to a Black woman would have led to unprecedented turbulence in the fandom:

> Going from a white guy to a black woman is such a 180 that the show would have imploded. Even the most die-hard fans would have had this embedded, visceral reaction to it, even if they don't think they're racist, even if they think they're wonderful people. Because of the way they are socialized, they are going to recoil. (Tia, 34, Black African American, USA)

Two years after the debut of the first woman Doctor, the show did include an incarnation of the Doctor in the form of a Black woman, played by actress Jo Martin. The participants were excited about having a woman *Doctor who* was more similar to them. For example, Gabby (37, Black, USA) shared:

> There's just something about seeing someone who looks like you and having that representation. It makes me feel so great. I'm thinking, "man, I need to learn how to sew, so I can like, perfect some kind of cosplay" (laughing).

Nevertheless, as the interviewees anticipated, adding a second woman *Doctor who* was also Black was met with yet another pushback against "the PC brigade" (Charles, 2020), which argued that the show was going too far with its "woke" agenda. Jenny (31, Chinese, UK) regarded the backlash as an effort to preserve the "natural order" of science fiction content that had been maintained for decades before:

> I can understand why people respond like that. For example, *Doctor Who* is something that is so familiar. Having your favorite blankie, it's like coming home to feel this comfort in your own home. As a white, cis, heteronormative man, which is predominately, I would assume, the demographic audience, you're challenged even in your own house, your own home [...] I just

don't want to engage with that s*** (laughing). I think that it translates to a lot of backlash and anger.

As Boeckner et al. (2020), some white men cannot associate Black people or women and the world of fantasy and science fiction. Following up on this argument and on Thomas' (2019) analysis of *Merlin* that was presented above, I claim that the conventional tropes that have been established in science fiction throughout the years have asserted whiteness as the norm. Based on this logic, any character who is not the traditional white masculine protagonist is retaliated against in some sectors because it appears antithetical to and even a betrayal of the traditional essence of the diegesis.

The cases of the two women Doctors demonstrate how the interviewees see representation in fandom as a source of joy and empowerment, as well as disappointment and disturbance. Having a character with whom the fan can identify cultivates a sense of belonging and enforces the tie between the fan and the object of her fandom. Still, as demonstrated throughout this chapter, "good" representation is not easy to achieve. Over the years, various women characters were added to *Doctor Who* and *Star Wars* to rejuvenate the franchises and diversify their ensemble. Many of these attempts faltered in their executions as such characters ended up serving as tokens with limited depth or developed storylines. Therefore, the reception of such representations was ambivalent, as feminist women fans had to navigate between their own expectations of such characters and the backlash they frequently received.

5.4   Conclusions: Does Representation Matter?

In this chapter, I have explored feminist women fans' engagement with the *Star Wars* and *Doctor Who* diegesis through four main characters: Leia, Martha, Rose, and the 13th Doctor. These characters were invaluable to the participants. They served as a canvas on which the fans projected and shaped their perceptions of and attitudes toward feminism, gender, ethnicity, and the fan community. Furthermore, such characters embodied the women fans' status in their communities. On the one hand, they were a source of inspiration and provided recognition of women audiences' existence and value. On the other hand, they mirrored the participants' disenfranchisement.

Characters such as Martha, Rose, and the 13th Doctor carry the "burden of representation" (Hall, 1996; Tagg, 1993). As the first of their kind in their respective franchises, they were expected to represent *all* women and embody *every* woman viewer's expectations. When they were not portrayed as multi-dimensional or influential women, they let down their audience who looked for role models to identify with and be inspired by. Given their rarity in the science fiction genre, these characters served as punching bags for fans who were aggressively opposed to the expansion of their beloved franchise into stories of marginalized individuals. The women fans' exposure to toxic online discourse regarding such characters was yet another blow to their sense of belonging in fan communities.

The discussion of *Star Wars'* and *Doctor Who's* characters also provides a platform for investigating the importance of representation in the media. When I discussed this issue with the participants, they identified three main justifications for promoting representation in popular culture: inspiring children, creating encounters with unfamiliar identities, and providing an economic incentive for the industry. The first motivation, inspiring children, featured prominently in many interviews. The participants referred to their own children or relatives, and their intentions of sharing their fandom with them and exposing them to positive role models:

I think representation is all about all the little kids out there being able to see "I can do that." I got a niece who I love, she's six and half, I'm always looking for stories with great female role models that I could show her. To show her, "you could be strong, you can be smart, you can be whatever you want to." (Sheela, 49, Indian-Anglo Saxon, Australia)

I don't have children, but I have lots of nieces and nephews, and I think it's important for them. I never... I only had so much to work with as a kid (laughing) I had to use my imagination and put myself in these situations. I feel like when there's just one view, it makes it really difficult, especially for young people, to see themselves in those possibilities. (Gabby, 37, Black, USA)

Being exposed to different types of human beings is an extraordinary force in shaping people's psyches and perceptions of certain demographics. I would even argue that while positive representation is so crucial, negative representation is even more powerful than that [...] The root of the problem goes so deep. It's very formative, especially for children, who look to see themselves in stories. (Daniela, 23, Latina, USA)

The participants emphasized that representation is vital for children who are still forming their identities and perceptions of the world. They maintained that being exposed to powerful, intelligent, capable characters who look like them was a major catalyst for children to explore their own abilities and become the best version of themselves. Moreover, as per Daniela, exposure to characters who represent unfamiliar social categories is an educational mechanism that might cement children's positive or negative attitudes toward such individuals.

The interviewees also talked about encounters with foreign identities through popular culture as a positive outcome of representation in the media. They maintained that such a motivation was not only important for children but also for the general society. For instance, Jenny (31, Chinese, UK) referred to the frequent negative or belittling depiction of Asian characters in the media:

> It f****** matters, media representation. We don't get represented in Anglophone media at all. But then, when it's something s*****, it's all Asian people. It f****** pisses me off.

For some people, popular culture is one of the only gateways to becoming acquainted with marginalized individuals. Therefore, when such characters are the villains, the sidekicks, or the butt of the joke, such stereotypical tropes are engrained in the viewers' psyche and later become difficult to shake. Therefore, the interviewees argued that representations that shed a positive light on an excluded identity have the power to break the stigma and build bridges between individuals and communities.

Lastly, some of the participants also claimed that diverse representation is or could be motivated by simple financial considerations. Providing a varied ensemble of characters could potentially attract viewers from different communities and social backgrounds, thus making more profits for producers. For example, Sheela (49, Indian-Anglo Saxon, Australia) asserted:

> I think the biggest rise in audience of science fiction has been women in the last few years. Any kind of producer of science fiction would be an idiot not to do something about it. That just makes common economic sense, basically.

While the interviewees supported this line of reasoning if it meant an improvement in the inclusion and diversity in mainstream media, they were also aware of the hazards in using marginalized characters as a marketing strategy:

> I just think, unfortunately, it's done wrong so many times. I love it, I think it's needed, but it shouldn't be such a forced situation. I just feel like there's so much force behind it. There's so much "hey, look, we're being politically correct" or "hey, look, we're being inclusive." Yeah, but not because you want to be, it's because you're literally getting marketing off of it (laughing). (Jessica, 32, biracial white-Jamaican, USA)

Jessica acknowledged that characters of marginalized identities are often used as mere tokens to demonstrate inclusion and a desire for social equality, when in fact these characters are abused and misused, much like Martha (*Doctor Who*) or Rose (*Star Wars*).

Indeed, Banet-Weiser's (2018) concept of the "economy of visibility" underscores the potential risks of seeing representation as the end goal. Banet-Weiser depicted a cultural industry that promotes representation for the sake of representation while potentially abandoning the motivation to achieve substantial, long-lasting social change. As Shaw (2015) stated, "Representation in popular media does not correct the lived experiences of oppression, nor does it necessarily reorganize the structures of power that have maintained inequality" (p. 148). Thus, when producers are adamant about diversifying their cast, they often neglect thinking about how they are presenting such characters. They turn a blind eye when actors are attacked, and they disregard the consistent white, male-dominated work environment behind the scenes that is still difficult to break through for marginalized individuals.

The findings reviewed in this chapter demonstrate the nuanced ways in which representation can be scrutinized and evaluated. On its own, representation is not enough. It is potentially a dangerous distraction from "real-life" conflicts and struggles. Avid consumers of popular culture should not rest on their laurels simply because more marginalized identities appear onscreen. "Good" representation portrays marginalized characters as fully fleshed-out individuals and provides them with opportunities to tell their stories from their own perspectives. As feminist women fans' biographical narratives demonstrate, representations *can* significantly influence viewers' lives and shape their identities, perceptions, and goals.

Therefore, debates on representation should not dismiss it or belittle it as a mere diversion from a more substantial form of activism. Nevertheless, the emphasis on representation should never be the end goal or examined in isolation from broader social processes and inequalities.

Through the discussion on representation, this chapter also indicates the fractures in the feminist women fans' identity. It demonstrates the difficulty of enjoying content while acknowledging its dismissal and belittlement of its women characters, as well as the viewers who love and promote them. As the participants explicitly articulated earlier in the chapter, such infrequent depictions of women in *Doctor Who* and *Star Wars* indicate that these are not feminist franchises. Having scrutinized the various arenas in which feminist women fans experience retaliation, frustration, and inner tensions, the last chapter reviews the tactics that feminist women fans develop in order to reconcile feminism and fandom.

REFERENCES

Alemoru, K. (2018, March 12). The Wakanda salute is becoming a symbol of black solidarity. *Dazed*. Retrieved May 6, 2021, from https://www.dazeddigital.com/film-tv/article/39357/1/the-wakanda-salute-is-becoming-a-symbol-of-black-solidarity

Banet-Weiser, S. (2018). *Empowered: Popular feminism and popular misogyny*. Duke University Press.

Besana, T., Katsiaficas, D., & Loyd, A. B. (2019). Asian American media representation: A film analysis and implications for identity development. *Research in Human Development, 16*(3–4), 201–225.

Boeckner, M. J., Flegel, M., & Leggatt, J. (2020). "Not my Captain America": Racebanding, reverse discrimination, and white panic in the Marvel Comics Fandom. In R. Pande (Ed.), *Fandom, now in color* (pp. 231–249). University of Iowa Press.

Bowman, C. (2005). Pregnant Padmé and slave Leia: Star Wars' female role models. In K. S. Decker & J. T. Eberl (Eds.), *The ultimate Star Wars and philosophy: You must unlearn what you have learned* (pp. 159–171). Open Court.

Brown, J. A. (2013). Panthers and vixens: Black superheroines, sexuality and stereotypes in Contemporary comic books. In S. C. Howard & R. K. Jackson II (Eds.), *Black comics: Politics of race and representation* (pp. 133–150). Bloomsbury Publishing.

Charles, A. (2020, February 3). Doctor Who: Fan reaction to first black Time Lord exposes Britain's deep divisions on race and gender. *The Conversation*.

Retrieved April 21, 2021, from https://theconversation.com/ doctor-who-fan-reaction-to-first-black-time-lord-exposes-britains-deep-divisions-on-race-and-gender-130962

Chichizola, C. (2018, August 21). Star War's Kelly Marie Tran opens up about leaving social Media after Last Jedi backlash. *Cinema Blend.* Retrieved April 17, 2021, from https://www.cinemablend.com/news/2456089/star-wars-kelly-marie-tran-opens-up-about-leaving-social-media-after-last-jedi-backlash

Cicci, M. A. (2017). The invasion of Loki's Army? comic culture's INCREASING awareness of female fans. In M. A. Scott & S. Scott (Eds.), *The Routledge companion to media fandom* (pp. 193–201). Routledge.

Dubrofsky, R. E., & Ryalls, E. D. (2014). The Hunger Games: Performing not-performing to authenticate femininity and whiteness. *Critical Studies in Media Communication, 31*(5), 395–409.

El Mahmoud, S. (2019, December 12). Star Wars: The Rose of Skywalker's Kelly Marie Tran went into therapy after Last Jedi online harassment. *Cinema Blend.* Retrieved April 17, 2021, from https://www.cinemablend.com/ news/2486675/star-wars-the-rise-of-skywalkers-kelly-marie-tran-went-into-therapy-after-last-jedi-online-harassment

Fürsich, E. (2010). Media and the representation of Others. *International Social Science Journal, 61*(199), 113–130.

Geena Davis Institute on Gender in Media. (n.d.). *The Scully effect: I want to believe in STEM.* Retrieved May 6, 2021, from https://seejane.org/research-informs-empowers/the-scully-effect-i-want-to-believe-in-stem

Gray, H. (2015). The feel of life: Resonance, race, and representation. *International Journal of Communication, 9,* 1108–1119.

Hall, S. (1993). What is this "Black" in Black popular culture. *Rethinking Race, 20*(1), 104–114.

Hall, S. (1996). The after-life of Frantz Fanon: Why Fanon? Why now? Why Black skin, white masks? In A. Read (Ed.), *The fact of Blackness: Frantz Fanon and visual representation* (pp. 12–38). Bay Press.

Hall, S. (1997). The spectacle of the other. In S. Hall (Ed.), *Representation: Cultural representations and signifying practices* (pp. 223–290). SAGE in association with The Open University.

Harrison, B. (2020). *The empire strikes back.* Bloomsbury.

hooks, b. (1992). Yearning: Race, gender, and cultural politics. *Hypatia, 7*(2), 177–187.

hooks, b. (2019). *Black looks: Race and representation.* Routledge.

Hooton, C. (2018, October 8). Jodie Whittaker's first full Doctor Who episode: What the critics are saying. *Independent.* Retrieved October 8, 2018, from https://www.independent.co.uk/arts-entertainment/tv/news/doctor-who-jodie-whittaker-series-11-episode-1-review-reaction-critics-a8573696.html

Howard, S. C., & Jackson, R. L., II (Eds.). (2013). *Black comics: Politics of race and representation.* Bloomsbury Publishing.

Jenkins, H. (1992). *Textual poachers.* Routledge.

Jowett, L. (2014). The girls who waited? Female companions and gender in Doctor Who. *Critical Studies in Television, 9*(1), 77–94.

Kligler-Vilenchik, N. (2015). From wizards and house-elves to real-world issues: Political talk in fan spaces. *International Journal of Communication, 9,* 2027–4046.

Lapointe, C. (2020). Understanding the good and the evil: The influence of fandom and overcoming reductive racial representation. In R. Pande (Ed.), *Fandom, now in color* (pp. 179–192). University of Iowa Press.

Mangan, L. (2018, October 7). Doctor Who review: Great Jodie Whittaker debuts in new series with heart(s) and soul. *The Guardian.* Retrieved October 8, 2018, from https://www.theguardian.com/tv-and-radio/2018/oct/07/doctor-who-review-great-jodie-whittaker-debuts-in-new-series-with-hearts-and-soul

Martin, A. L., Jr. (2019). Fandom while black: Misty Copeland, Black panther, Tyler Perry and the contours of US black fandoms. *International Journal of Cultural Studies, 22*(6), 737–753.

Mulvey, L. (1975). Visual pleasure and narrative cinema. In M. Merck (Ed.), *The sexual subject: Screen reader in sexuality* (pp. 6–18). Taylor and Francis.

Nadkarni, S., & Sivarajan, D. (2020). Waiting in the wings: Inclusivity and the limits of racebanding. In R. Pande (Ed.), *Fandom, now in color* (pp. 159–176). University of Iowa Press.

Pande, R. (2018). *Squee from the margins: Fandom and race.* University of Iowa Press.

Pande, R., & Moitra, S. (2020). Whose representation is it anyway? Contemporary debates in femslash fandoms. In R. Pande (Ed.), *Fandom, now in color* (pp. 194–209). University of Iowa Press.

Phillips, A. (2018). Game studies for great justice. In J. Sayers (Ed.), *The Routledge companion to media studies and digital humanities* (pp. 117–127). Routledge.

Phillipson, D. (2020, August 29). Black Panther's 'Wakanda Forever' salute continues to inspire people across the world. *LAD Bible.* Retrieved May 6, 2021, from https://www.ladbible.com/entertainment/tv-and-film-black-panthers-wakanda-forever-salute-continues-to-inspire-worldwide-20200829

Powell, T., & Spencer, M. (2017, July 16). Doctor Who fanatics in meltdown after BBC reveals new female Time Lord. *Evening Standard.* Retrieved September 24, 2018, from https://www.standard.co.uk/showbiz/doctor-who-fanatics-in-meltdown-after-bbc-reveals-new-female-time-lord-a3589086.html

Reinhard, C. D. (2018). *Fractured fandoms: Contentious communication in fan communities.* Lexington Books.

Said-Moorhouse, L. (2015, December 30). Carrie Fisher shuts down body-shamers over "Star Wars: The Force Awakens" appearance. *CNN*. Retrieved July 10, 2019, from https://edition.cnn.com/2015/12/30/entertainment/carrie-fisher-star-wars-aging-response-twitter/index.html

Sandvoss, C. (2005). *Fans: The mirror of consumption*. Polity Press.

Shaw, A. (2015). *Gaming at the edge: Sexuality and gender at the margins of gamer culture*. University of Minnesota Press.

Sobande, F. (2020). *The digital lives of Black women in Britain*. Palgrave Macmillan.

Szalai, G. (2017, July 17). 'Doctor Who' fans divided over first female time lord. *The Hollywood Reporter*. Retrieved September 24, 2018, from https://www.hollywoodreporter.com/heat-vision/doctor-who-fans-divided-first-female-time-lord-1021648

Tagg, J. (1993). *The burden of representation: Essays on photographies and histories*. University of Minnesota Press.

Thomas, E. E. (2019). *The dark fantastic*. New York University Press.

Thomas, E. E., & Stornaiuolo, A. (2019). Race, storying, and restorying: What can we learn from Black fans? *Transformative Works and Cultures, 29*. https://doi.org/10.3983/twc.2019.1562

Toliver, S. R. (2018). Alterity and innocence: The hunger games, Rue, and Black girl adultification. *Journal of Children's Literature, 44*(2), 4–15.

Tonic, G. (2015, December 30). Why Carrie Fisher's stance against ageism is a body positive action we need more of. *Bustle*. Retrieved July 10, 2019, from https://www.bustle.com/articles/132695-why-carrie-fishers-stance-against-ageism-is-a-body-positive-action-we-need-more-of

Tyree, T. C. M. (2013). Contemporary representations of black females in newspaper comic strips. In S. C. Howard & R. K. Jackson II (Eds.), *Black comics: Politics of race and representation* (pp. 45–64). Bloomsbury Publishing.

Walter, S. (2017, December 4). Steven Moffat defends his casting of male Doctor Who as he says: 'This isn't a show exclusively for progressive liberals'. *The Telegraph*. Retrieved July 1, 2019, from https://www.telegraph.co.uk/news/2017/12/04/steven-moffat-defends-casting-male-doctor-says-isnt-show-exclusively

Wanzo, R. (2009). *The suffering will not be televised: African American women and sentimental political storytelling*. Suny Press.

Wanzo, R. (2015). African American acafandom and other strangers: New genealogies of fan studies. *Transformative Works and Cultures, 20*(1), n.p.

Wanzo, R. (2020). *The content of our caricature: African American comic art and political belonging*. New York University Press.

Wood, M. (2016). Feminist icon needed: Damsels in distress need not apply. In P. W. Lee (Ed.), *A galaxy here and now: Historical and cultural readings of Star Wars* (pp. 62–83). McFarland Publishing.

CHAPTER 6

Reconciling Feminism and Fandom

After the participants shared their frustration with fandom and the frictions between their fan and feminist identities, at the conclusion of each interview, we discussed how the two could be managed. One of the responses that encompassed the tensions, dilemmas, and efforts of reconcilement was that of Olivia (40, white, UK):

> We're full of contradictions. I can't watch James Bond with the way he treats women, but I love Flash Gordon, and it's exactly the same. I do the thing we're not supposed to do, "oh, it was done in the 80s, I'm allowed to enjoy problematic representations of women." There are moments where it feels very important to make those decisions and times when it's not. I think it's different when people need to make a stance in terms of not watching *House of Cards* on Netflix,[1] and I think it's important. There is something active in resisting, in such a pathetic little thing, whereas not turning the TV on Christmas day because *Flash Gordon* is on, I don't think it is political in the same way. I guess I want a "Get out of Jail" card to consume things that are problematic sometimes. I'm not sure it's about levels of passion, I think it's about levels of attachment, and those attachments are historical, stuff I had most of my life like *Flash Gordon*. I don't want to give them up because I

---

[1] The interview was conducted shortly after Kevin Spacey, the then star of *House of Cards*, was accused of numerous sexual assaults.

© The Author(s), under exclusive license to Springer Nature   141
Switzerland AG 2022
N. Yodovich, *Women Negotiating Feminism and Science Fiction Fandom*, Palgrave Fan Studies,
https://doi.org/10.1007/978-3-031-04079-5_6

have had them in my life for 30+ years, whereas resisting something I haven't seen is easier. I have less of an emotional attachment to it. Part of it is letting myself off. If it's pre my feminist timeline or political timeline, maybe I'm allowed to have it.

Olivia's decision-making process in determining which popular culture content to boycott or spare is complex and nuanced. Her contradictory and ambivalent relationship with popular culture, in which she rejects *James Bond* due to its misogynist depictions of women, but enjoys *Flash Gordon*, describes the intricate negotiation process between fandom and feminism, which will be unpacked throughout this chapter.

The interviewees acknowledged that identifying as feminists hinders their enjoyment of popular culture. For instance, Olivia's quote illustrates that feminist consumers feel obligated to either rebuff "problematic" content or provide rational justifications when supporting it. Ally (39, white, UK) also referred to this tension when she commented, "Being a feminist can't stop me from enjoying things; you have to live as well. If I decide to boycott everything that's problematic, there's nothing left at all." As I established in earlier chapters, the participants regarded their feminist identities as arduous and rarely satisfying. In the same manner, Phillips (2020) asserts that "one does not become woke; one must stay woke. It's a process without end [...] staying woke is particularly exhausting when you are also committed to pleasure" (p. 3). The accounts reviewed in this chapter align well with Phillips' sentiment. The findings reveal the difficulty of continuously fine-tuning one's feminist identity while simultaneously holding on to cultural content and fan communities that are exclusionary, unwelcoming, and toxic.

This chapter elaborates on the tactics that feminist women fans have developed to reconcile their identities and alleviate inner tensions. When using the term "tactic," I am drawing from de Certeau's (1984) notable works. De Certeau distinguished between strategies, which serve the strong, and tactics that are used by the disenfranchised. Due to their lack of means, the marginalized, or "others" as de Certeau (1984) dubs them, manipulate everyday "events in and turn them into 'opportunities'" (p. xix). Using tactics, they transform daily practices into fleeting moments of power and agency. De Certeau's conceptualization of tactics provides a suitable prism through which to observe how, despite their inferior position in the science fiction fandom community, feminist women fans find opportunities to exercise their agency and push for change in their object of fandom and fan communities.

Two clusters of tactics emerged from this research: "narrative" and "practice." When using "narrative tactics," the participants created justifications for and rationalizations of their fandoms, which allowed them to ignore or accept aspects of the fandom that clashed with their feminist perspectives. Through narrative tactics, feminist fans continued to enjoy their fandoms while preserving their feminist identities. "Practice tactics" reintroduce fannish practices, which were reviewed in Chap. 2. This time, these practices are redefined as channels through which women fans practice their feminist identity while pushing their fan community and its content toward a more equal, inclusive representation of women. The tactics discussed in this chapter do not stand alone. No tactic is efficient on its own. It joins with others in order to ensure that feminism and fandom are reconciled. As I will indicate, these tactics are not peripheral to feminist women fans' experiences. Indeed, they are crucial because without them, the interviewees would not be able to remain fans. I begin by reviewing feminist women fans' narrative tactics.

6.1 "NOTHING IS PERFECT": RECONCILING FANDOM AND FEMINISM THROUGH NARRATIVE TACTICS

The interviewees used three narrative tactics: "imperfect feminism," "compartmentalization," and "guilt-free feminism." I categorized these methods as narrative tactics because they all incorporate various rationalizations and justifications that the participants created to reconcile their fandom and feminism. In addition, they encompass the stories that feminist fans tell about their identities, in contrast to what they do, which will be developed in the discussion about "practice" tactics.

Tia (34, Black African American, USA) provided an example of the first tactic, "imperfect feminism." When asked how she deals with the faults she finds in *Doctor Who*, she responded:

I know that nothing is perfect. I'm not perfect. The shows I love are not going to be perfect. We are never going to be one hundred percent on point all the time. That is a completely unrealistic expectation to have. I think that by being a fan, I can see when things aren't... when they are missing the mark, and say something, and encourage them when they do hit it, so they keep working toward doing better. [...] That's kind of how I navigate it. I understand that none of us is perfect, no one in that writing room is perfect, but they're trying.

Fans like Tia who espoused "imperfect feminism" acknowledged the flaws in their beloved content but commended efforts to improve. Tia's appreciation of the attempt that *Doctor Who*'s team put into creating a more inclusive series helped her acknowledge her own attempts to improve and become a "better" feminist.

Olivia also used this tactic, as she explained in the quote that opened this chapter: "I do this thing we're not supposed to do 'oh, it was done in the 80s.' " As an older fan, Olivia accepted that popular culture texts are created in particular historical and social contexts and include representations and storylines that might have been acceptable at the time of their creation but are frowned upon today. She questioned if the content she grew up adoring is still appropriate to endorse as an adult feminist woman. Similarly, Justine (43, Lebanese-Maltese-English, Australia) also acknowledged that she tended to be less critical of fandoms she had been part of for a long time: "If I'm being honest, I am more forgiving of *Star Wars* because I am a fan, and I have been a fan for so many years." Thus, by using the "imperfect feminist" tactic, the fans were able to forgive older and dated material, especially ones with such longevity like *Star Wars* and *Doctor Who*, and justified their imperfections as a sign of the times.

Fans who adopted this approach not only were more tolerant but also generally described themselves as "easier to please." For example, Ramona (31, white, Ireland) stated:

> My bar is really low, as long as you have female characters that are well written, I'd be very happy as a feminist.

Another example was Jane (46, white, UK), who was pleased with *Doctor Who*'s traditional formula of a male Doctor and a female companion, asserting "the alternative of having a male Doctor and male companion could have been worse (laughs)."

Similar to "imperfect feminism," the respondents deliberately focused on positive aspects of their fandoms when using the second tactic, "compartmentalization." Stephanie (29, white, UK) adopted this tactic as well, explaining, "I think there are fans, like myself, who compartmentalize, 'I like X, Y, Z, but not A, B, C.'" Likewise, Anna (27, white, France) shared: "Even if there are little things that I don't like, I can put it aside and watch the show." Here, the participants did not praise efforts to improve, as they did in "imperfect feminism," but acknowledged their fandom's faults. Despite their awareness, the participants chose to put aside any annoyance they might experience to keep enjoying their favorite content without destabilizing their identities as feminists. As Cristina (34, Latina, USA) noted, "People can cherry-pick the Bible; we can cherry-pick *Star Wars.*" Compartmentalization "involves willful ignorance," reckoned Sharon (39, white, UK). It includes "ignoring the non-feminist elements [...] recognizing their part in a set of institutions that are deeply flawed, but still enjoying the story." Compartmentalization relates to the hierarchies of belonging discussed previously. Chapter 3 demonstrated that the participants were frequently required to prioritize their identities and choose which community and cause was their primary preference. In a similar manner, some interviewees decided to focus on particular aspects of the franchise and intentionally downplay the gravity of others. Such a tactic allowed them to keep from jeopardizing their feminist identity and continue to enjoy their fandom.

The last tactic, "guilt-free feminism," contrasts with the previous ones in this cluster. In the first two approaches, the interviewees created narratives that justified and rationalized the tensions they experienced between fandom and feminism. With the third tactic, "guilt-free feminism," the participants did not try to produce a cohesive narrative about their identities:

> I feel like I'm at this point in my life where I don't want to have internal conflicts anymore, I'm just going to say who I am, and like what I like, and if they don't fit together—too bad, they're both there (laughs). I'm not going to have this internal struggle about "can I still like whatever and call myself that." (Eve, white, 30, UK)

The interviewees who utilized this method stressed that human beings are meant to be complicated and contradictory. Therefore, they did not express guilt for enjoying popular culture texts they were "supposed" to rebuff. Olivia's rationale also contained elements of this rationale. Like Eve, when justifying rejecting *James Bond* while enjoying *Flash Gordon*, Olivia noted that human beings are "full of contradictions."

Feminist fans also used this tactic when retaliating against what I call "guilt culture." Guilt culture permeates the social and cultural worlds of feminists who are constantly faced with questioning if "they can be a feminist and still do X" (Favaro & Gill, 2018, p. 61). In fandom, "guilt culture" was evident in cases where fans, especially feminist female fans, were exhorted to feel guilty for enjoying content that did not align with their social values. For example, Jamie (39, white, UK) stated:

There are conferences that have seminars about 'why women should hate Joss Whedon', or 'what to do if your fave [short for favorite] is problematic' and things like that.[2]

Favaro and Gill assert (2018) that debates about feminist guilt do not target patriarchy as women's greatest enemy but instead blame feminism itself for "trying to ruin your fun!" (p. 61). In Chap. 4, I related their argument to the generalized other. Feminist women in general and feminist fans specifically internalize the normative understanding that a "good" feminist should not consume or take pleasure in certain content. Feminism itself becomes an enemy they need to appease. Even if feminist fans have never faced actual scrutiny and criticism of the franchises they enjoy, they still feel policed and monitored by other, "imagined" feminists. They feel the need to justify themselves in order to avoid feeling guilty or ashamed of their feminist generalized other. However, the participants who endorse "guilt-free feminism" reject this burden, dismiss these debates, and push for more pluralism and less puritanism in fandom.

The "guilt-free feminism" narrative tactic is consistent with postfeminist values and current trends (Budgeon, 2011; Genz, 2009; McRobbie, 2004; Walker, 1995). Postfeminism encourages women to exercise their agency and individualism through freedom of choice. The mere act of choosing for oneself is empowering and liberating, regardless of what one chooses to do. The postfeminist woman, therefore, celebrates her freedom while shaking off feelings of guilt and shame that might accompany her actions (ibid.). As McRobbie describes (2020), after having to succumb to pressures of perfectionism, women in the new millennium are resisting stringent demands by accepting imperfections. Embracing imperfection is considered a new form of self-care and an accepted form of ameliorating tension.

To further define and conceptualize "guilt-free feminism," it is important to differentiate it from the "imperfect feminism" tactic, which might appear equivalent. Both tactics echo Roxane Gay's work, *Bad Feminist* (2014), which depicted Gay's acknowledgment of her "flawed" feminist identity. In accordance with Gay's depiction of the "bad" feminist, the participants who espoused these tactics reckoned that enjoying certain

---

[2] This quote is taken from an interview that was conducted several years before stars from *Buffy the Vampire Slayer* and *Angel* openly came out and discussed the abuse and toxicity they endured on set because of Joss Whedon.

popular culture content harmed their feminist identities. The difference between "imperfect feminism" and "guilt-free feminism" is that the first has in it the implied aspiration to improve and become a "better" feminist. The interviewees who espoused "guilt-free feminism," however, were uninterested in reconciling fandom and feminism. They were indifferent about being regarded as "bad" feminists.

The three narrative tactics seemingly correspond with the notion of the "problematic fave" (Knox & Schwind, 2019; Salter, 2020; Schwartz, 2019; Stitch, 2015). In general terms, a "problematic fave" is a character or celebrity who has controversial attitudes or partakes in behaviors that inflict pain on others (verbally, physically, or sexually). Nevertheless, fans are unable to "let them go" or defend their behaviors. In such cases, fans settle for a "happy medium" by openly acknowledging that an artist or a fictional character is problematic, but still regard them as their favorites. Warner (2018) explains that when fans acknowledge their inability to reject a character or celebrity despite their inappropriate behaviors, they openly abdicate their agency. While this could be true to an extent, the interviewees demonstrated a more complex form of negotiating with their problematic faves. Being conscious of their fandom's flaws led them to actively tailor narratives that allowed them to reconcile conflicts and fractures. Such narratives sustained their love of their fandom and kept their sense of agency.

The narrative tactics described here indicate how the interviewees perceived their identities. These tactics, especially "imperfect feminism," connote the impression of identity as an ongoing project (Bauman, 2004; Beck & Beck-Gernsheim, 2001; Lawler, 2014). For instance, using the tactic of "imperfect feminism" led feminist fans to accept that they had yet to become the "perfect" or "good" feminists they wish to be; they were as imperfect as their fandoms. Their comments are, nevertheless, evidence of their belief that they can keep improving their feminist identity and perfect it.

"Imperfect feminism," as well as "compartmentalization," attempts to construct a cohesive, tensionless identity. Traditional approaches assess authentic identity through the correlation between one's set of values and beliefs and their expression and performance in one's daily life (Erickson, 1995; Kernis & Goldman, 2006). Observing the interviewees' tactics using this definition crystalizes their attempts to create a coherent narrative about their feminist and fan identities that reconciles the tensions between them. Comparing "imperfect feminism" and "compartmentalization" with "guilt-free feminism" reveals the difference in the latter's attitude toward identity. While the first two tactics push for a coherent identity, "guilt-free feminism" sees identity as a messy, complex, dialectic construct (Bauman, 2004; DeNora, 1999; Giddens, 1991). The participants who employed this tactic were not concerned with reconciling feminism and fandom because they accepted that their identities did not have to coexist or be justified.

Another insight gleaned from narrative tactics deals with the interviewees' normative approach to feminist identity. Each narrative tactic incorporated the understanding that feminist identity could be evaluated on a scale ranging from "bad" feminism to "good" feminism. Even "guilt-free" feminists acknowledged the existence of such a scale but rejected taking part in this evaluation system. Returning to my earlier claim about the feminist generalized other, it appears that the interviewees internalized the standards according to which one's feminist identity is assessed and evaluated their own feminist identities even without being scrutinized by others. This phenomenon was evident, for instance, when Olivia (40, UK) used an apologetic tone when trying to defend why she still enjoys *Flash Gordon*, saying, "I do this thing we're not supposed to do."

6.2   "Bloody patriarchy, let's write some fanfic to correct it": Reconciling Feminism and Fandom Through Practice Tactics

While the participants used the first cluster of tactics to navigate between feminism and fandom through what they *said*, practice tactics incorporated feminism and fandom through what they *did*. More so than narrative tactics, practice tactics not only reconcile feminism and fandom but also are used to demonstrate that these identities can flourish alongside each other. For example, Zoe (34, white, UK) claimed: "Being part of fandom has made me a better feminist […] it's always part of how I see culture but made it something I express more explicitly than I did before." Driven by the understanding that fandom and feminism can complement each other, this section explores the practice tactics with which the interviewees reinforced their feminist perspectives and values. They used these tactics to tackle discrimination in the fandom and the object of the fandom by lobbying actively for change and recognition.

Jenkins (2012) defines fan activism as "forms of civic engagement and political participation" (n.p.), where fans unite in order to influence the fandom community and beyond. Practices of intra-fandom activism include, among others, pushing for diversity and representation and preventing cancellations of series (or bringing them back on air). In contrast, inter-fandom activism involves fundraising for "real-world" causes. An example is the fundraiser for women's rights that fans of *Firefly* (cult science fiction series, 2002–2003) launched (Bourdaa, 2018; Brough & Shresthova, 2012; Jenkins, 2012; Lopez, 2011). Through practice tactics, the interviewees took part in various forms of fan activism, which enabled them to articulate and execute their feminist identities. In this section, I revisit the fannish practices developed in Chap. 2. While these practices were initially introduced as a labor of love and source of frustration, they are reframed here as a form of activism through which the respondents practice feminism within their fandom. These practice tactics include (1) community-focused practices, (2) content producing, (3) consumption, and (4) intellectual engagement.

The first cluster of practice tactics, community-focused practices, includes two main spaces: conventions and online communities. Some participants shared that they merge feminist activism and fandom by organizing panels at conventions to promote values that are dear to them. One interviewee took part in a panel on sexual harassment in fannish spaces. Another participant gave talks on mental health and bullying in fandom:[3]

> We do panels that are specifically about mental health and being well aware of the other people around you and how you can not only respond to your own needs but also respond to other people's needs. Anti-bullying, which definitely leads to a lot of what I feel feminism is about [...] just talking about different things you can do, how you can help other people, how you can advocate for other people.

Such self-organized colloquia provided the participants with the opportunity to promote equality, kindness, and ethics of care in fandom while staying true to their feminist standpoint.

Fan communities, especially online ones, were another venue in which the interviewees combined their fandom and feminism. Scholars such as

---

[3] This chapter includes several occasions in which details about the participants, their activities, and their fandoms are intentionally vaguely written or left out in order to ensure their anonymity.

Bury (2005) and Larsen and Zubernis (2011) argue that fan communities could provide women with solace, a space to discuss gender, sexuality, and intimacy, issues they might not be able to develop or express outside the fan community. Yet, as Chap. 4 revealed, feminist women fans are frequently policed in fan spaces and are subject to implicit or explicit pressures to adjust themselves to rigid rules of conduct. To avoid such frictions and surround themselves with like-minded people, the participants turned to alternative communities.

The communities that accommodated the interviewees' needs and values were those that were established for women, people of marginalized ethnicities, and feminists. For instance, while studying for her BA, Ally (39, white, UK) joined a university society dedicated to women fans of *Star Wars*, where they could discuss women characters in *Star Wars*, a negligible and contested topic among some men fans. In another example, Tia (34, Black African American, USA) was part of several Facebook groups that were more compatible with her identity:

> One is just for Black nerds. I'm also part of a book group that a friend of mine started, and it's predominately female. There are a few men. It's very well-run. I can't stand the ones that are toxic. I don't need that in my feed.

Due to their experiences of conditional belonging in traditional science fiction communities, the participants also reported on their efforts to create inclusive fandom environments:

> When you start saying, "you're a fan, you're not a good fan," it starts becoming elited and snobbish. I don't like that idea of kind of disregarding people's opinions, disregarding them as people, just because they don't have the same knowledge. I mean, I love Doctor Who, I really do, but if someone says they have no idea who Jon Pertwee[4] was, I'll just say, "ok, they're that type of fan, more new Who than classic Who." There's enough room for any kind of fan. (Stephanie, 29, white, UK)

Participants reported that they opposed interrogation and discrimination. Instead, they encouraged newcomers to engage with their fandom. For example, Samantha (46, white, UK) maintained: "You should be welcoming to fans; if they don't know the details, teach them the details." The interviewees also declared that they were aware of discrimination against other sectors in the fandom, based on their own experiences. When Anita

[4] The 3rd Doctor, 1970–1974.

(35, white, Italy), for instance, encountered a gay player in a role-playing event, she encouraged him to join her:

> He never felt like he could come out as gay in the community. When he saw me, we clicked: 'You're a woman, I'm a gay man, we're both minorities in this situation.'

She carried on describing her eagerness to interact with women at such events, sharing: "Every time in a convention here, I see women, girls, coming up, wanting to play a game […] I jump up, 'Here! Come here.'"

At the same time, as previous chapters demonstrated, some women fans had to look further and deeper to find a community that embraced them. For example, Lily (31, white, UK), who has a physical disability, is frequently marginalized and overlooked. Lily often finds herself unable to participate in inaccessible science fiction conventions, events, and meetups. According to Lily, even though awareness of intersectionality and inclusion has increased in recent years, not much has changed in practice. Of course, we cannot generalize based on only one participant with a physical disability. Nevertheless, Lily provided an important insight into her experiences in the fandom as a person living with a physical disability. Similarly, the interviewees from marginalized ethnicities did not automatically search for an all-women's fan group because they were not necessarily inclusive either. Tia's quote above shows that some women fans from marginalized ethnicities chose communities similar to them based on their ethnicity rather than their gender.

I frame the participants' turn to alternative, more niche fan communities in the broader debate on assimilation versus multiculturalism (Ashcroft & Bevir, 2018; Greenman & Xie, 2008; Mansouri & Modood, 2021; Parekh, 2001; Ponzanesi, 2007; Wildsmith, 2004). In light of growing immigration in many Western countries since the twentieth century, scholars and policymakers alike have reflected on the methods of integrating newcomers into their new country. In general, the concept of assimilation envisions immigrants gaining access to a new community by becoming similar to its veteran members (Greenman & Xie, 2008; Wildsmith, 2004). Those who oppose such a notion argue that assimilation forces marginalized individuals to shed their own culture, forgo the habits and rituals that are essential to them, and adopt the norms and lifestyles of the dominant group (Parekh, 2001; Wildsmith, 2004). Seeking an alternative gateway for immigrants without erasing their identity led to the development of multiculturalism. Theoretically, multiculturalism provides more diversity and inclusion in society as it allows all cultures to exist simultaneously (Mansouri & Modood, 2021; Parekh, 2001). However, critics of multiculturalism assert that there is a limit to a society's capacity for pluralism without fractures and tensions between cultures developing. Thus, multiculturalism is perhaps good in theory, but it does not necessarily exist in reality (Ashcroft & Bevir, 2018; Okin, 1999; Ponzanesi, 2007).

The debate on assimilation and multiculturalism is helpful in the analysis of feminist women fans' community of choice. Such concepts indicate the difficulty in achieving visibility and a sense of belonging while staying faithful to one's marginalized culture and values. Feminist women fans prefer to turn to smaller communities that do not require them to surrender their agency at their gates. Daniela (23, Latina, USA) explained why she favored niche fan communities and referred to the complexity of such a decision:

> Truly, marginalized people creating their own spaces is a reaction, not a solution. It's a coping mechanism. If that is forced to be a solution, then it is what it is. A lot of times, the way things start is, a lot of us try to do option A, right? We try, while we're in these toxic spaces, to undergo that wave and educate and broaden all these spaces. Almost without fail, it just doesn't work. And so, I think, from what I have seen, fan spaces and even on social justice spaces [...], the responsibility falls on the disprivileged. It cannot be up to the marginalized to defend their right to exist in these spaces [...] The solution is for the privileged to do work with their peers. Until then, fandom spaces at large will continue to be profoundly unsafe to the underprivileged.

Daniela's argument in favor of moving to smaller spaces echoes Lorde's opposition (2003) to the contention that women of marginalized ethnicities must educate white women regarding their particular struggles and challenges. According to Lorde, "This is a diversion of energies and tragic repetition of racist patriarchal thought" (p. 27).

Assimilating into large communities that reject diversity and feminism and trying to change them from within is an excessive, even damaging demand made of feminist women and women of marginalized ethnicities (Stitch, 2021a, 2021b). Cristina (34, Latina, USA) articulated this perpetual sense of threat and unease in large, mainstream fan spaces when she shared:

I think there's this sort of myth that there aren't Black cosplayers, and there are tons of Black cosplayers. They have a whole convention in Atlanta, they had Wakanda Con. It was incredible. It was packed. It's not that POC and Black cosplayers and queer cosplayers, that we're not out there, it's just that because nobody really caters to us, we seem so invisible [...] it's not only that we feel excluded; we feel like if we go, it's going to be an unsafe experience for us. It doesn't just mean physical threat. It can be people coming up to you and saying racist things to you. That's compromising my safety.

Finding their own communities within the fandom provided the interviewees with solace from the toxicity in other fan spaces.

As the last quote by Cristina indicates, community-focused experiences are frequently intertwined with content producing. Several interviewees are members of fan fiction communities that promote their feminist identities. For instance, Zoe (34, white, UK) is a member of a fan fiction community inspired by a television series with a woman protagonist. Feeling unsettled by *Doctor Who*'s gender politics in recent years with the love-struck companions and blasé Doctors made Zoe turn to fan fiction in order to "fix" *Doctor Who*. When the first woman Doctor was announced, Zoe decided to write a cross-over fan story between *Doctor Who* and her other fandom, a more feminist series (according to Zoe):

I wanted to set it up as a slightly antagonistic, sisterly relationship between them, where the Doctor has all the knowledge of time and space but has never experienced things like gender oppression before [...] X's entire shtick is that she uses her femininity and her sexuality to be able to do what she damn well pleases, which is to fight crime [...] I thought it would be a nice thing to have that kind of setup where she has that kind of aspect of knowledge about what it's like to be female, the positive section of it, and the Doctor has knowledge about everything else. And they have a male companion that they rarely ever listen to.

In another example, an interviewee published two novels based on a famous men-led franchise. Her books, however, focus on woman characters who played minor roles in the original franchise:

To me, personally, what I like to do is tell stories about women, people of color that are oppressed, being pushed down. History has been told by white straight men [...], so I tell stories about people who are not white straight men [...] that's my own personal feminist interest, stories about women that need to be told and not ignored anymore, need to be brought forward so that people know them.

The notion of "improving" the object of fandom through fan fiction is a common practice among women fans, queer fans, and fans of marginalized ethnicities who attempt to imbue the object of their fandom with more social, emotional, and sexual depth (Busse & Hellekson, 2006; de Kosnik, 2013; Jung, 2002; Larsen & Zubernis, 2011; Pande, 2018; Salter & Blodgett, 2017). The participants who took part in fan fiction writing infused their content with feminist perspectives and values. As feminists, the interviewees found their fan fiction work an important contribution to the franchise by "fixing" badly written characters, storylines, and relationships: "If *Doctor Who* does something problematic, I know I can go to them [her fan fiction community] [...] 'yes, bloody patriarchy, let's write some fanfic to correct it'" (Zoe, 34, white, UK).

Fan fiction is not the only content-producing practice through which the participants expressed their feminist values. Lucia (39, white, Spain) used her YouTube channel, which analyzed various popular culture content, to present a feminist critique. Given the policing and silencing that feminist fans experience in men-dominated fandoms (Chap. 4), Lucia was conscious of the need to soften her feminist arguments for some of her viewers:

I had to find a way to avoid a feminist explanation, not because I was afraid of the hate, but because I was afraid that if I use this terminology, men won't listen to that. So, if I didn't make it easy for them, they wouldn't want to watch it [...] I try to avoid feminist vocabulary, I try to think of other ways to say the same, in a different way.

Lucia's quote exemplifies the subtle negotiations in which feminist women fans must engage when operating within a monolithic, men-dominated community. Moreover, Lucia's experience provides an insight into gendered fannish practices and their relationship with feminism. Given that fan fiction is accepted as a feminine fannish practice (Bacon-Smith, 1992; Larsen & Zubernis, 2011; Scott, 2017a), the interviewees expressed their feminist identities openly through it. Thus, when Lucia takes part in forensic fandom through her YouTube channel, a traditionally masculine practice, she feels pressured to soften her feminist critique.

The last content-producing practice in which the interviewees merged their identities instead of experiencing tension between them was cosplaying. The interviewees who participated in cosplaying could be grouped into those whose cosplay corresponded with their identities and those who took part in race-bending and gender-bending (Gackstetter Nichols, 2019; Gn, 2011; Kirkpatrick, 2019). In accordance with their views on their representation in mainstream media (Chap. 5), the participants felt empowered when cosplaying a character who looked like them:

> One of the greatest feelings I have ever got to experience, being in one of those costumes. I was Storm[5] at the time, and I was just walking through the hall, this group of young kids, they had to be junior high, maybe high school, younger than I was, they freaked out. They hadn't seen a Storm the entire time. Everybody is everyone else. They were all like, most of them were Black, some other races, I wasn't sure exactly. Most of them were obviously not white. They had this moment of being able to see, like, their hero, that looks like them, in real life [...] I do like to go with the character I enjoy, but there is a moment where sometimes you gotta do what you kinda look like because you may be inspiring other people who don't think they have the option. I feel like that that right there is a huge reason why I cosplay. (Jessica, 32, biracial white-Jamaican, USA)

Warner (2015) maintains, "Producing content is a necessary act of agency for women of color who strive for visibility" (p. 34). Unpacking Jessica's remark illustrates how her embodiment of Storm provided the opportunity to extend her feelings of empowerment and inspiration to others who also experienced marginalization. In a sea of white cosplayers, Jessica, dressed as Storm, was a testament to the existence of marginalized ethnicities in fandom.

The interviewees also perceived cosplay as an experience that allowed them to experiment with identities that were typically more foreign to them. As an example, Angela (55, white, UK) cosplayed for the first time as the 10th Doctor (played by David Tenant, 2005–2010) for the show's 50th anniversary event. Anaya (19, Indian, UK), a more frequent cosplayer, cosplayed as different *Doctor Who* characters over the years, such as the 11th Doctor's companion, Amy Pond (played by Karen Gillan, 2010–2013). Angela's and Anaya's choices provide compelling examples of race and gender-bending through cosplaying. Angela dressed as a male Doctor, while Anaya, originally from India, cosplayed as a white companion. Lamerichs (2011) argues that cosplaying is a performance of one's

---

[5] Woman character of African descent, X-Men franchise

identity: "On the one hand, players actualize a narrative and its meaning; on the other hand, they actualize their own identities" (n.p.). Through cosplaying, fans not only embody a beloved character but also represent themselves. However, as Gn (2011) demonstrates, cosplaying does not have to align with one's gender or any other social category. It can allow the fan to add additional layers of meaning to his/her interpretation of the character.

Cosplaying provided participants such as Angela and Anaya with opportunities to express their perspectives and values. In their interviews, Angela stressed the importance of leading a gender-neutral lifestyle, while Anaya explained that she attaches little significance to ethnicity. Through cosplaying, Anaya and Angela were able to appropriate their favorite characters and provide different interpretations of them by conveying their own social perspectives. Nevertheless, it is also possible that due to the scarcity of Indian or older women characters in *Doctor Who* specifically and popular media in general, Anaya and Angela had no choice but to cosplay as characters who had a different social background than their own.

Moving to the third tactic, consumption, I review the participants' push for recognition in the fan community and expression of their agency through their consumption of merchandise and content. To start, many interviewees described having a complicated relationship with fannish merchandise since their childhoods. For example, Samantha (46, white, UK) stated:

> I got Barbies, my brother got the sci-fi toys [...] It was me who loved it, I was the actual fan [...] I understood that it was boys who get these toys, and the girls steal the toys.

Indeed, the manufacturers of *Star Wars* paraphernalia traditionally ignore women consumers (Brown, 2018; Jowett, 2019; Scott, 2017b). The reluctance to acknowledge women fans through merchandising has two crucial meanings. First, women are assumed to be uninterested in science fiction and are therefore not recognized as potential consumers. Second, operating under the premise that only men engage with science fiction, women characters are underrepresented in merchandise because, as one Disney executive was rumored to suggest, "no boy wants to be given a product with a female character on it" (as cited in Boehm in Salter & Blodgett, 2017, p. 198). Samantha and other participants realized that the production and consumption of merchandise are gendered and are just one more area in which they are overlooked. With this in mind, the interviewees reported practicing their feminist identities through consumption.

The case of the #WheresRey (where's Rey) controversy is a fitting example of women fans' exclusion when it comes to the production of merchandise and the feminist backlash against it (Brown, 2018; Jowett, 2019; Scott, 2017b). After the release of the new *Star Wars* trilogy, featuring a female protagonist for the first time (Rey), fans were flabbergasted and enraged over her absence from most promotional marketing, such as toys and clothing. The lack of Rey merchandise was followed by a massive Twitter campaign (#Wheresrey) in which fans demanded Rey-centered merchandise. In the wake of this campaign, many interviewees reported intentionally seeking out merchandise with women characters from *Star Wars*. For example, Donna (46, white, UK) stated that:

> We bought as many female characters merchandise we could get our hands on. It is obviously frustrating and infuriating that there is so little. We only have a small Lego set with Jyn.[6]

Donna also expressed frustration over gendered marketing. Not only was most merchandise targeted at men fans, but also the products that were made for women were stereotypically "girly":

> It's frustrating that everything has to be so genderized [...] if you find a t-shirt with Rey on it, it's for girls and usually pink. I can wear a shirt with Harrison Ford because masculinity is something to aspire to.

Donna's example illustrates that even once manufacturers acquiesce to demands for merchandise with female characters, they keep a traditionally gendered approach to the products: "girly" for women, "cool" for men (de Bruin-Molé, 2018). This type of segregation also discourages men fans from engaging with women characters due to their "feminine" branding.

The interviewees were motivated to purchase merchandise featuring women characters in order to gain visibility in what appeared to be men-dominated fandoms and prove that women characters are marketable. While Linden and Linden (2016) argue that fans use their power as consumers to increase their share of the bounty, this study demonstrates that

---

[6] Jyn Erso is another woman protagonist in the *Star Wars* franchise.

this contention is only partly true. The participants sincerely wanted to own merchandise featuring women characters, but this was not just a personal whim; to them, it was activism. As Brown argues (2018), "*Star Wars* merchandising is not a mere fannish obsession [...] it is a recognition that political elements worth fighting over permeate every facet of our modern culture" (p. 338). For feminist fans interviewed in this study, fannish consumption has a political meaning that goes beyond fandom. Women are tired of being ignored and demand to be acknowledged and included in the public sphere.

In a different example, the interviewees actively searched for and wanted to support creators and content that were sincerely committed to promoting diversity and inclusion. Camila (33, Latina, Australia), for instance, shared, "I only try to buy books by female authors. Some authors don't know how to write female characters, so what's the point?" As an avid comic-books consumer, Camila decided to purchase only the ones that write women characters as multifaceted individuals:

> I discovered Greg Rucka; he writes very good female characters. He wrote *The Old Guard*. He has a whole series of *Wonder Woman* books and *Catwoman books*. I would try to focus on those authors that give the characters justice [...] I really didn't care if he wrote for DC or Marvel, I just looked for his books.

As feminists, the participants acknowledged their power as consumers. They framed their engagement with popular culture as an arena in which they can hone their sense of agency and take a moral stand. In parallel, scholars such as Wanzo (2009, 2015), Sobande (2020), and Martin (2019) commented on the ways in which consumerism in general, and fandom specifically, could be considered acts of activism and resistance. Especially among marginalized communities, purchasing tickets for a movie that tells their story or features them in leading roles is almost a moral obligation. By doing so, they can ensure the success of the film, which might lead to the production of similar content. Martin (2019) calls this commitment the "politics of responsibility," wherein people's consumerism patterns contribute to help ameliorate social inequalities. Nevertheless, such a responsibility might then become a burden when enjoying "flawed texts that allow for attachment to quality despite the text's problematic content" (Wanzo, 2015, n.p.).

The interviewees expressed their feminist identity not only through the products they chose to consume but also through the products and content they chose *not* to consume. They commented on rejecting popular culture texts that do not align with their values. Returning to the excerpt from the beginning of the chapter, Olivia (40, white, UK) was interviewed shortly after the news broke regarding Kevin Spacey's sexual misconduct. In the wake of the announcement, Olivia asserted: "I think it's different when people need to make a stance in terms of not watching *House of Cards* on Netflix, and I think it's important." In a more recent example, Daniela (23, Latina, USA) talked about having to stop consuming new *Harry Potter* content after its creator, J.K. Rowling, openly expressed transphobic attitudes (Ennis, 2019; Gardner, 2021; Kirkpatrick, 2020):

> *Harry Potter* was the most near and dear to me. It had a formative impact. Thus, the fall of its creator was the most heart-breaking. As J.K. Rowling has got more violent with her bigotry, I've had to sort of let go. I keep the books that I loved. I keep the stories that I loved. But I can no longer engage in further content that comes from her pen at this time.

For instance, Daniela referred to the upcoming release of a new *Harry Potter* video game, *Hogwarts Legacy*. Despite its appeal, Daniela had no intention of purchasing the game in order to ensure that Rowling would not profit from it.

A recent prominent phenomenon associated with the morality of consumption and the importance of boycott and resistance is "cancel culture." Cancel culture originated in Black communities, especially among Black women who chose to "withdraw one's attention from someone or something whose values, (in)action, or speech are so offensive, one no longer wishes to grace them with their presence, time, and money" (Clark, 2020, p. 88). Consumers recognize their integral role in "making or breaking" an artist or franchise. Thus, once a celebrity expresses controversial ideas, antagonizes a marginalized community, or physically and sexually abuses them, audiences have the power to end their engagement with such figures and damage their ability to profit from their craft. Cancel culture has become even more widespread after the MeToo movement erupted online (Berg, 2017; Boyle, 2019; Hagi, 2019). Since then, viral campaigns have been launched against artists who express or act in an abusive, misogynist, homophobic, transphobic, or racist manner (Bishop,

2018; Clark, 2020; Pereira de Sa & Pereira Alberto, 2021; Romano, 2020, 2021).

Daniela's tactic is, related to cancel culture. As Daniela explains, she is keeping the books she had already purchased in her childhood, from which Rowling has already profited. From now on, however, she will no longer consume new content and will not make Rowling any richer. Thus, feminist fans saw boycotting popular culture content, similar to consuming merchandise, as an activist, political act with the power to influence the fandom community and beyond.

While cancel culture is helpful in framing feminist women's interaction with their fandom, such a phenomenon is not always compatible with their experiences because the interviewees did not want to turn their backs on any beloved content. One might ask why the interviewees chose to boycott certain content, but not *Star Wars* or *Doctor Who*, despite their discontent with them. During the interviews, some respondents shared they indeed no longer follow new episodes of *Doctor Who*: "I stopped watching *Doctor Who* when I was more angry than happy. I am happy with things not being perfect, but I have limits" (Ruby, 38, white, UK). As Jenkins explains (1992), fandom relies on a mixture of fascination and frustration. Fans need to be simultaneously enamored and angry with the object of fandom in order to feel motivated to engage with it. The participants remained fans of *Doctor Who* and *Star Wars* as long as their enjoyment surpassed their frustration. While every fan's threshold is different, once the balance between fascination and frustration tilted, fans like Ruby could no longer follow their fandoms.

Like Olivia's quote from earlier, Daniela (23, Latina, USA) asked for leniency when consuming popular culture texts:

> We are small facets of a very structurally oppressive world, hyper capitalistic one, violently capitalistic one. Truly, there is no ethical consumption under capitalism. Capitalism is intersectional as well, it perpetuates misogyny, it profits out of it. So, I think that as feminists we should extend grace to ourselves because if we chose not to consume content that is not feminist, we would be left with nothing (laughing).

Understanding the small role she plays as a consumer in a capitalist system, Daniela sought comfort and escapism without feeling a constant moral obligation to exercise her feminist identity. Thus, Daniela, as well as other participants, maneuvered between rejecting and embracing content based on the level of its toxicity and the potential destructive outcome of consuming it.

The participants also transformed the last fannish practice, intellectual engagement, which includes curating trivia and theoretical analysis of the text, into a feminist tactic to develop and refine feminist critical thinking. Contrary to stigma-driven assumptions regarding women fans' lack of critical thinking (Ali, 2002; Fan, 2012), the interviewees proved that they were not only critically engaged with their fandoms but could also incorporate feminist thought into their critique and apply it to broader issues beyond their fandom. Providing critical feminist theory of their beloved content played a significant role in reinforcing the interviewees' identities. The respondents found fandom a platform that enabled them to polish their feminist perspectives of the world and develop their identities. As Zoe (34, white, UK) stated:

> Being part of a fandom has made me a better feminist [...] it's always been part of how I view culture but made it something I express more explicitly than I did before.

In another example, Lucy (41, white, UK) shared a similar sentiment:

> That's where all the fun is, in those tensions, hacking those tensions [...] I feel that thinking about these conflicts makes me a better person.

I assert that practicing feminist intellectual engagement resembles consciousness-raising (Chesebro et al., 1973; Green, 1979; Sowards & Renegar, 2004). Sowards and Renegar (2004) argued that popular culture and feminist content, in particular, can inspire viewers to develop feminist thinking. While Sowards and Renegar focused on explicitly feminist content, it appears that polysemic texts, even those that are not considered feminist, can also promote feminist thinking. For instance, Pough (2002) acknowledged that her engagement with hip-hop music, which is sometimes regarded as sexist and misogynist, enhanced her feminist identity by her engagement in critical thinking about her fandom. Likewise, even though the interviewees did not see *Doctor Who* and *Star Wars* as feminist franchises, they established their feminist identities by engaging in feminist critiques of their fandoms.

Parallel to the practices of consumption, the interviewees maintained that feminist intellectual engagement has implications that go beyond the fandom realm:

It's the classical argument about "you shouldn't complain about this thing happening when there are girls in Africa who are experiencing the most intense, horrible things because they're female." But I can be pissed off about how Padmé[7] is used very poorly in the films. I'm not going to say it's as important as other things in the world, but it's also a way of practicing your arguments… basically Padmé was in an abusive relationship that was romanticized. They [young feminist fans] can then take it to their lives and articulate it when they see it applied to real people when the newspaper is making up that some guy killed his girlfriend as a twisted romantic thing. I get uncomfortable when people try to minimize that kind of thing. You know it's not that important in the great scheme of things, it's just something you do for fun, but it's the same argument, really. (Ally, 39, white, UK)

The crux of Ally's claim is that fandom specifically and popular culture in general serve as fertile ground for social and political discussions that could later be reproduced in other, broader contexts (Kligler-Vilenchik, 2015; McManus, 2020; Petersen, 2011; Wood, 2016).

Another example of fandom as a platform to ponder "real-life" political issues was also evident in Ramona's (31, white, Ireland) critique of one of *Doctor Who*'s companions' departure. Donna, a fans' favorite, had a poignant ending to her run on the show. After absorbing the Doctor's DNA to save him, Donna's brain had to be wiped to prevent it from bursting. Despite her pleas not to erase the special memories she shared with him, the Doctor made it so that Donna completely forgot him and their adventures together. Irish Ramona criticized the Doctor's decision, explaining she felt strongly against it, "especially with being Irish, the March of Choice, and everything." From Ramona's perspective, Donna's right to her own body and mind was taken away, parallel to the pro-choice movement in Ireland. Although other fans complained about Donna's fate, none linked it to abortions but to the general patronizing, patriarchal superiority over women in Western society. Ramona's remark demonstrates that fans' critiques are situational and context-based. As Morimoto and Chin (2017) argue, "Fandom is always performed against a backdrop of real-world events" (p. 181).

---

[7] The main woman character in the second *Star Wars* trilogy.

To conclude, the interviewees who utilized intellectual engagement in order to develop their feminist identities were not burdened by guilt for enjoying non-feminist content. On the contrary, the participants could detect misogynist, sexist undertones in the diegesis and critique it. Doing so reinforced their sense of being "good" feminists. As Zoe (34, white, UK) expressed: "I don't see a contradiction [between fandom and feminism]. The feminist aspect is expressed through critique."

6.3   CONCLUSIONS: LIVING A FANNISH, FEMINIST LIFE

This chapter unpacks the tactics that feminist women fans developed and employed in order to reconcile and marry feminism and fandom. Seven tactics emerged from the interviews: three "narrative tactics," which included what women *say* in order to reconcile their fandom and feminism, and four "practice tactics," which encompassed what women *do* to navigate feminism and fandom. The four primary purposes for feminist women fans' tactics were as follows: (1) reconciling tensions between fandom and feminism, (2) protecting their identities from being threatened, (3) enjoying fandoms even while criticizing them, and (4) incorporating feminism and fandom in order to promote equality in the beloved content and fandom community.

Through the examples I provided in this chapter, I demonstrated how feminist fans oscillate between the different tactics, providing alternative rationales and justifications to support or boycott content. The participants expressed feeling guilty, unapologetic, powerful, powerless, fascinated, and frustrated, sometimes all at the same time. Such expressions ultimately illustrate that the feminist existence in fandom is an ambivalent one.

Even though the interviewees adopted feminism as part of their identity, it often disturbed their enjoyment of their fandoms. In the prioritization of their identities, fandom ultimately took precedence over feminism. Despite their struggles with exclusion and policing in their fandoms, fandom was a fun identity that brought them joy. Feminism, on the other hand, frequently felt constraining. Even though the interviewees were committed to the feminist project, identified as feminists, and promoted feminist values, they acknowledged feminism as a burden that required constant reconciliation and management with other identities and practices they enjoyed more. Utilizing the tactics I identified reduced their frustration and kept their identities as fans and feminists unharmed. In some cases, it even allowed both identities to coexist harmoniously.

Having reviewed the tactics that feminist women fans used, I then discussed their significance. As debates on representation (Chap. 5) and cancel culture have shown, actions that see popular culture as an end goal are in danger of neglecting "real-life" struggles and inequalities. In parallel, the interviewees' tactics might also seem inconsequential. Some might argue that buying Rey merchandise or writing fan fiction about the 13th Doctor will not make an impact on the object of fandom, the fan communities, or society as a whole. Science fiction content will continue to include stereotypical women characters, some men fans will continue to exclude fans who are different from them, and women of marginalized ethnicities will continue to experience racism on the street, in academia, and in the workplace. In her book on self-perceptions of inequality, Bottero (2020) maintained, "People constantly seek to adapt their circumstances to their own practical purposes, but, their ability to do so depends on the situational constraints they encounter" (p. 208). She argued that individuals vary in the resources and opportunities they have to bring about actual social change. "People are not wrong if they feel their social relations are external and constraining," Bottero said (ibid.). In accordance with Bottero's approach, I argue that as avid consumers, feminist women fans make the most of the resources they have: they protest against misogyny, racism, homophobia, and transphobia by creating their own content and organizing public talks. They tune in to shows and movies that make an effort to be inclusive and tune out those who do not. Such fandom-focused forms of activism also permeate other arenas, as the interviewees attested. Feminist fans use the critique they developed with other women in the fandom in "real life": from talking about politics and current events to how they raise their children (Yodovich, 2022). As Frisina (2010) described, such tactics are "adopted by social actors who insist on hoping that, by accepting some direct responsibility, by doing their little bit, social change becomes possible" (p. 569).

While indeed there are other causes to which feminist women fans could devote their effort and resources, such women are striving to make a change in a community that is significant to their sense of self and worth. By developing tactics to maneuver in communities and texts that could be toxic and dangerous to them, feminist women fans find ways to empower themselves, exercise their agency, and perhaps even make a change:

It's easier to just roll over and say "fine, this is what the fandom is, and if I like the fandom, I have to concede that", but why should you? I'm sorry, I love *Star Wars*, I love *Doctor Who* because the heroes come in and they defy the odds. I will defy the odds too. Even if I failed, at least I tried. (Jessica, 32, biracial white-Jamaican, USA)

REFERENCES

Ali, S. (2002). Friendship and fandom: Ethnicity, power and gendering readings of the popular. *Discourse: Studies in the Cultural Politics of Education, 23*(2), 153–165.

Ashcroft, R. T., & Bevir, M. (2018). Multiculturalism in contemporary Britain: Policy, law and theory. *Law and Theory, 21*(1), 1–21.

Bacon-Smith, C. (1992). *Enterprising women: Television fandom and the creation of popular myth.* University of Pennsylvania Press.

Bauman, Z. (2004). *Identity: Conversations with Benedetto Vecchi.* Polity Press.

Beck, U., & Beck-Gernsheim, E. (2001). *Individualization.* SAGE.

Berg, M. (2017, November 10). Louis C.K.'s losses: How much the sexual misconduct scandal may cost the comedian. *Forbes.* Retrieved August 10, 2021, from https://www.forbes.com/sites/maddieberg/2017/11/10/louis-c-k-s-losses-how-much-the-sexual-misconduct-scandal-may-cost-the-comedian/?sh=4801ff075801

Bishop, B. (2018, July 20). Writer-director James Gunn fired from Guardians of the Galaxy vol. 3 over offensive tweets. *The Verge.* Retrieved August 10, 2021, from https://www.theverge.com/2018/7/20/17596452/guardians-of-the-galaxy-marvel-james-gunn-fired-pedophile-tweets-mike-cernovich

Bottero, W. (2020). *A sense of inequality.* Rowman & Littlefield Publishers.

Bourdaa, M. (2018). "May we meet again": Social bonds, activities, and identities in #clexa fandom. In P. Booth (Ed.), *A Companion to media fandom and fan studies* (pp. 385–400). John Wiley & Sons.

Boyle, K. (2019). *# MeToo, Weinstein and feminism.* Palgrave Pivot.

Brough, M. M., & Shresthova, S. (2012). Fandom meets activism: Rethinking civic and political participation. *Transformative Works and Cultures, 10,* 1–27.

Brown, J. A. (2018). #WheresRey: Feminism, protest, and merchandising sexism in Star Wars: The Force Awakens. *Feminist Media Studies, 18*(3), 335–348.

Budgeon, S. (2011). *Third-wave feminism and the politics of gender in late modernity.* Springer.

Bury, R. (2005). *Cyberspaces of their own: Female fandoms online.* Peter Lang.

Busse, K. & Hellekson, K. (2006). Introduction. In K. Hellekson & K. Busse (Eds.), *Fan fiction and fan communities in the age of the internet: New essays* (pp. 5–32). McFarland.

Chesebro, J. W., Cragan, J. F., & McCullough, P. (1973). The small group technique of the radical revolutionary: A synthetic study of consciousness raising. *Communications Monographs, 40*(2), 136–146.

Clark, M. D. (2020). DRAG THEM: A brief etymology of so-called "cancel culture". *Communication and the Public, 5*(3-4), 88–92.

de Bruin-Molé, M. (2018). 'Does it come with a spear?' Commodity activism, plastic representation, and transmedia story strategies in Disney's Star Wars: Forces of Destiny. *Film Criticism, 42*(2): n.p.

de Certeau, M. (1984). *The practice of everyday life*. University of California Press.

de Kosnik, A. (2013). Interrogating 'free' fan labor. http://spreadablemedia.org/essays/kosnik/index.html#.X4IQvdBKhPZ

DeNora, T. (1999). Music as a technology of the self. *Poetics, 27*(1), 31–56.

Ennis, D. (2019, December 19). J.K. Rowling comes out as a TERF. *Forbes*. Retrieved August 1, 2021, from https://www.forbes.com/sites/dawnstaceyennis/2019/12/19/jk-rowling-comes-out-as-a-terf/?sh=5a5def4e5d70

Erickson, R. J. (1995). The importance of authenticity for self and society. *Symbolic Interaction, 18*(2), 121–144.

Fan, V. (2012). The poetics of addiction: Stardom, "feminized" spectatorship, and interregional business relations in the Twilight series. *Camera Obscura, 27*(1), 31–67.

Favaro, L., & Gill, R. (2018). Feminism rebranded: Women's magazines online and 'the return of the F-word'. *Revista Dígitos, 4*, 37–66.

Frisina, A. (2010). Young Muslims' everyday tactics and strategies: Resisting Islamophobia, negotiating Italianness, becoming citizens. *Journal of Intercultural Studies, 31*(5), 557–572.

Gackstetter Nichols, E. (2019). Playing with identity: Gender, performance and feminine agency in cosplay. *Continuum, 33*(2), 270–282.

Gardner, A. (2021, July 20). A complete breakdown of the J.K. Rowling transgender-comments controversy. *Glamour*. Retrieved August 1, 2021, from https://www.glamour.com/story/a-complete-breakdown-of-the-jk-rowling-transgender-comments-controversy

Gay, R. (2014). *Bad feminist*. Harper Collins.

Genz, S. (2009). *Postfemininities in popular culture*. Palgrave Macmillan.

Giddens, A. (1991). *Modernity and self-identity: Self and society in the late modern age*. Stanford University Press.

Gn, J. (2011). Queer simulation: The practice, performance and pleasure of cosplay. *Continuum, 25*(4), 583–593.

Green, P. (1979). The feminist consciousness. *The Sociological Quarterly, 20*(3), 359–374.

Greenman, E., & Xie, Y. (2008). Is assimilation theory dead? The effect of assimilation on adolescent well-being. *Social Science Research, 37*(1), 109–137.

Hagi, S. (2019, November 21). Cancel culture is not real – At least not in the way people think. *Time*. Retrieved August 10, 2021, from https://time.com/5735403/cancel-culture-is-not-real

Jenkins, H. (1992). *Textual poachers*. Routledge.

Jenkins, H. (2012). Cultural acupuncture: Fan activism and the Harry Potter Alliance. *Transformative Works and Cultures, 10*. http://journal.transformativeworks.org/index.php/twc/article/view/305

Jowett, L. E. (2019). Rey, Mary Sue and Phasma Too: Feminism and fan responses to The Force Awakens merchandise. In W. Proctor & R. McCulloch (Eds.), *Disney's Star Wars: Forces of production, promotion, and reception* (pp. 192–205). University of Iowa Press.

Jung, S. (2002). Queering popular culture: Female spectators and the appeal of writing slash fan fiction. *Gender Forum, 2*, 30–50.

Kernis, M. H., & Goldman, B. M. (2006). A multicomponent conceptualization of authenticity: Theory and research. *Advances in Experimental Social Psychology, 38*, 283–357.

Kirkpatrick, E. (2019). On [dis] play: Outlier resistance and the matter of race-bending superhero cosplay. *Transformative Works and Cultures, 29*, 1–17.

Kirkpatrick, E. (2020, September 14). J.K. Rowling proves her commitment to transphobia in her new novel. *Vanity Fair*. Retrieved August 1, 2021, from https://www.vanityfair.com/style/2020/09/jk-rowling-transphobia-new-novel-troubled-blood-controversy

Kligler-Vilenchik, N. (2015). From wizards and house-elves to real-world issues: Political talk in fan spaces. *International Journal of Communication, 9*, 2027–2046.

Knox, S., & Schwind, K. H. (2019). The one with the emblematic problematic Fave: Friends and the politics of representation. In *Friends* (pp. 169–221). Palgrave Macmillan.

Lamerichs, N. (2011). Stranger than fiction: Fan identity in cosplay. *Transformative Works and Cultures, 7*(3). https://doi.org/10.3983/twc.2011.0246

Larsen, K., & Zubernis, L. (2011). *Fandom at the crossroads: Celebration, shame and fan/producer relationships*. Cambridge Scholars Publishing.

Lawler, S. (2014). *Identity: Sociological perspectives*. Polity Press.

Linden, H., & Linden, S. (2016). *Fans and fan cultures: Tourism, consumerism and social media*. Springer.

Lopez, L. K. (2011). Fan activists and the politics of race in The Last Airbender. *International Journal of Cultural Studies, 14*, 1–15.

Lorde, A. (2003). The master's tools will never dismantle the master's house. In R. Lewis & S. Mills (Eds.), *Feminist postcolonial theory: A reader* (pp. 25–28). Routledge.

Mansouri, F., & Modood, T. (2021). The complementarity of multiculturalism and interculturalism: Theory backed by Australian evidence. *Ethnic and Racial Studies, 44*(16), 1–20.

Martin, A. L., Jr. (2019). Fandom while black: Misty Copeland, Black Panther, Tyler Perry and the contours of US black fandoms. *International Journal of Cultural Studies, 22*(6), 737–753.

McManus, K. (2020). Hidden transcripts and public resistance. *Transformative Works and Cultures, 32.* https://journal.transformativeworks.org/index.php/twc/article/view/1713/2359

McRobbie, A. (2004). Post feminism and popular culture: Bridget Jones and the new gender regime. *Feminist Media Studies, 4*(3), 255–264.

McRobbie, A. (2020). *Feminism and the politics of 'resilience': Essays on gender, media and the end of welfare.* Polity Press.

Morimoto, L., & Chin, B. (2017). *Reimagining the imagined community: Online media fandoms in the age of global convergence.* In J. Gray, C. Sandvoss, & C. L. Harrington (Eds.), Fandom: Identities and communities in a mediated world – Second edition (pp. 174–188). New York University Press.

Okin, S. M. (1999). *Is multiculturalism bad for women?* Princeton University Press.

Pande, R. (2018). *Squee from the margins: Fandom and race.* University of Iowa Press.

Parekh, B. (2001). Rethinking multiculturalism: Cultural diversity and political theory. *Ethnicities, 1*(1), 109–115.

Pereira de Sa, S., & Pereira Alberto, T. (2021). Bigmouth strikes again: The controversy of Morrissey and cancel culture. *American Behavioral Scientist.* https://doi.org/10.1177/00027642211042291

Petersen, A. H. (2011). That teenage feeling: Twilight, fantasy, and feminist readers. *Feminist Media Studies, 12*(1), 51–67.

Phillips, A. (2020). *Gamer trouble.* New York University Press.

Ponzanesi, S. (2007). *Feminist theory and multiculturalism. Feminist Theory, 8*(1), 91–103.

Pough, G. D. (2002). Love feminism but where's my hip hop?: Shaping a black feminist identity. In D. Hernandez & B. Rehman (Eds.), *Colonize this! Young women of color on today's feminism* (pp. 85–95). Seal Press.

Romano, A. (2020, August 25). Why we can't stop arguing about cancel culture. *Vox.* Retrieved August 10, 2021, from https://www.vox.com/culture/2019/12/30/20879720/what-is-cancel-culture-explained-history-debate

Romano, A. (2021, May 5). The second wave of "cancel culture". *Vox.* Retrieved August 10, 2021, from https://www.vox.com/22384308/cancel-culture-free-speech-accountability-debate

Salter, A. (2020). #RelationshipGoals? Suicide Squad and fandom's love of "problematic" men. *Television & New Media, 21*(2), 135–150.

Salter, A., & Blodgett, B. (2017). *Toxic geek masculinity in media: Sexism, trolling, and identity policing*. Springer.

Schwartz, D. (2019, December 23). Where were you when you found out your fave was problematic? *Glamour*. Retrieved July 20, 2021, from https://www.glamour.com/story/problematic-fave-trend-decade

Scott, S. (2017a). Modeling the Marvel everyfan: Agent Coulson and/as transmedia fan culture. *Palabra Clave, 20*(4), 1042–1072.

Scott, S. (2017b). # Wheresrey?: Toys, spoilers, and the gender politics of franchise paratexts. *Critical Studies in Media Communication, 34*(2), 138–147.

Sobande, F. (2020). *The digital lives of Black women in Britain*. Palgrave Macmillan.

Sowards, S. K., & Renegar, V. R. (2004). The rhetorical functions of consciousness-raising in third wave feminism. *Communication Studies, 55*(4), 535–552.

Stitch. (2015, December 9). Problematic fave – The authority: Human on the inside. *Stitch's Media Mix*. Retrieved July 20, 2021, from https://stitchmediamix.com/2015/12/09/problematic-fave-the-authority-human-on-the-inside

Stitch. (2021a, April 30). Facing backlash for anti-racism... It's more common than you think. *Stitch's Media Mix*. Retrieved July 24, 2021, from https://stitchmediamix.com/2021/04/30/facing-backlash-for-anti-racism-its-more-common-than-youd-think

Stitch. (2021b, May 27). What fandom racism looks like: No safe space/"curate your space". *Stitch's Media Mix*. Retrieved July 24, 2021, from https://stitchmediamix.com/2021/05/07/wfrll-curate-your-space

Walker, R. (Ed.). (1995). *To be real: Telling the truth and changing the face of feminism*. Anchor.

Wanzo, R. (2009). *The suffering will not be televised: African American women and sentimental political storytelling*. Suny Press.

Wanzo, R. (2015). African American acafandom and other strangers: New genealogies of fan studies. *Transformative Works and Cultures, 20*(1), n.p..

Warner, K. J. (2015). ABC's Scandal and Black women's fandom. In E. Levine (Ed.), *Cupcakes, Pinterest and ladyporn: Feminized popular culture in the early twenty-first century* (pp. 32–50). University of Illinois Press.

Warner, K. J. (2018). JunexNick: The quietest ship in the Handmaid fandom. *Communication, Culture and Critique, 11*(1), 198–200.

Wildsmith, E. (2004). Race/ethnic differences in female headship: Exploring the assumptions of assimilation theory. *Social Science Quarterly, 85*(1), 89–106.

Wood, M. (2016). Feminist icon needed: Damsels in distress need not apply. In P. W. Lee (Ed.), *A galaxy here and now: Historical and cultural readings of Star Wars* (pp. 62–83). McFarland Publishing.

Yodovich, N. (2022). Like father, like daughter: The intergenerational passing of Doctor Who and Star Wars fandoms in the familial context. In: B. Kies & M. Connor (Eds.), *Fandom, the next generation* (pp. 57–67). owa City, IA: Iowa University Press.

CHAPTER 7

Finding a Space(ship) of One's Own

On 21 January 2017, a day after President Donald Trump's inauguration, women marched across the USA. These women, who were later joined by others worldwide, protested against sexism and misogyny and demanded equal rights and governance over their bodies. The Women's March took place merely a month after Carrie Fisher's untimely death. Countless women who participated in the various events of the Women's March honored their beloved feminist symbols, Fisher and Princess Leia, as they fought for equality and justice. These women marched with banners, t-shirts, and buttons featuring an image created by graphic designer, Hayley Gilmore, that featured Princess Leia in her white dress, holding an Imperial Blaster. Leia's image was accompanied by the sentence: "A woman's place is in the resistance." This sea of Leia posters decorating the marches received media attention with headlines such as "How Princess Leia Became an Unofficial Symbol for the Women's March" (Gibson, 2017) or "Princess Leia Gave the Women's March a New Hope" (Watercutter, 2017). Since then, Princess Leia has become an honorary symbol in many protests for women's rights, not only as a quirky pop culture reference but also as an emblem of hope, resistance, and resilience.

I conclude this book with the Women's March because it exemplifies the potential symbiosis between fandom and feminism, even though it is not necessarily the perfect exemplar of feminist action. As I demonstrated

© The Author(s), under exclusive license to Springer Nature Switzerland AG 2022
N. Yodovich, *Women Negotiating Feminism and Science Fiction Fandom*, Palgrave Fan Studies,
https://doi.org/10.1007/978-3-031-04079-5_7

earlier in the book, and as other scholars have established, despite raising awareness about gender inequality and gaining prominence in mainstream media, the march was also commercialized and marginalizing (Gomez Sarmiento, 2020; North, 2018). Nevertheless, it is a suitable demonstration of the ways in which feminist women drew upon references from their fandoms to convey their message as they protested for social change. By doing so, they not only promoted their feminist causes but also demonstrated that fandom is not a mindless hobby. It is a platform that develops and articulates feminist critiques. Through Leia, women expressed frustration with their marginalized and disregarded position in fan communities and society as a whole.

Despite this example of synergy between feminist protests and *Star Wars* fandom, as I noted, women still negotiate their fan and feminist identities in a tense and confusing social climate. Fandom has gradually shifted to the mainstream and now appears more accessible and open. However, as the participants of this research testified, many fan communities remain exclusionary, toxic, and policing. The ostracism of women, people of marginalized ethnicities, members of the LGBTQ+ community, older individuals, and the disabled from fan communities and popular culture texts can create inner conflicts among those who are interested in being part of these fan communities. Given this situation, I was curious to learn about feminist women fans' experiences in white, men-dominated communities and their efforts to reconcile their identities.

In this concluding chapter, I review the main arguments and key findings of this book and discuss the larger debates that have emerged. I reflect on what we can learn from the case of feminist women fans, but also on the limitations of this study. I conclude with final thoughts about the pressures of fitting oneself into limiting definitions of identities such as being a fan.

7.1   WHAT CAN WE LEARN FROM THE CASE OF FEMINIST WOMEN FANS?

The experiences of feminist women fans were anchored by the concept of "identity" and its various stages of development and different aspects: becoming, being, belonging, representing, and reconciling. Chapter 2, "Becoming a Feminist Fan," detailed the biographical narratives provided by the interviewees in which they described how they came to identify as fans and feminists. This chapter revealed the feminist women fans' feelings of illegitimacy and inauthenticity, regardless of the quality or quantity of the practices in which they took part. Chapter 3, "Being a Feminist Fan," added the prisms of gender, ethnicity, and age. The chapter explored the women's self-categorization processes after experiencing marginality and exclusion in both fan and feminist communities. Being perceived as and feeling like outsiders in fandom and feminism led some of the participants to prioritize their identities. Chapter 4, "Belonging as a Feminist Fan," introduced the concept of conditional belonging, which captured the liminal state of feminist women fans in their respective fandoms. The constant scrutiny and the burden to prove that they "deserved" to belong disrupted the feminist women's ability to see themselves as genuine fans and led to feelings of self-doubt and self-policing practices. Chapter 5, "Representing Women and Feminism in Fandom," scrutinized the ways in which the participants negotiated the representation of women characters in their favorite franchises. This chapter discussed the importance of representation in popular culture as an indication to the feminist women fans' of their own position in the fan community and beyond. Lastly, Chap. 6, "Reconciling Feminism and Fandom," reviewed the narrative and practice tactics feminist women fans use in order to harmonize their feminist and fannish inclinations.

Simply phrased, the crux of this book is that identifying as a feminist fan is hard work. The interviewees expressed their constant frustration and unease with their fan identity, the object of their fandom, and the fan community. They described becoming fans as an organic process that was motivated by their attraction to the diegesis and the women characters that it featured. However, as they delved deeper into the world of fandom, the participants felt inauthentic and not "good enough." They also described a similar process with regard to becoming feminists, wherein their instinctive inclination to identify as feminists was quickly replaced by self-doubt and hesitations. Unpacking the experience of being a feminist fan revealed the participants' challenge of managing their various identities in conjunction with one another. Moreover, in parallel to Cooley's "the looking-glass self" (1992), feminist women fans saw themselves through the perspective of others. They internalized the frequent criticism and scrutiny they were exposed to in offline and online spaces and judged themselves harshly as a result.

Despite encountering frictions and threats, the participants were motivated to reconcile feminism and fandom. In order to marry their two identities and allow themselves to continue to enjoy their fandoms without feeling guilty and conflicted, feminist women fans developed tactics that relieved inner contradictions and allowed them to exercise their agency and use their voice. These tactics were imperative for feminist women fans. They would not be able to keep both identities without them. While most tactics focused on the object of the fandom and the fan community, I argued that these were not trivial acts. By promoting change in their fandom, feminist women fans operated as agents of change who pushed for diversity and inclusion and fought against bigotry and toxic behaviors. The toolkit that feminist women fans created when protecting a fictional character under attack could also be implemented in other, broader social contexts. Such tactics provide feminist women fans with a sense of worth and capability while advocating for identities and communities that are vital to them.

It is important to note that the challenges and barriers that feminist women fans faced varied in intensity and severity depending on their social baggage. Throughout this book, I explored gender, feminism, and fandom, while being conscious of ethnicity and age. By doing so, I captured the difficulty that women of marginalized ethnicities face in fully engaging with both feminism and fandom. Feminist thought and practice are still primarily motivated and dictated by white, middle-class women, who do not do enough to make space for marginalized women. In fan communities, women of marginalized ethnicities are constantly attacked and verbally abused. What some fans absentmindedly regard as an acceptable argument against "PC culture" or "social justice warriors" is, in fact, quite frequently, an inherently racist and misogynist discourse. Ageism is also prevalent in fan communities. The participants noted the shift in fandom where spaces that were once more inviting and accessible became hostile and gated as they grew older and were considered less appealing. They found their struggles embodied in the scrutiny of women who grew old in Hollywood, such as Carrie Fisher. It was particularly interesting to observe the rapidity with which a woman becomes "old" in fan communities, where turning 30 is already considered "old age."

The accounts of feminist women fans and the negotiation of their identities are especially telling in light of the accepted narrative about fandom and resistance. Despite the romanticized portrayal of fandom in the early days of the scholarly field (Abercrombie & Longhurst, 1998; Jenkins, 1988, 1992; Scodari, 2003), fandom is sometimes quite the opposite of a resistance-focused community. Strict regulations on what is and what is not fandom, who is a "good" fan, and what is "good" content are policing and restricting. As some scholars have argued (Pande, 2018; Salter & Stanfill, 2020; Scott, 2019; Wanzo, 2015), the more marginalized the fan is, the less power they have to promote substantial change or to enjoy being non-conforming. The critical lesson to be learned from the interviewees is that even though it is crucial that they actively push back against toxicity, racism, and misogyny, it is even more imperative that the privileged, and those in a position of power in fandom, join this effort. The striving for inclusivity and the fight against bigotry should not be the burden of the marginalized and the silenced alone. Therefore, while feminist women fans have created vital tools to manage their day-to-day interactions in the fan community, privileged fans, producers, and creators need to step up and contribute their part to eradicating toxicity in fannish spaces and popular culture content.

My study contributes to the scholarship on fan studies by directly examining women who explicitly identify as fans and feminists. In light of the historical link between fan studies and feminist thought (Bacon-Smith, 1992; Hannell, 2020; Penley, 1992; Scott, 2019; Woo, 2018), I have demonstrated and emphasized the merits of exploring feminist women fans who avidly support franchises that are not necessarily feminist. Studies that focus only on one identity or infer that their research subjects are feminists miss the heightened tension that arises when feminism and fandom are coalesced, the burden of carrying the stigma of both identities, and the dual silencing of women and feminists in men-dominated fan communities.

This research on feminist women fans is set in the particular context of lively discussions on cancel culture and representation. Indeed, such topics deserve academic endeavors of their own. Nevertheless, it is essential to acknowledge how this study relates to such broader debates. The act of cancellation and rejection of a text or an individual is complex for those who support them. Cases such as celebrities who took part in sexual harassment or transphobia, and the content that features them, usually appear more clear-cut and are deemed deserving of cancellation (Gardner, 2021; Kirkpatrick, 2020; Potton, 2021; Silva, 2021). In this research, however, I was interested in gray areas, in franchises that are not expressly misogynist but are not necessarily celebrated as feminist either.

This study revealed that fans would go to great lengths before parting ways with their fandom. They develop rationales to explain their attraction, attempt to "fix" storylines, and campaign for change and improvement. They turn their favorite celebrities into "problematic faves" to indicate their acknowledgment of their imperfections. I claim that such efforts demonstrate the fans' willingness to exercise their agency, pursue their hobby, and assert their identity. As long as the fans' fascination surpasses their frustration, they will continue to support their fandom while developing various methods to rationalize, defend, and improve it.

7.2   LIMITATIONS

The findings of this research are based on 40 in-depth interviews I conducted with self-identified fans and feminists. This method led to a comprehensive, substantial, and nuanced depiction of the lives of feminist women fans. It is a method that provided the interviewees with a platform to talk about their encounters with exclusion, toxicity, and racism, as well as share their hopes, loves, and excitement in their own words. Such a method is rigorous, yet limiting, nonetheless.

Despite the exhaustive findings included in this research, the conclusions might not apply to each and every feminist woman fan's experience. Due to the conscious decision to focus on the intersection of gender, ethnicity, and age, some crucial identities did not receive critical and intellectual engagement and were not fully represented by the pool of interviewees I gathered. Therefore, members of the LGBTQ+ community or disabled individuals did not receive sufficient exposure and academic attention. Nevertheless, I attempted to incorporate glimpses into the lives of the interviewees who were, for instance, asexual, working-class, or disabled, identities that also came into play when they engaged with fandom and feminism. Future research should be mindful of diversifying fan studies and their research subjects and exploring identities that did not receive sufficient attention in this book.

Even though this research focused on ethnicity, I am hesitant to make generalizable claims about feminist women fans who identify with a marginalized ethnicity. Of the 40 interviewees, 11 identified with a marginalized ethnicity, such as Latinas, African American/Black, Chinese, and Indian. In some cases, only one interviewee "represented" a particular ethnicity, like Jenny (31, Chinese, UK) and Anaya (19, Indian, UK). Moreover, including all interviewees of marginalized ethnicities under the same umbrella term is also potentially risky, as women of different ethnic identities experience different forms of marginalization and discrimination in varying degrees. Despite a somewhat limited pool of interviewees, I based this study on a close and nuanced reading of their accounts. The participants reported on experiences and struggles that were significant to their identities as women of marginalized ethnicities who also identify as fans and feminists. Based on these reports I established my theory of conditional belonging and the rest of the findings presented in this book. I hope that the reports provided in this book are intellectually and emotionally stimulating and inspire researchers to delve deeper into the study of fandom and ethnicity.

Another limitation is the participants' nationality. Most participants were from Anglophone countries, such as the UK and the USA, while others were from various European countries. Besides Spain and Australia, where I was able to interview several participants, every other country (Switzerland, Italy, Germany, France, and Ireland) was "represented" by only one interviewee. Therefore, I did not draw conclusions about the perceptions, practices, or challenges particular to feminist fans from each country. In a few rare cases, the participants provided specific examples from their own cultural and social contexts, such as Ramona's referencing of the March of Choice in Ireland. Still, they all ultimately echoed each other's narratives. Many participants encountered exclusion and shared feeling guilty and inadequate, regardless of their nationality or their native language. I demonstrated that women fans' conditional belonging is not limited to a particular country. It is a prevalent phenomenon in fan communities of different nationalities. This finding also indicates how fandom operates as a global community, which transcends national and cultural boundaries, primarily through online spaces.[1]

Lastly, because the interest in feminist women fans was the driving force of this study, I did not capture men fans' side of the story. Certainly, men fans also encounter gatekeeping in science fiction fandom, as their identities also intersect with categories such as ethnicity, age, disability, or sexuality, which could contribute to their exclusion. Much like women fans, men fans should also not be regarded as a homogeneous group wherein every member is socially privileged and takes part in toxic behaviors. Needless to say, not every white, cishet, abled man is toxic or abusive. If anything, it is the loud minority of men who take part in toxic geek masculinity practices that dominate the community and dictate to it. The quiet majority is silent, silenced, or not loud enough to drown out the ear-deafening bigotry. Therefore, I encourage future research to explore men fans' experiences of gatekeeping, frictions, and inner contradictions through an intersectional lens.

---

[1] Nevertheless, this, of course, does not mean that a global community is egalitarian, as the findings presented in this book have attested.

7.3   LOOKING FORWARD

Based on my findings, I suggest three main avenues for future research: a discussion on the importance of fandom and cultural engagement for the fabric of social life, an invitation to expand on the concept of conditional belonging, and a reconsideration of the insistence on coherent, consistent identities in fandom, feminism, and beyond.

I begin by suggesting that this book serves as an important illustration of the importance of fan studies. Going back to the question that sparked this research, I asked: "How do feminist women fans of science fiction reconcile and negotiate their identities?" In other words, "Can one be a feminist and a fan of content that is not necessarily feminist?" Such questions are all too often deemed trivial distractions from more pressing current affairs (Gay, 2014; Mahoney, 2020; Redfern & Aune, 2010). However, I stress that the identities discussed in this book have proven to play a significant role in the ways in which women construct and perceive themselves and their social worlds. Fandom provides a fascinating microcosm of society at large, where we can find racism, sexism, and ingroup-outgroup tensions, as well as activism, solidarity, and creativity. In a nutshell, fandom matters. It is significant academically, socially, and individually.

Second, I invite scholars to use the concept of conditional belonging as a helpful theoretical framework to explore intricate communal relationships in fandom and similar communities characterized by gatekeeping. Through this study, I defined conditional belonging as a liminal state in which individuals are neither complete outsiders nor insiders. In this position, individuals are policed and expected to conform to the perceptions, values, and behaviors dictated by those in power. For example, the notion of conditional belonging helped depict the state of feminist women fans of science fiction. To avoid ostracization, they were required to refrain from externalizing their gender, ethnicity, age, and feminist identities. Since such expectations are made of those with other identities in fandom (disabilities or LGBTQ+ identities) and other communities in general, I hope to see scholars implementing the term in their work and assessing its potency in different social groups and other identities.

Lastly, based on the case of feminist women fans, I also encourage a further examination of complex identities. I find it intellectually intriguing and socially imperative to scrutinize questions about personal choice and conflicted identities because of what lies beneath them: the persistent requirement to establish a contradiction-free, flawless identity. Such demands are made of fans and feminists, who are expected to be fully immersed in and committed to fandom and feminism. These expectations render criticism or discontent an act of disloyalty to the community. It turns feminist women fans into a "fifth column," when they "dare" to care about social equality more than their beloved franchise. It also belittles feminist women who focus their efforts on changing their fandom instead of working for broader social change.

The demand of women to be "proper" fans, or any fan for that matter, is indicative of the hazards of the attempt to keep fandom under a strict and binding definition. The notion that fans have to be actively engaged in various fannish practices in order to be defined as such leaves them with either one of the two options: strive to become "superfans" (Baym et al., 2018; Hills, 2019) or be in jeopardy of not being acknowledged as fans at all. As fandom scholars, it is understandable that we attempt to define what makes one a fan. Doing so is easier by using quantifiable, visible practices. However, fandom is not only what we do, but also what we feel (Grossberg, 1992; Larsen & Zubernis, 2013; Sandvoss et al., 2017; Stein, 2015). As some of the interviewees articulated, fandom is very much emotive. This aspect of fandom is easy to neglect or dismiss, especially when trying to turn fandom into a legitimate identity, or when it is associated with women. The emphasis on practices also fails to acknowledge that marginalized individuals are unable to take part in certain activities. Economically disadvantaged fans, for instance, simply cannot consume merchandise or frequent expensive conventions, and fans of marginalized ethnicities cannot attend some fannish communities due to racism and toxicity.

As I look ahead and envision avenues that could be developed further, I argue that we should continue to unpack the demands of fans and other individuals alike to develop cogent, indisputable, unshakeable identities. Such a demand leaves very little room for self-growth and self-examination. It also limits our ability to stretch boundaries and redefine them. As scholars, we should allow ourselves to feel more comfortable or at ease with leaving the fan as a nebulous identity because when we try to define it, we are also taking part in gatekeeping. Indeed, this approach might "compromise" the clarity of the term, but it will also turn it into a more inclusive one. Instead of defining, we should continue examining how our participants and communities define fandom and the kinds of justifications they use to identify fandom as one thing and not the other.

Although I have yet to fully untangle some of the paradigms I have presented here, I hope I have demonstrated the potential of fan studies to contribute to larger sociological debates on identity, belonging, and everything in between. Until more is done to broaden our framing of the fan and feminist identities, or identities in general, and allow for more ambivalence and fuzziness, I hope you found yourself in this book. I hope this book helped you learn about other women's experiences and maybe resolve some conflicts you had yourself. So, shall we rewatch *Buffy* now?

References

Abercrombie, N., & Longhurst, B. J. (1998). *Audiences: A sociological theory of performance and imagination*. SAGE Publications Ltd.

Bacon-Smith, C. (1992). *Enterprising women: Television fandom and the creation of popular myth*. University of Pennsylvania Press.

Baym, N., Cavicchi, D., & Coates, N. (2018). Music fandom in the digital age: A conversation. In M. A. Scott & S. Scott (Eds.), *The Routledge companion to media fandom* (pp. 141–152). Routledge.

Cooley, C. H. (1992 [1902]). *Human nature and the social order*. Transaction Publishers.

Gardner, A. (2021, July 20). A complete breakdown of the J.K. Rowling transgender-comments controversy. *Glamour*. Retrieved August 1, 2021, from https://www.glamour.com/story/a-complete-breakdown-of-the-jk-rowling-transgender-comments-controversy

Gay, R. (2014). *Bad feminist*. Harper Collins.

Gibson, C. (2017, January 23). How Princess Leia became an unofficial symbol for the Women's March. *The Washington Post*. Retrieved July 25, 2019, from https://www.washingtonpost.com/news/arts-and-entertainment/wp/2017/01/23/how-princess-leia-became-an-unofficial-symbol-for-the-womens-march

Gomez Sarmiento, I. (2020, January 17). After controversial leaders step down, the women's march tries again in 2020. *NPR*. Retrieved September 23, 2021, from https://www.npr.org/2020/01/17/797107259/after-controversial-leaders-step-down-the-womens-march-tries-again-in-2020?t=1632391075092

Grossberg, L. (1992). Is there a fan in the house? The affective sensibility of fandom. In L. A. Lewis (Ed.), *The adoring audience: Fan culture and popular media* (pp. 50–65). Routledge.

Hannell, B. (2020). Fan studies and/as feminist methodology. *Transformative Works and Cultures, 33*. https://doi.org/10.3983/twc.2020.1689

Hills, M. (2019). When the Pet Shop Boys were 'imperial': Fans' self-ageing and the neoliberal life course of 'successful' text-ageing. *The Journal of Fandom Studies, 7*(2), 151–167.

Jenkins, H. (1988). Star Trek rerun, reread, rewritten: Fan writing as textual poaching. *Critical Studies in Media Communication, 5*(2), 85–107.

Jenkins, H. (1992). *Textual poachers.* Routledge.

Kirkpatrick, E. (2020, September 14). J.K. Rowling proves her commitment to transphobia in her new novel. *Vanity Fair.* Retrieved August 1, 2021, from https://www.vanityfair.com/style/2020/09/jk-rowling-transphobia-new-novel-troubled-blood-controversy

Larsen, K., & Zubernis, L. S. (2013). *Fangasm: Supernatural fangirls.* University of Iowa Press.

Mahoney, C. (2020). Is this what a feminist looks like? Curating the feminist self in the neoliberal visual economy of Instagram. *Feminist Media Studies.* https://doi.org/10.1080/14680777.2020.1810732

North, A. (2018, December 21). The women's march changed the American left. Now anti-semitism allegations threaten the group's future. *Vox.* Retrieved September 23, 2021, from https://www.vox.com/identities/2018/12/21/18145176/feminism-womens-march-2018-2019-farrakhan-intersectionality

Pande, R. (2018). *Squee from the margins: Fandom and race.* University of Iowa Press.

Penley, C. (1992). "Feminism, psychoanalysis, andpopular culture," pp. 479–94 in L. Grossberg, C. Nelson, and P. Treichler (eds.), Cultural Studies Now and In the Future. Routledge.

Potton, E. (2021, April 9). Armie Hammer and the trouble with Hollywood men: How he joined the long list of cancelled stars. *The Times.* Retrieved September 23, 2021, from https://www.thetimes.co.uk/article/armie-hammer-and-the-trouble-with-hollywood-men-kdmwhbn53

Redfern, C., & Aune, K. (2010). *Reclaiming the f word: The new feminist movement.* Zed.

Salter, A., & Stanfill, M. (2020). *A portrait of the auteur as fanboy: The construction of authorship in transmedia franchises.* University Press of Mississippi.

Sandvoss, C., Gray, J., & Harrington, C. L. (2017). Introduction. Why still study fans? In J. Gray, C. Sandvoss, & C. L. Harrington (Eds.), *Fandom: Identities and communities in a mediated world* (pp. 1–26). New York University Press.

Scodari, C. (2003). Resistance re-examined: Gender, fan practices, and science fiction television. *Popular Communication, 1*(2), 111–130.

Scott, S. (2019). *Fake geek girls: Fandom, gender, and the convergence culture industry.* NYU Press.

Silva, C. (2021, July 28). Celebrities, activists condemn rapper DeBaby's homophonic comments. *NBC News.* Retrieved September 23, 2021, from https://

www.nbcnews.com/nbc-out/out-news/celebrities-activists-condemn-rapper-dababys-homophobic-comments-rcna1535

Stein, L. E. (2015). *Millennial fandom: Television audiences in the transmedia age.* University of Iowa Press.

Wanzo, R. (2015). African American acafandom and other strangers: New genealogies of fan studies. *Transformative Works and Cultures, 20*(1): n.p.

Watercutter, A. (2017, January 23). Princess Leia gave the women's march a new hope. *Wired.* Retrieved July 25, 2019, from https://www.wired.com/2017/01/princess-leia-womens-march

Woo, B. (2018). *Getting a life: The social worlds of Geek culture.* McGill-Queen's Press.

INDEX[1]

[1] Note: Page numbers followed by 'n' refer to notes.

© The Author(s), under exclusive license to Springer Nature
Switzerland AG 2022
N. Yodovich, *Women Negotiating Feminism and Science Fiction
Fandom*, Palgrave Fan Studies,
https://doi.org/10.1007/978-3-031-04079-5

Printed by Printforce, United Kingdom